Sermons on the Beatitudes,

WITH OTHERS MOSTLY PREACHED BEFORE

THE UNIVERSITY OF OXFORD:

TO WHICH IS ADDED

A PREFACE RELATING TO THE VOLUME OF

"Essays and Reviews."

BY GEORGE MOBERLY, D.C.L.

FORMERLY HEAD MASTER OF WINCHESTER COLLEGE;
NOW LORD BISHOP OF SALISBURY.

THIRD EDITION.

WIPF & STOCK · Eugene, Oregon

Wipf and Stock Publishers
199 W 8th Ave, Suite 3
Eugene, OR 97401

Sermons on the Beatitudes, 3rd Edition
By Moberly, George
Softcover ISBN-13: 978-1-7252-8988-8
Hardcover ISBN-13: 978-1-7252-8989-5
eBook ISBN-13: 978-1-7252-8990-1
Publication date 10/29/2020
Previously published by James Parker and Co., 1870

This edition is a scanned facsimile
of the original edition published in 1870.

PREFACE.

SINCE the first Edition of these Sermons was put to press, the volume of Essays and Reviews, which I had taken occasion to notice in the preface, has reached its eighth edition, and the strong and general disapprobation with which it has been received among Church-people of all shades of opinion, and the weighty expressions of condemnation on the part of all the bishops, and both Houses of the Convocation of the clergy of the province of Canterbury,—not to speak of various Reviews of greater and less importance,—might seem to make it less necessary, perhaps hardly seemly, for a private clergyman to offer observations of his own, as if he had any right by position, or claim from learning or ability, to be heard separately among so many voices.

But I shall venture, not indeed to reprint exactly my former preface, but to recast it in some degree, with reference to the more advanced state in which the controversy, so to call it, now stands. I also wish to explain myself more fully on some points on which my meaning seems to have been somewhat misunderstood. The particular line which I may reasonably take seems to me to be the one of suggesting *per contrâ* topics of strength and helpfulness to my own pupils. I feel that those who have been bred up under my own care, and taught, as I hope, the sober faith of the Church of England, are seriously endangered by finding themselves launched into an ocean of speculation and free-thinking, particularly in the University. Men whom they cannot but admire for their ability, and some whom they know to be most warmly loved for their kindness, write and print various things which, to say the least, are widely different from what they have been taught, and what has been authoritatively taught in any age of the Christian Church. It is true that these things are not new. They have been taught in Germany for many years, and speculations of the same kind have been floating in the minds of many persons in England for a considerable time. But this is the first time in which they have been put forward in so connected a shape, and by men of station and ability, holding in various parts of the country important offices as teachers. The few observations which I propose to make, I wish to be understood as addressed to my own pupils. If they are of any weight, others will read them. If they are not, I shall be well content to hope that they may have done no harm to the sacred cause of Holy Scripture and Catholic truth, and to trust that others may come forward with more power to vindicate them against what one of these writers well calls the "negative theology" of the present generation, the most dangerous, because the most insidious, form of attack upon the truth, as I think, to which it has yet been subject.

In the Advertisement prefixed to the volume the Essayists claim to be "responsible for their respective articles only. They have written in entire independence of one another, and without concert or comparison." Not at all doubting of the fact stated in the latter of these sentences, I demur to the claim of freedom from mutual responsibility made in the former of them. Why do the Essays appear thus together? Why are the writers thus associated in "an attempt to illustrate," &c. ? If the seven stars be, as they say, wholly separate and unconnected with one another, by whose doing is it that they appear to us in the form of a constellation of no good omen to the cause of Christian truth? If the seven musicians play each his own instrument "without concert or comparison," is it surprising that we perceive a distinct harmony among them, set as they are in one key, and taking different notes in the same chord? I cannot think that any wrong is done to any one of the writers, though their book be regarded as one book, their view as one view, their design (according to their own advertisement) as a joint "attempt to illustrate the advantage" (if advantage it be) "derivable to the cause of religious and moral truth" from so free a handling, in what they think "a becoming spirit," of the subjects of Christian religion. Take, for instance, the first Essay. The view which it suggests of the parallel between the education of the world, and that of an individual man, is slight, fanciful, and obviously untrue if it be pressed seriously, or far. The Essayist himself cannot suppose it to bear more than such slight approximation to truth as may serve as a peg to hang a few suggestive reflections on. Had this Essay stood alone, had it remained the "University Sermon" on which, as we are told by high authority, it was based, no person would have thought it of sufficient consequence to call for objection or remark. It is not a serious statement of what even the author can think important truth. It contains a clever, suggestive *view*, which will not hold water,—and that is all. But the writer of it is the man of most reputation of the seven. His name gives more weight to the book than that of any of the other contributors. His "view," slight and unimportant as it is in itself, is found to blend very intimately with the more serious teachings that follow. If the education of the world be really so analogous to that of an individual, as that mankind *has* outlived the age of *examples* [a] (i.e. the age of the Apostolic teaching) and of *creeds* (i.e. the age of the early Church [b]) and reached a further age of *principles*, and if this

[a] p. 28.   [b] p. 44.

teaching be really intended to be serious, and gravely true, then the further Essays may well be understood to supply a large number of the very principles to which the full-grown world has now attained. Thus the first Essay seems at once to introduce the other six, and to receive illustration from them. If, then, this connexion of meaning be one which the writer of the first Essay repudiates, he is bound, as I think, to disavow it, and withdraw his Essay from a neighbourhood where it seems to bear so close a relation to all that follows it. But if he leaves it in the same connexion through eight large editions, how can he complain if the world attributes to him his share of the responsibility of the whole volume? I am perfectly certain that the writer neither intended beforehand, nor approves subsequently of the use which his words are thus made to subserve, and I can quite enter into the difficulties of feeling which beset his position, particularly since so extensive and authoritative disapprobation has been expressed respecting the whole book:—but the question is really not one of any man's feelings. In the interest of the souls of the young and the unstable,—the *vital* interest of the souls of the young and the unstable,—it appears to me to be absolutely necessary that he should withdraw from an apparent co-partnery, which, as I fully believe, he does not intend. While the work is selling by thousands, and doing direct mischief wherever it sells, it is comparatively little to the purpose to speak or write other words, though they be of sounder or less dangerous character, which cannot spread so far, or prevent the joint-essays from doing their own evil work. What would the writer do, if he had written a theoretical essay on *politics*, and found his lucubrations unawares made to usher in six other essays, containing unmixed and undoubted *treason*, to the views of which his own speculations bore a most awkward, though, as I fully grant, an unintended resemblance?

It is urged more than once in the course of these Essays, that it is unreasonable on the part of such as are satisfied with the Christian truth as they have learned and believe it, to be uneasy at finding others offering objections and stating difficulties which they themselves do not feel. It is implied continually that these discussions are designed to help doubters and obviate difficulties, and, as such, ought to be welcomed rather than discouraged by such as desire to see union among Christians on such points as can stand the test of unlimited discussion, and be ultimately agreed upon as the essence, the real, central, vital essence of sacred truth [c]. Indeed, the very captiousness with which, it is not denied, such objections are sometimes urged, is partly to be laid, they tell us, to the blame of those who ignore the difficulties of others, because they may not feel any for themselves [d]: and we are warned that

[c] pp. 95, 96. p. 178.

by so doing we run great risk of turning into bitterness the sincerity of those who should be our best allies as friends of truth [c].

The persons on whose behalf these charitable discussions of difficulties are provided, are, according to Mr. Wilson, many indeed. "It may not be very easy, by a statistical proof," he tells us, "to convince those whose preconceptions indispose them to admit it, of the fact of a very wide-spread alienation, both of educated and uneducated persons, from the Christianity which is ordinarily presented in our churches and chapels. Whether it be their reason or their moral sense which is shocked by what they hear there, the ordinances of public worship and religious instruction provided for the people of England, alike in the endowed and unendowed Churches, are not used by them to the extent we should expect, if they valued them very highly, or if they were really adapted to the wants of their nature as it is. And it has certainly not hitherto received the attention which such a grave circumstance demanded, that a number equal to five millions and a quarter of persons should have neglected to attend means of public worship within their reach on the census Sunday in 1851; these five millions and a quarter being forty-two per cent. of the whole number able and with opportunity of then attending. . . . This," i.e. "the wide spread of what has been

[c] p. 174.

called the negative theology," "is rather owing to a spontaneous recoil on the part of large numbers of the more acute of our population, from some of the doctrines which are to be heard at church or chapel, to a distrust of the old arguments for, or proofs of, a miraculous revelation, and to a misgiving as to the authority, or extent of the authority, of the Scriptures. In the presence of real difficulties of this kind, probably of genuine English" (i.e. not German) " growth, it is vain to seek to check that open discussion out of which alone any satisfactory settlement of them can issue [f]."

Mr. Jowett, it must be confessed, seems hardly disposed to go to the census of the non-Church-goers on a certain Sunday in 1851, for the "measure of public opinion [g]" respecting such difficulties: but he too, acknowledging (what is more near the truth) a sort of smouldering scepticism, particularly, it would seem, among able and highly-educated young men, anticipates in glowing terms the possible result of such a reconcilement or restoration of belief as discussions of this nature, fully and satisfactorily concluded after the elimination of all difficulties, might be expected to effect. "No one," he says, "can form any notion from what we see around us, of the power which Christianity might have, if it were at one with the conscience of man, and not at variance with his in-

[f] pp. 150, 151. [g] p. 373.

tellectual convictions. There, a world weary of the heat and dust of controversy,—of speculations about God and man,—weary, too, of the rapidity of its own motion, would return home, and find rest [h]."

Are then the "difficulties" which we are thus urged, under penalty of bitterness on the part of our adversaries, to consider with tender respect, which interfering thus with man's conscience, and being at variance with his intellectual convictions, impede this blessed union and peace of minds,—few, slight, or unimportant?

Let us gather a few of them up, as they are scattered over the pages of this volume. *Specimen-difficulties* indeed, only, they are: for from the unsystematic nature of essay-writing, as well as from the other published writings of many of the Essayists, we may be perfectly sure that they are only a few of the difficulties which they really feel. Yet these may at least serve to shew us to what sort of extent the ordinary belief of Christian people requires to be shaken to pieces before such happy consent of consciences and intellectual convictions as several of the Essayists are sanguine enough to expect, can be attained.

It is difficult to know where to begin. Perhaps we may begin with Holy Scripture, and first with the Old Testament.

The first chapter of Genesis may best be regarded

[h] p. 376.

"as the speculation of some Hebrew Descartes or Newton, promulgated in all good faith as the best and most probable account that could be then given of God's universe [i]."

There are many indications in various parts of the volume of doubt respecting the descent of mankind from a single pair [k].

The following are specimens of Baron Bunsen's teaching, adopted and improved by Dr. Williams.

"The historical portion" of the Old Testament, "as opposed to the legendary, begins with Abraham;" yet, adds Dr. Williams, "a sceptical criticism might indeed ask by what right he (Baron Bunsen) assumes that the moral dimensions of our spiritual heroes cannot have been idealized by tradition [l]."

In the passage of the Red Sea, the description may be interpreted with the latitude of poetry [m].

As to the Pentateuch in general, "Numerous fragments of genealogy, of chronicle, and of spiritual song go up to a high antiquity, but are imbedded in a crust of later narrative, the allusions of which betray at least a time when kings were established in Israel [n]."

"That there was a Bible before our Bible, and that some of our present books, as certainly Genesis and Joshua, and perhaps Job, Jonah, Daniel, are expanded from simpler elements, might be proved [o]."

[i] p. 252.   [k] pp. 221, 129.   [l] p. 97.
[m] p. 59.   [n] p. 60.   [o] p. 62.

PREFACE. xiii

"The famous Shiloh in Genesis xlix. 10 is (to be) taken in its local sense as the sanctuary where young Samuel was trained [p]."

The book of Isaiah is composed of elements of different eras. No one is to be listened to who pretends that the maiden's child in Isaiah vii. 16 was not to be born in the reign of Ahaz as a sign against the kings Pekah and Rezin. If any single person is to be selected as the person to whom the 52nd and 53rd chapters of Isaiah refer, the arguments of Baron Bunsen prove (Dr. Williams thinks) that Jeremiah must be the man. But he prefers to believe that "collective Israel" is meant in them [q].

The book of Zechariah is of three dates.

The prophecy of Micah (understood by the Jewish Scribes of the birthplace of the Messiah, St. Matt. ii. 6) signifies that the deliverer to come from Bethlehem was to be a contemporary shield against the Assyrian.

"It provokes a smile on serious topics," with Dr. Williams, "to observe the zeal with which our critic (Baron Bunsen) vindicates the personality of Jonah, and the originality of his hymn [r]."

Two things, in the case of Daniel, are clear beyond fair doubt, that the period of the seventy weeks ended in the reign of Antiochus Epiphanes, and that those portions of the book which are supposed to be specially

[p] p. 62.   [q] pp. 68, 73.   [r] p. 77.

predictive, are a history of past occurrences up to that reign.

"When so vast an induction on the destructive side has been gone through, it avails little that some passages" (of the Prophets) "may be doubtful, one perhaps in Zechariah, and one in Isaiah capable of being made directly Messianic, and a chapter possibly in Deuteronomy, foreshadowing the final fall of Jerusalem. Even these few cases, the remnant of so much confident rhetoric, tend to melt, if they are not already melted, in the crucible of searching enquiry [s]."

Yet Baron Bunsen is far from satisfying Dr. Williams in his views of prophecy. "Why" (after excluding from prophecy everything that is divine and supernatural) "he should add to his moral and metaphysical basis of prophecy a notion of foresight by vision of particulars, or a kind of *clairvoyance*, though he admits it to be a natural gift, consistent with fallibility, is not so easy to explain. One would wish he might have intended only the power of seeing the ideal in the actual, or of tracing the divine government in the movements of men [t]."

Mr. Wilson, too, feels much comfort in the fact that the Holy Scriptures are not in the sixth Article called "the Word of God," "a phrase which begs many a question when applied to the Canonical Books of the Old and New Testament;" so that "under the

[s] pp. 68, 70. [t] p. 77.

terms of the sixth Article one may accept literally or allegorically, or as parable, or poetry, or legend, the story of a serpent-tempter, of an ass speaking with man's voice, of an arresting of the earth's motion, of a reversal of its motion, of waters standing in a solid heap, of witches, and a variety of apparitions. So under the terms of the sixth Article, every one is free in judgment as to the primeval institution of the Sabbath, the universality of the deluge, the confusion of tongues, the corporeal taking up of Elijah into heaven, the nature of angels, the reality of demoniacal possession, the personality of Satan, and the miraculous particulars of many events [u]."

Mr. Jowett believes that the prophecies (Jer. xxxvi. 30; Isa. xxiii.; Amos vii. 10—17) have failed of their accomplishment. He also complains that "the mention of a name" (the name of Cyrus in Isa. xlv. 1) "later than the supposed age of the prophet is not allowed, as in other writings, to be taken in evidence of the date [v]."

As to the New Testament, Mr. Wilson speaks of "the difficulty, if not impossibility, of reconciling the genealogies of St. Matthew and St. Luke, on the chronology of the holy week, or the accounts of the resurrection;" and "of the uncertainty in which the New Testament writings leave us as to the descent of Jesus Christ according to the flesh, whether by His mother

[u] p. 177.   [v] p. 343.

He were of the tribe of Judah, or of the tribe of Levi [w]." He also tells us that "the ideologian is evidently in possession of a principle which will enable him to stand in charitable relation to persons of very different opinions from his own, and of very different opinions mutually. For relations which may repose on doubtful grounds as matter of history, and, as history, be incapable of being ascertained or verified, may yet be equally suggestive of true ideas with facts absolutely certain. The spiritual significance is the same of the Transfiguration, of opening blind eyes, of causing the tongue of the stammerer to speak plainly, of feeding multitudes with bread in the wilderness, of cleansing leprosy, whatever links may be deficient in the traditional record of particular events." Accordingly, "it need not trouble us, if in consistency we should have to suppose both an ideal origin, and to apply an ideal meaning to the birth in the city of David, and to other circumstances of the infancy. So, also, the incarnification of the divine Immanuel remains, although the angelic appearances which herald it in the narratives of the evangelists may be of ideal origin according to the conceptions of former days [x]."

Does my memory deceive me in thinking that this gentleman is the same H. B. Wilson, Fellow and Tutor of St. John's College, Oxford, who was one of the four tutors who signed the famous protest against the "non-

[w] p. 180.   [x] pp. 202, 203.

PREFACE.   xvii

natural" interpretations of the Articles suggested in Tract 90?

"The Gospel of St. John cannot by external evidence be attached to the person of St. John as the author [y]."

"The verse, 'And no man hath ascended up into heaven, but He that came down,' is intelligible as a free comment near the end of the first century, but has no meaning in our Lord's mouth at a time when the Ascension had not been heard of [z]."

The Epistle to the Hebrews, so different in its conception of faith and in its Alexandrine rhythm from the doctrine and language of St. Paul's known Epistles, has its degree of discrepance explained by ascribing it to some companion of the Apostle, probably Apollos, though in Dr. Williams's own judgment it is probably post-apostolic [a]. The interpretation of the types of the Mosaic Law, as contained in that Epistle, is treated with scorn by several of the Essayists [b].

"The second of the Petrine Epistles, having alike external and internal evidence against its genineness, is necessarily surrendered as a whole [c]."

Miracles, i. e. infringements of the universal laws of nature for purposes of evidence or the like, are, in the strong and repeated language of the late Professor Powell, wholly inconceivable to a scientific mind [d].

[y] p. 161.   [z] p. 84.   [a] Ibid.
[b] pp. 419, &c.   [c] p. 84.   [d] pp. 109, 110, &c.

b

As to doctrine, I find the following words in the essay of Mr. Wilson, (the protester against non-natural interpretations of the Articles) :—" Forms of expression partly derived from modern modes of thought on metaphysical subjects, partly suggested by a better acquaintance than heretofore with the unsettled state of Christian opinion in the immediately post-apostolic age, may be adopted with respect to the doctrines enunciated in the first five Articles, without directly contradicting, impugning, or refusing assent to them, but passing by the side of them,—as with respect to the humanifying of the divine Word, and to the divine Personalities [e]." Mr. Jowett, too, on the subject of the Personality of the Holy Spirit, tells us that "the words in St. John xiv. 26, xvi. 15, are mysterious, and seem to come out of the depths of a divine consciousness; they have sometimes, however, received a more exact meaning than they would truly bear: what is spoken in a figure is construed with the severity of a logical statement, while passages of an opposite tenour are overlooked or set aside [f]."

Thus the details of the doctrine of the Holy Trinity disappear; and Mr. Wilson assures us, in general, that " those of the clericalty do wrong who consider the Church of Christ to be founded, as a society, on the possession of an abstractedly true and supernaturally

[e] p. 186.   [f] p. 360.

communicated speculation concerning God, rather than upon the manifestation of a divine life in man [g]."

Thus speaks the same writer on the subject of a future life and eternal punishment:—"We must entertain a hope that there shall be found, after the great adjudication, receptacles suitable for those who shall be infants, not as to years of terrestrial life, but as to spiritual developments,—nurseries, as it were, and seed-grounds, where the undeveloped may grow up under new conditions, the stunted may become strong, and the perverted be restored. And when the Christian Church, in all its branches, shall have fulfilled its sublunary office, and its Founder shall have surrendered His kingdom to the great Father, ALL, both small and great, shall find a refuge in the bosom of the universal Parent, to repose, or be quickened into higher life, in the ages to come, according to His will [h]."

On original sin, and the resurrection of the flesh, I must be content with a reference [i].

Creeds and Sacraments fare no better:—"There succeeded to the fluid state of Christian opinion in the first century a gradual hardening and systematizing of conflicting views; and the opportunity of reverting to the freedom of the apostolic and immediately succeeding periods was finally lost for many ages by the sanction given by Constantine to the decisions of

[g] p. 195. [h] p. 206. [i] pp. 88—90.

Nicæa[k]." "Our own Churchmen ... should endeavour to supply to the negative theologian some positive elements in Christianity, on grounds more sure to him than the assumption of an objective 'faith once delivered to the saints,' which he cannot identify with the creed of any Church as yet known to him[l]."

"In the present day ... nothing is allowed in the Church of England but the formulæ of past thinkings, which have long lost all sense of any kind[m]." "Some expressions" of the Articles "may appear superstitious, such as those which seem to impute an occult operation to the Sacraments[n]."

On the subject of the non-Christian races, Mr. Wilson has written the following audacious words:—"As to the necessity of faith in a Saviour to those peoples, when they could never have had it, no one, upon reflection, can believe in any such thing. And when we hear fine distinctions drawn between covenanted and uncovenanted mercies, it seems to be either a distinction without a difference, or to amount to a denial of the broad and equal justice of the Supreme Being. We cannot be content to wrap this question up and leave it for a mystery, as to what shall become of those myriads upon myriads of non-Christian races. First, if our traditions tell us that they are involved in the curse and perdition of Adam, and may justly

[k] p. 166; cf. 420.
[l] p. 174.
[m] p. 297; cf. p. 41.
[n] p. 182.

PREFACE.

be punished hereafter individually for his transgression, not having been extricated from it by saving faith, we are disposed to think that our traditions cannot herein fairly declare to us the words and inferences from Scripture: but if on examination it should turn out that they have, we must say that the authors of the Scriptural books have, in these matters, represented to us their own inadequate conceptions, and not the mind of the Spirit of God; for we must conclude with the Apostle, 'Yea, let God be true, and every man a liar[o].'"

Not many very definite statements as to inspiration are to be found in the Essays, though it is abundantly clear, from the way in which they treat the holy volume, how little the Essayists believe in it. "To the question," says Mr. Jowett, "what is inspiration? the first answer" (rather a misty one though, as it seems,) "is, That idea of Scripture which we gather from the knowledge of it." Again he writes: "There is no foundation in the Gospels or Epistles for any of the higher or supernatural views of inspiration[p]." "The continuous growth of revelation which the interpreter of Scripture traces in the Old and New Testament, is a part of a larger whole," (including, it would seem, "Luther and Milton[q]," and many others,) "extending over the earth, and reaching to another world[r]." "To attribute to St. Paul or the Twelve the

[o] p. 154. [p] pp. 347, 345. [q] p. 78. [r] p. 389.

abstract notion of Christian truth which afterwards sprang up in the Christian Church, is the same sort of anachronism as to attribute to them a system of philosophy. Still greater difficulties would be introduced into the Gospels by the attempt to identify them with the Creeds. We should have to suppose that our Lord was and was not tempted; that when He prayed to His Father, He prayed also to Himself; that He knew and did not know 'of that hour' of which He, as well as the angels, were ignorant. How could He have said, 'My God, My God, why hast Thou forsaken Me?' or, 'Father, if it be possible, let this cup pass from Me?' How could He have doubted whether, 'when the Son cometh, He shall find faith upon the earth?' These simple and touching words have to be taken out of their natural meaning and connexion to be made the theme of apologetic discourses, if we insist on reconciling them with the distinctions of later ages [s]."

These may be regarded as a specimen of the difficulties of the new, or "negative theology." They are, indeed, only specimens; not only because, as I before observed, the same writers, as well as others of their school, have given utterance to many other, and very grave ones, in other publications; but even in this unhappy volume, with its guerilla warfare of essays, hundreds of points are touched, none completed. A

[s] p. 355.

general loosening of all that has been hitherto held sacred seems to be intended rather than a grave discussion of any particular difficulty. There is a wide and very random scattering of uneasiness. The writers may possibly hold some things in religion sacred affirmatively, (though it is difficult to conceive what these things, in respect of four at least of the seven, may be); but in the present case they seem to have met, like the triumvirs of old, and drawn up a list of proscriptions. Each, for the sake of destroying his own enemies, has left his friends to the mercy of his colleagues. If such proscription ever led in history to a peaceful harmony and secure tranquillity among the survivors, then may it be expected that this jointstock of negatives may leave behind it an affirmative Christianity in which two men may agree.

The writers claim consideration, tenderness, respect. Is this a well-founded claim? If the forty-two per cent. who stayed away from church on a particular Sunday in 1851 are distressed in their intellectual depths by all these "difficulties," (which, however, is surely an absurd supposition,) is it quite fair to scatter these wild firebrands of infidelity among the fifty-eight per cent., who, with much greater reason, may be counted as contented with the Christianity of their fathers? May not they more reasonably claim consideration and respect? Is it reasonable to demand the respect of believers, very many of them unable from want of leisure and learning to examine such deep questions for themselves, for men who, not in the way of serious and complete discussion of single points, but in the assumption of superior intellect, knowledge, and love of truth, throw random discredit upon every point of that holy faith wherein they have their peace in life, and their hope in death? I desire to speak with all caution and self-restraint, but may I not reasonably ask this question? Suppose, for a moment, that the Holy Scriptures *are* [t] the Word of the Spirit of God, —that the miracles [u], including the resurrection of Christ, are actual objective facts, which have really happened,—that the doctrines of the Church are true [x], and the Creeds [y] the authoritative expositions of them,—and that men are to reach salvation through faith in Christ Virgin-born, according to the Scriptures, and making atonement [z] for their sins upon the cross. On this supposition, is not the publication of this book an act of real hostility to God's truth, and one which endangers the faith and salvation of men? and is this hostility less real, or the danger diminished, because the writers are, all but one, clergymen, some of them tutors and schoolmasters; because they wear the dress, and use the language of friends, and threaten us with bitter opposition if we do not regard them as such?

[t] p. 177. [u] cf. p. 109. [x] p. 195.
[y] p. 355. [z] cf. p. 87.

It is quite possible,—it is more than possible, I believe it to be the actual state of the case,—that the writers themselves, or, at least, some of them, are eagerly desirous of an affirmative standing-place of faith. They, it is very probable, feel the pressure of infidel argument so strongly as to be unable to retain any Christian faith at all, except such shadowy residue as this "negative theology" might leave unassailed. They may, in their intellectual search for truth, have lost various powers of attaining truth which intellects such as they deem feebler may retain. But the movement itself is one of hostility, and the manner of it is one of insidious hostility; and the movement and the manner of it seem to me to be no more defensible than the scattering of poison in the wells of a city would be defensible, and the defending of such an act on the ground of personal taste, or peculiarity of constitution, or the search after chemical truth. And therefore I am struck almost more with what seems to me the hardheartedness and exceeding unkindness of this book, than with its unsoundness. Have the writers considered how far the suggesting of innumerable doubts,—doubts unargued and unproved,—will check honest devotion, and embolden timid sin? For whom do they intend this book? Is it written for the mass of general readers? Is it designed for students at the Universities? Do they suppose that this multitude of random suggestions will be carefully wrought out by these readers, and be rejected if unsound, so as to leave their faith and devotion untarnished; or that they will be lightly taken up by light and conceited brains, to the ruin of all humility and simplicity of faith, and the encouragement of all kinds of sin? Have they reflected how many souls for whom Christ died may be slain in their weakness, by their self-styled strength? Yet let me not be mistaken. Unmerciful as I think this book, I do not plead for mercy. Those who have the means of knowing must not be content with a religion on sufferance. The difficulties must be solved, and the objections must be met, when they are produced in a serious and argumentative form. When so offered they will not lack their answer. What I am now principally objecting to in this unhappy book is the random, and, as I think it, cruel way in which these things are thrown out in it, unargued and unproved, to the certain injury of the faith of many.

We are often told that the book has not been answered; and a general demand for an answer rather than a condemnation, or loud expression of disapprobation, is heard on all sides. I venture to think, in opposition, I am sorry to say, to many of my friends, that an answer, in any such form as should be complete, crushing, and co-extensive with the attack, is not to be expected, at least in the readable size and effective shape which would carry it home to the minds which have been, and are likely to be, injured by the Essays themselves. The great number of the points of the faith assailed or glanced at, the wide scattering of doubt, the underlying assumptions which shew themselves in so many slighting words in the midst of other discussions, offer very little opportunity for coming to a fair issue on any definite field. You might as well attempt to do battle against a swarm of gnats, as to meet this sort of guerilla warfare in direct and solemn encounter. Add to which, that real answers must, if they are to be of any weight, be long, learned, and, compared with the smartness of an essay-attack, somewhat ponderous. Dr. Williams, for instance, may in less than fifty pages tell us how *another person* has proved that almost everything which we believe of the Old Testament and its contents is unfounded and mistaken. How many pages will it take to go fully into the proof of all the various things which Baron Bunsen has mischievously taught, together with all the still more mischievous comments of his reporter? I might add other considerations, which are many, bearing in the same direction, but it is not needful. I only trust that no evil will result from the well-meant efforts now making on various sides to give the whole book a final and crushing answer. For, before one line of such answer is put to paper, I venture to express a fear that the slightness of Dr. Temple's Essay, the historical gravity of much of Mr. Pattison's, the real difficulty of subject which pervades Mr. Goodwin's, the amiable spirit and commixture of truth which are to be found in the midst of much and very dangerous error in Mr. Jowett's, will still remain when all the projected answers are written and read, and, remaining, will be thought by those who are already struck and pleased with them, to remain as masters of the field.

Indeed, I believe that the true method of replying to such objections as these is not to waive the vantage-ground of assured belief in the great Christian verities, nor to consent to regard each "difficulty," with all its train of consequences running up into total unbelief, as an open question to be argued without reference to those consequences, but rather, holding fast the great affirmative certainties of Christian religion, to regard from thence these which then appear comparatively insignificant questions. It makes a wonderful difference in the apparent magnitude and importance of a difficulty, whether it be regarded as the possible entrance to an entire unbelief, or an acknowledged perplexity on the fringe or edge of a strong and impregnable faith. We should therefore, in my humble judgment, do more wisely to take our stand on our well-established faith, and while we repel and reply to any definite attacks, or defend any distinct points on which that faith has been assailed, (and there are many such in this book capable of most

PREFACE.

distinct and crushing reply,) to decline meeting so vague, and loose, and multifarious a scattering of objections as is here brought together, *en champ clos*, and going down into the field for a great pitched battle, on an issue so indeterminate, and so little likely to be satisfactory.

My object in these few pages is of a different kind. I wish rather, noticing some of the views which seem to underlie the particular arguments and statements of these writers, to suggest a few thoughts on the other hand, affirmatively, for the support, if it may be, in the faith of such as are in danger of being shaken by these speculations. To me by far the most melancholy thought connected with this unhappy book, and that which moves my indignation most, is the thought of the effect it is likely to have upon young and unstable minds. As an attack upon Christianity itself, the Christianity of the Church of eighteen centuries, I regard it as wholly innocuous. But as a means of shaking the faith, the personal faith of such as are imperfectly grounded in Christian truth, I fear that it will be, and has proved to be, very dangerous. Faith is a very delicate thing, and on Christian faith depends Christian living. If you shake young people's faith to pieces, and offer them nothing else to put into its place, if you teach them to set at nought all that they have heard and read from the beginning of the Bible to the end, altering, distorting, depreciating, denying every single point on which the faith of the millions who have fallen asleep in Jesus has happily rested, and built up such a life as they have had grace to lead of self-mastering goodness, what is likely to be the consequence upon their habits of holiness, and of the love and obedience of God? Will these last on, endangered as they are by temptations of every kind, when you have shaken down the pillar of faith on which they have been built up, and learned to rest? Do not even older people, and those whose faith may be more firmly established, feel, after reading a few pages of such a book as this, as if they needed a lustration, some ceremonial purgation as it were, to clear their faith and comfort from the poisonous haze which begins to gather over them, and bring them meekly back to their insulted Lord? The Christianity of eighteen centuries needs no defence against these things, but the faith of our young and unstable people, the faith of those whom Christ tenderly calls His "little ones," is a matter of great and pressing consequence, and a fearful woe is denounced against those who would offend them in respect of it.

In the first place, then, I observe throughout the Essays an uniform and continual consent to eliminate from religion everything that is *supernatural*, whether in miracle, in prophecy, in inspiration, in narrative, or in doctrine.

The leader in the attack upon supernaturalness is

undoubtedly the late Professor Powell, who holds that the omnipotence of God is "entirely an inference *from the language of the Bible*, adopted on *the assumption* of a belief in revelation [a]," and that "creation"—not meaning to limit that term, so far as I can understand his words, to *continual* creation, but including original creation as well,—is an exploded idea among men of science [b]. He also tells us that Mr. Darwin's [c] masterly volume on the origin of species must "soon bring about an entire revolution of opinion in favour of the

[a] p. 113.   [b] pp. 129, 134, 139.

[c] The acceptance of the *extreme theory* of Mr. Darwin by a large part of the scientific world appears to me to be a phenomenon deserving of very particular remark. That the patient and extensive observation of facts by so accomplished a naturalist should be received with the utmost attention and respect is most just; that an individual philosopher should construct an extravagant theory upon a very imperfect basis is nothing very wonderful or unprecedented; but that scientific men in general should be ready to accept that theory at once, and believe that not only all plants and animals, but that man also, with his mind and conscience, with his gift of government and sense of immortality, are all derived by natural selection from a common parentage, — to accept that theory in spite of the experience of at least some thousands of years of history, in defiance of the pretty well established law of hybrid infertility, on the ground of imagined millions of years during which the requisite changes *may* have taken place, even though there be a contemporary record in the earth's crust, which cannot be so properly said to omit the confirmation, as absolutely to contradict the conclusions of the theory, seems to me to be unaccountable, except as shewing an eager avidity to seize upon anything or everything, under the sanction of a great name, which assails the authority of Holy Scripture.

grand principle of the self-evolving powers of nature."
"Every truly inductive enquirer has the grand truth of the universal order and constancy of natural causes so strongly entertained and fixed in his mind, that he cannot even conceive the possibility of its failure [d]." Miracles are consequently, to a scientific enquirer, "simply incredible, unless"—strange! that so universal a proposition should admit of an "unless"— "as connected with a religious doctrine, regarded in a sacred light, asserted on the authority of inspiration. In this case, it" i.e.—the miraculous narrative —"ceases to be capable of investigation by reason, or to own its dominion: it is accepted on religious grounds, and can appeal only to the principle and influence of faith. Thus miraculous narratives become invested with the character of articles of faith, if they be accepted in a less positive and certain light, as requiring some suspension of judgment as to their nature and circumstances, or perhaps as involving more or less of the parabolic or mythic character, or at any rate as received in connexion with and for the sake of the doctrine inculcated [e];"— which last sentence seems, if I understand it, to say, that a scientific man (to whom all miraculous infringements of the order of nature are simply inconceivable) may nevertheless accept a miraculous narrative in any of three ways: 1st,

[d] p. 109.   [e] p. 142.

as incorrectly recorded; 2ndly, as parabolic or mythic; 3rdly, "*for the sake of the doctrine inculcated;*" the logic and common sense of which third alternative is altogether beyond my comprehension.

But I have no need to dwell upon Professor Powell's Essay. The denial of the Divine Omnipotence and of the idea of creation is not dangerous.

Miracles gone, prophecy and inspiration, ("in any higher or supernatural sense," in any sense beyond such as was possessed by "Luther or Milton,") and, by consequence, the divine character of the Old Testament, naturally go too, and in the hands of Messrs. Williams, Wilson, and Jowett they almost totally disappear.

Almost totally; for, in respect to prophecy, Dr. Williams tells us that there is "one perhaps in Zechariah, and one in Isaiah, capable of being made directly Messianic, and a chapter possibly in Deuteronomy foreshadowing the final fall of Jerusalem [f]."

Not being informed which passages of Isaiah and Zechariah are intended, I may be allowed to make a few observations on the single definite prophecy thus graciously left to us by Dr. Williams, the prophecy contained in the 28th chapter of Deuteronomy; for I will venture to assert with confidence that that prophecy alone is sufficient to supply at least the foundation of an answer to the criticism which thus

[f] p. 70.

audaciously denies the supernatural inspiration of the Old Testament.

Nearly 1,500 years before Christ this prophecy was spoken. It declared the promises of God to the children of Israel in the case of their obedience, and His judgments if they should prove finally disobedient. It was spoken when the people still wandered in the wilderness, homeless and landless, and before yet even the sight of their promised inheritance was allowed to Moses. "The Lord shall bring a nation against thee from far, from the end of the earth, as the eagle flieth [g], a nation whose tongue thou shalt not understand; a nation of fierce countenance, which shall not regard the person of the old, nor shew favour to the young." Had Moses mentioned the Romans *by name*, this would have proved, according to Mr. Jowett's view of prophecy, that the words were spoken after the event,—but can *description* of a nation be more precise or unmistakeable than the description here given by Moses of the Romans, some seven centuries before Romulus? Are they not, as it were, *photographed*, though not named, in these words? "And he shall besiege thee in all thy gates, until thy high and fenced walls come down, wherein thou trustedst, throughout all thy land: and he shall besiege thee in all thy gates throughout all thy land, which the Lord thy God hath given thee. And thou shalt eat

[g] ὡσεὶ ὅρμημα ἀετοῦ.—LXX.

the fruit of thine own body, the flesh of thy sons and of thy daughters, which the Lord thy God hath given thee, in the siege, and in the straitness, wherewith thine enemies shall distress thee. . . . The tender and delicate woman among you, which would not adventure to set the sole of her foot upon the ground for delicateness and tenderness, her eye shall be evil toward the husband of her bosom, and toward her son, and toward her daughter, and toward her young one that cometh out from between her feet, and toward her children which she shall bear: for she shall eat them for want of all things secretly in the siege and straitness wherewith thine enemy shall distress thee in thy gates."

Need I refer to the horrid tale of " Mary the daughter of Eleazar" told by Josephus, which makes the siege of Jerusalem by Titus,—Jerusalem which did not belong to the children of Israel for some 500 years after this prophecy was uttered,—conspicuous for "tribulation such as was not since the beginning of the world to this time, no, nor ever shall be," among all nations?

Is this a case of *clairvoyance not supernatural*, according to Baron Bunsen, or of " *seeing the ideal in the actual*," according to his improver, Dr. Williams?

We shall probably be told that siege of cities and famine even to so dreadful an extent are not so strange or unusual incidents in the history of a nation as to require us to suppose supernatural prescience in the lawgiver, even though the words were spoken long before the children of Israel possessed either land or city. And we shall be reminded that precisely the same horrible fact is recorded in the siege of Samaria by Benhadad [h], and again in that of Jerusalem by Nebuchadnezzar [i]; and that it is referred to by Baruch as expressly fulfilling the prediction of Moses in Deut. xxviii. Most true. The specially predicted judgment of God did come in part upon either portion of the nation before the final fulfilment, but it came in part only. The ten tribes, so distressed in Benhadad's reign, and subsequently led captive by the Assyrians, without, so far as we read in Scripture, the repetition of this precise incident of suffering in the siege, were so lost among the nations, that to this day it is impossible to recognise with certainty either the country to which they were carried, or the nations which are descended from their blood. The two tribes visited by God with this terrible affliction in Nebuchadnezzar's reign,—so that Baruch might well dwell upon it as fulfilling that portion of the prophecy of Moses,—were yet allowed a further trial and another hope; and there can, I suppose, be no doubt that had they repented after their return from the seventy years' captivity, and had they accepted and submitted to the

[h] 2 Kings vi. 28.
[i] Lam. iv. 10; ii. 20; Jer. xix. 9; Baruch ii. 2—5.

divine mission of the Messiah, the remaining part of the judgment denounced by Moses would never have fallen upon them. But when they "filled up the measure of their fathers" by slaying the Son of God, and thus brought upon their heads the full severity of the woe long since predicted, how can any man deny the supernatural knowledge of the prophet who had declared it with so wonderful particularity above a thousand years before? I do not now urge the photographic description of the conquerors, nor the language of the historian who plainly believed that the characteristic horror of Titus's siege was unprecedented in the sufferings of other times and people [k], but I confidently ask whether the wonderful sequel of this prophecy does not absolutely fix its meaning to the final destruction of the city, and prove beyond a doubt, to all who are not wedded to scepticism, the supernatural prescience of the prophet:—"And the Lord shall scatter thee among all people, from the one end of the earth, even unto the other; and there thou shalt serve other gods, which neither thou nor thy fathers have known, even wood and stone. And among these nations shalt thou find no ease, neither shall the soul of thy foot have rest: but the Lord

---

[k] τί δεῖ τὴν ἐπ' ἀψύχοις ἀναίδειαν τοῦ λιμοῦ λέγειν; εἶμι γὰρ αὐτοῦ δηλώσων ἔργον, οἷον μήτε παρ' Ἕλλησι, μήτε παρὰ Βαρβάροις ἱστόρηται, φρικτὸν μὲν εἰπεῖν, ἄπιστον δὲ ἀκοῦσαι· καὶ ἐγὼ δὲ μὴ δόξαιμι τερατεύεσθαι τοῖς αὖθις ἀνθρώποις, κἂν παρέλιπον τὴν συμφορὰν ἡδέως, εἰ μὴ τῶν κατ' ἐμαυτὸν εἶχον ἀπείρους μάρτυρας.—*Joseph. de Bello Jud.* vi. 111.

shall give thee there a trembling heart, and failing of eyes, and sorrow of mind: and thy life shall hang in doubt before thee; and thou shalt fear day and night, and shalt have none assurance of thy life. In the morning thou shalt say, Would God it were even! and at even thou shalt say, Would God it were morning! for the fear of thine heart wherewith thou shalt fear, and for the sight of thine eyes which thou shalt see."

There is no vagueness here. The judgment denounced against the nation after the destruction of its city, is one most signal, definite, and unexampled. "Slay them not, lest my people forget it, but scatter them abroad, O Lord our defence!"

The Jewish nation has now been scattered for near 1,800 years. They have had neither land nor city, neither temple nor daily sacrifice in all that time. They ceased to be a nation near 500 years before any of the existing nations of Europe began to be; above 700 years before England was united as a single nation under one ruler. They have suffered precisely such unspeakable distresses in their scattered state as their lawgiver above 3,000 years before denounced in such striking and wonderful terms. Yet they are found, and have been found, in every land; present, yet never blending; suffering, pillaged, yet ever rising again to wealth and affluence,—better known, at this moment, to all men by feature, by character, than the natives of any other country upon earth.

Is this a case of *natural clairvoyance,* or the *sight of the ideal in the actual?* Perish the miserable, self-styled philosophy which would dare to call it so! No! It is the finger of God making good in history and life the Word of God. Many miracles may be of temporary evidential force, many prophecies may be of doubtful interpretation,—but every city of Europe with its "Jews' quarter," its "Old Jewry," and the like, every Jewish face with its unmistaken features, every fact in ordinary life which testifies to the continued existence of "the Jews" among us, as in the midst of us, yet distinguished from us, not by dress, not by colour, not by rank, not by habits, but by the unextinguishable nationality of God's scattered wanderers, is a continued witness, addressed to the mind of every single man among us, of the truth of God, of the divine inspiration of His servant Moses, and, *pro tanto,* of the supernatural character of Holy Scripture.

This is a specimen of the argument *à priori* for the supernatural inspiration of the Old Testament, and it is obvious that it is only one out of a very large number of similar cases which might be, and often have been, adduced out of the Old Testament in proof of the same thing.

But the argument *à priori* is only half, or not half, of that on which we ground our belief of the writings of the Old Testament being divinely inspired.

The Jewish Church, which was entrusted with the oracles of God, and in which there was a series of divinely inspired prophets, held not only that the writers of these books were men inspired by the Holy Spirit of God, but that the books also were the faithful and true expositions of the Divine mind in them.

The providential history of the Jewish nation also combines itself throughout with the sacred books, and furnishes a continual witness to them; so that, whatever there is of wonderful and out of the ordinary course of nature in the maintenance of the worship of the true God, and of exalted morality in one only nation in a remote corner of the earth, in their escape from Egypt, their wandering in the wilderness, their return from captivity, their hard-hearted, but predicted, rejection of Christ, and the subsequent fall of their nation and dispersion of their people, re-acts in the way of argument upon the books, and confirms their claim to a divine original.

These confirmations are great; and they sufficed during all the ages of the continuance of the Jewish Church and nation to establish in the minds of all that people the divine authority of the books of the Old Testament. If the fact of superhuman prescience, or any other grounds with which the generation was acquainted, proved that in this or that prophet there resided the gift of divine assistance, or inspiration, in the fact that the Jewish Church did in all its history receive the books as inspired, there was the sufficient proof that not the men only were so gifted, but that these particular writings also were to be acknowledged as the genuine and true expressions of the mind of the Holy Spirit within them.

But to these grounds of confirmation *à posteriori* of the sacred writings of the Old Testament, we Christians have to add another, which appears to be absolutely final and not to be gainsaid, at least by such as acknowledge the Divine authority of the Lord Himself. I mean the sanction which He has given by His own words, not to one nor two only of the writings of the Old Testament, but to the whole volume in general, and to many books of it in particular. Indeed, it seems to me to be a remarkable thing, and one of the many indications of the loving providence of God with which Holy Scripture[1] abounds, that the Lord did give so singularly complete and at the same time minute confirmation to the books, and to the contents of the books of the Old Testament. Not only did He in terms speak of Daniel, Jonah, and

[1] As like specimens of this loving providence, I should wish to refer to St. Luke xi. 28, viii. 21, in connexion with the late-appearing *cultus* of the Blessed Virgin; St. Matt. xxvi. 29, ("this fruit of the Vine,") in connexion with the doctrine of Transubstantiation; and St. Matt. xxvi. 27, ("Drink ye all of it,") in connexion with the withholding of the Cup from the laity. Yet these very sayings would be in danger of being adduced, on the critical principles of pp. 60, 343, in proof that the ancient record is interpolated with passages referring to comparatively modern controversies!

Isaiah as prophets, and quote from them predictions as divine words necessary to be fulfilled, (and let it be observed that these are precisely three of the prophets whose authority the criticism of our Essayists assails,) but in speaking of David, He distinctly attributed to him the divine inspiration of the Holy Ghost. For when He asks the Pharisees, "How then doth David in spirit call Christ Lord [m]?" and both by this expression, and by the form of the interrogatory, plainly shews that David's appellation is one that is not to be gainsaid, it cannot be denied that the Lord attributes "supernatural" illumination to David in the 110th Psalm. Moreover, the report of the same saying in St. Mark leaves no room for cavil as to the meaning of the words "in spirit:"—"For David himself said by the Holy Ghost [n]." Then, if it be doubted how far such reference to particular books is to be understood to guarantee them to the full extent of these words, that is, beyond their general truth, or the divineness of the precise passages to which the Lord makes actual and literal reference, I ask, what conclusion is to be drawn from His words as recorded in St. John x. 34,—"Is it not written in your law, I said, ye are gods? If He called them gods unto whom the word of God came, and the Scripture (οὐ δύναται λυθῆναι) cannot be broken, diluted, done away with,"—does He not attribute not

[m] St. Matt. xxii. 43.   [n] St. Mark xii. 36; cf. 2 Sam. xxiii. 2.

only to the 82nd Psalm, but to "the Scripture" also, a sacredness and stedfastness, and that verbal rather than ideal or general, and belonging to the writings as well as to the writers, which is only intelligible on the supposition of that Psalm and "the Scripture" being written with supernatural light? Add, then, to these more particular considerations the fact that He did more than once speak of the whole of the ancient Scriptures in terms which notoriously cover the entire body of the Old Testament as it was received by the Jews of His age,—"O fools, and slow of heart to believe all that the prophets have spoken, ought not Christ to have suffered these things, and to enter into His glory? and beginning at Moses, and all the Prophets," (observe that He makes no exception of Jonah, Daniel, Zechariah, or "the later Isaiah,") "He expounded to them in all the Scriptures the things concerning Himself," and again, "All things must be fulfilled which are written in the law of Moses, and in the Prophets, and in the Psalms concerning Me,"—and what remains to be desired as to the witness which the Lord gives *à posteriori* to the Old Testament? Does He not set His seal, absolutely, upon the whole volume? Can any man accept His testimony as divine, and reject any part of that Book? I confess that I do not see how the force of this argument can be evaded by any person who believes the Lord Himself to be divine, and His words the words of truth.

Now let me ask, what is to be alleged against all this, and what is the nature and what the weight of that criticism which, setting all this at nought, claims to re-adjust the history of these books, to deny their authenticity, to disallow the divine prescience exhibited in them, and dealing with them *de haut en bas,* to undervalue their authority, and disown their claim to be considered holy and true.

Who will tell us? Where are the principles of the new science to be seen? Are they established? Have they been fully discussed and allowed? What are they?

In the case of the science of geology we *are* so informed. We know the basis, the nature, and the extent of the difficulty which exists in the reconcilement of the discoveries of geology with the narrative of the creation in the Book of Genesis: and while we esteem it highly unphilosophical, in the present state of the science, to assume its conclusions as so certain as to warrant us in withdrawing one jot or tittle from the authority of the Book of Genesis, and while we look upon the various suggestions made (as by Chalmers, Hugh Miller, and others) for the purpose of shewing, as the science of geology advances further and further, that the two records are not inconsistent with each other, as useful and good in their time, without binding ourselves to accept their theories as offering that which will be found at last to be the real solution of the difficulty,—we neither wish to check the onward progress of the science, nor complain if any person seriously endeavours to examine the subject of the two records, or of either separately, even though his conclusions may not be the same as we ourselves should draw.

But in the so-called science of criticism the case is different. Any person seems to be at liberty to throw out whatever disparaging remarks he thinks proper against ancient writings, sacred or profane, and, calling it "criticism," to turn round upon the supporters of that which he assails, as blind and prejudiced persons, who desire to stop the progress of human knowledge.

No person can doubt that good and sound criticism is of most real and precious value. But, on the other hand, none can doubt that the world owes so very much, in all sorts of ways, to the treasures which it inherits from old times in ancient books and records, that it is matter of the deepest importance that we should not yield them up, even the secular ones, without knowing why, or on what precise and irresistible grounds they are to be surrendered. But what I complain of now is, that without any scientific enunciation, or establishment of such principles, we are called upon, on the mere guesses of modern speculators, to abandon conclusions respecting the sacred books which we believe to be of the most inestimable preciousness, and to be fully established by their own legitimate proofs.

In the case of the Old Testament, however, the argument in favour of its inspiration, as I have sketched it above, appears to me irresistible to a Christian; and though I am far from intending to disallow all introduction of criticism into the interpretation and general understanding of the Old Testament, yet it seems to me not only that a Christian must so use it as to keep it in subordination to the Lord's own judgment of the character of the Old Testament writings, but also that we have a right to require some complete and scientific statement of the principles and procedure of that criticism which undertakes so great and momentous a task.

It will be observed that in thus tracing the argument for the inspiration of the Old Testament, I have distinguished between what I have called the *à priori* grounds of argument, and those which are *à posteriori;* and it seems to me to be highly important that this distinction should be carefully kept in mind.

A priori, there are many conceivable reasons for supposing a person to be endued with supernatural inspiration. The power of working miracles, the knowledge to foretell future events with prescience exceeding human foresight and skill in guessing, these, joined with various other grounds, such as of character, position, training, holiness, and the like, and the claim of divine help, may reasonably lead a generation to believe that in this or that man there resides a gift of the Holy Spirit of God, enabling him to speak with a power not his own. And it is plain that such supernatural inspiration may exist in different men in every variety of degree, from that of Caiaphas, the man officially inspired to utter words above his own meaning or intention, or of Balaam, the man of a single message, but a rebel and traitor in heart, to that of Elijah, the holy man of God, empowered to act, to work, to denounce and to foretell, but not to write books, and of Isaiah, the man whose lips were touched with the live coal from the altar of God, and whose book is full of the very truth of the Gospel of Christ. It is also plain, as I think, that however strong such *à priori* grounds may be in any case, yet, if they be alone, it can never be possible to pronounce that the speakers or writers are absolutely incapable of intermingling anything of their own, and therefore fallible matter, with that which is divine. We can neither say with certainty how the divine help blends with their own thoughts and powers, when it does exalt and enlighten them, nor how much of their own thoughts and powers is left unexalted and unenlightened. We may argue, and with great justice, that it is not likely that God would leave us in danger of being misled or deceived by the natural effect of His own gift, but we never can be absolutely certain that the gift, however completely proved and undenied, excludes the possibility of all commixture of human error in the words spoken or the books written. However, when, in the case of the books of the Old Testament, we add to all these *à priori* grounds the proof *à posteriori*, 1. the acceptance by the Jewish Church, 2. the confirmation imparted by the providential history, 3. the seal set upon the whole of the books by the Lord Himself and His apostles, the argument seems to be complete. The remaining possibilities of error are excluded as a matter of fact, and *the books* are seen to be as fully deserving of acceptance as the very Word of God, as *the writers* were already acknowledged to be men endued with divine inspiration.

Now let it be observed that (except in the single article of the fulfilment of prophecies) the *à priori* grounds of believing any person to be inspired, do, in the natural course of things, gradually disappear by lapse of time. Late generations are not, and cannot be, in possession of all, or most of the *à priori* grounds which once existed for believing the inspiration of many ancient writers,—say Job, Ezra, Moses,—or of many ancient books. Such proofs naturally die out with the ages to which they more immediately belong. But in the same proportion do the *à posteriori* proofs grow and strengthen. The acceptance of a hundred generations, and the growing authority arising from it, the institutions based upon such ancient writings, and the history into which they have entwined themselves indissolubly for many centuries,—all constitute a perpetually increasing and strengthening proof, which by degrees becomes the chief, and might conceivably become at last wellnigh the only one. How unreasonable, then, is that 'criticism' which in a late age ignores the whole mass of the *à posteriori* arguments altogether, and claiming to throw itself upon the *à priori* proofs with the searching cross-examination with which it would deal with contemporary writings, pronounces confidently against claims respecting which many of the *à priori* grounds have necessarily long since perished!

Now I would urge any candid person to consider very carefully what a great step, and, as I think, what a sure footing we have here gained towards the further argument of the inspiration of the New Testament. The whole Old Testament is but the anticipation of a divine sequel, and that sequel is furnished by the New. The whole Old Testament lays out, announces, prepares the way for something greater and diviner than itself. Either the New Testament is that diviner thing, or it has never been given. "If the ministration of death be glorious, how shall not the ministration of the Spirit be rather glorious?" The writers of the Old Testament are many and various; their writings extend over a thousand years. The Psalms, to take a single instance, nominally

David's, are yet notoriously the work of several writers: other books may probably have been put into their present shape by Ezra, or some other scribe of later days. But the New Testament, on the contrary, is the work of comparatively a very few years, of eight well-known men, (all but two, apostles,) and the others close companions and friends of the apostles. Moreover, the gift of the Holy Spirit, though He moved the old prophets to speak divine words at different times and in divers manners, was expressly given in a new, fuller, and more wonderful way to the Church of the apostles than ever it had been poured upon the Jewish Church. To this add the whole amount of the internal evidence which the New Testament offers of its own divineness,—its doctrines, its morality, its adaptation to men of all ages and circumstances and their wants, its style, so simple and so grand in its simplicity, so characteristic of its human penmen, and yet so unlike the work of men,—(witness the immeasurable gulf that separates the apostolic Epistles from the writings of the apostolic Fathers). Add, again, to all this the unimpeached holiness, the labours, the devotion even to death of these eight writers; the personal companionship of the greater part of them with the Lord Himself, and the claim which they lay to divine help and inspiration; and in these things we find the parallel, only in a vastly stronger form, to the *à priori* argument alleged above in favour of the inspiration of the writers of the Old Testament.

But strong as this argument is,—strong enough, without anything else, to establish the claim of the New Testament to the entire and submissive acceptance of all Christian people,—it is still *à priori* only. It is compatible with the fact that St. Peter and St. Barnabas were wrong at Antioch, that the apostles had recourse to conciliar action at Jerusalem on the subject of circumcising heathen converts, and that St. Paul communicated privately to them that were of reputation the Gospel which he preached among the Gentiles, lest by any means he should run, or have run in vain. It is compatible with the fact that neither the Epistle of St. Barnabas nor that of St. Clement of Rome form part of the canon, while the Gospels of St. Luke and St. Mark are admitted into it. It is conceivably compatible with error or mistake, not indeed in the main of their teaching, but in collateral and non-essential matter of fact °, or the like.

° For example, if there were supposed to be a mistake in history in the words of St. Stephen in Acts vii. 16, (though I entirely believe that those words are strictly true, and that there is no mistake at all in them,) yet I do not see that such mistake would be incompatible either with the real (*à priori*) inspiration of St. Stephen, as speaking before the Jewish Council, or with that of St. Luke, (confirmed *à posteriori* also,) as faithfully recording it. It is remarkable, however, how the 'mistakes,' as they have been sometimes called, in Holy Scripture, gradually disappear on more thorough examination and knowledge. The supposed mistake of St. Luke in attributing the

It is an argument which, strengthen it as you will, (and it is capable of almost unlimited strengthening,) can never, in its very nature, reach so far as utterly to exclude either the 'human element,' or, with it, the possibility of error.

But besides all the *à priori* reasons for thinking that apostles and apostolic men could not do otherwise than speak the very truth of God, we have *à posteriori* grounds of the greatest weight for feeling entirely assured that we may accept these particular writings as the very Word of the Holy Spirit.

The first and chiefest of these lies in the fact that the Church of God, the pillar and ground of the truth, did in the early ages, when the gifts of the Holy Spirit (and among them that of discerning spirits) were of ordinary occurrence, pronounce absolutely, though gradually, on the canonicity of the books of the New Testament; thereby adding to the personal weight and authority of the inspired men the further acceptance, by the divinely inhabited and guarded

---

holding of the census at the time of our Lord's birth to Quirinius has been satisfactorily disposed of by A. W. Zumpt, (*Commentationes Epigraphicæ*, part ii. p. 88—103,) who appears to me to have proved beyond reasonable doubt that before the appointment of Quirinius to the Proconsulate of Syria, A.D. 6, he had previously held the Proconsulate of Syria and Cilicia together, and had been in that office at the time of the Nativity. In like manner the difficulties felt about Zacharias, 'son of Barachias,' in St. Matt. xxii. 35, and in the text St. Matt. xxviii. 9, seem to disappear by the aid of the newly discovered *Codex Sinaiticus*. (Christ. Remembr., No. cxi., pp. 237, 238.)

Church, of these particular writings; which acceptance has been confirmed by the unhesitating voice of eighteen centuries, unanimous in this, however widely differing in many other things. If the arguments which I have hitherto alleged and spoken of as *à priori*, went very far towards proving that the writers of the New Testament *could not* err in what they wrote for the guidance and teaching of the Church, the scope of the present or *à posteriori* argument, is to shew that, as a matter of fact, they *did not*. To this may be added, as I observed in the case of the Old Testament, the evidence borne to the books by the providential facts of the history of the Gospel, its spreading among the nations, the amelioration [p] of faith and manners which has followed on its acceptance, and the faith of saints without number in every age; all which so blend themselves and are entwined with the belief in the divineness of the books, as to form a parallel line of divine facts, re-acting in the way of evidence on the books themselves.

And as in the case of the Jewish Church the words of the Lord Himself gave the final and most full seal and authority to the testimony in favour of the holy books of the Old Testament, so do I most faithfully believe that when His personal presence shall terminate this dispensation, as it terminated that one,

[p] Vid. the striking argument of "the Restoration of Belief," p. i.

PREFACE.

we shall find Him setting His seal in like manner to the authority of the books of the New Testament, and judging us according to the way in which we have received and obeyed them, or undervalued them and disowned their authority. For what less can we conclude from that saying of the Lord recorded in the 12th of St. John,—" He that rejecteth Me, and receiveth not My words, hath one that judgeth him: the word that I have spoken" (surely whether by His own holy lips or by the pens of His apostles) " shall judge him in the last day [q]."

I observe, further, that throughout these Essays, the nude Scripture, the merest letter of the sacred volume, is spoken of as if in it, and in it alone, resided the entire revelation of Christ, and all possible means of judging what that revelation consists of. But this is very far indeed from being the case. Every single book of the New Testament was written to persons already in possession of Christian truth,—of the nature of which we have a great deal of evidence independent of those books. It is no doubt true that, as to the events of our Lord's life and His actual words, though they were so many that if they should have been written every one, even the world itself would not have contained the books that should have been written, and though the first generation of Christians must needs have been in possession of a great

[q] St. John xii. 48.

number of them, none now remain but those which are recorded in the Gospels, except a word or two in the later Scriptures. But with respect to the Christian institution of the Church, and its doctrines as held from the beginning and traditionally known, it is quite erroneous, historically and notoriously erroneous, to suppose either that literally they were founded upon the written words of Holy Scripture, or that they can impart no illustration nor help in the interpretation of those written words. It might seem almost childish to urge that the three thousand who were baptized on the day of Pentecost, the five thousand of a later chapter of the Acts, the multitudes both of men and women, the people of Antioch, the proselytes and heathens of Ephesus, Thessalonica, Corinth, received the saving truth in its saving fulness without either Gospel or Epistle,—that the apostles set up bishops in separate cities and countries, such as Jerusalem, Ephesus, Crete, — that some of them, as St. John, lived on long, and left behind them, not writings only which have their place in the sacred canon, but pupils also who themselves were writers, and were succeeded by other pupils, writers also, as St. Polycarp and St. Irenæus,—if it were not that our Essayists simply disown everything except the merest letter of the New Testament as capable of throwing light upon the New Testament and its teaching, bid the interpreter, as a first principle of interpreting, "disengage himself from all that follows [r]," and thus obtain an unembarrassed opportunity of applying all the resources of a so-called criticism to discredit and destroy the written record itself.

That all the vital doctrines of the Christian revelation are contained in the New Testament, we do most thankfully acknowledge,—whereby the gracious providence of God has given to the truth a double support, the tradition for ever finding its due confirmation and proof in the written document, the written document blending with the perpetual tradition, and receiving continual illustration from it. But this *completeness* in the New Testament, composed as it is of several independent narratives, and a large number of, so to speak, casual letters, is a thing which had to be established and recognised as a *fact*, not one which was historically or *à priori* necessary as a *truth*. And a very wonderful and very providential fact it is, and one for which we never can be sufficiently thankful. Yet it became a fact by degrees and in lapse of time; whilst the complete possession of the saving truth belonged to the Christian Church not by degrees, nor in lapse of time, but from the first. Of that saving truth, thus taught and thus possessed, the Apostles' Creed, growing up as it did on every side of Christendom as the faithful record of the uniform oral teaching of the apostles, is the true and precious historical monu-

[r] p. 338.

PREFACE. lvii

ment, and I venture to say that if any person claims to reject the Apostles' Creed as an auxiliary, a great and invaluable auxiliary, in interpreting the writings of the Apostles, he shews himself to be very wanting indeed in appreciation of the comparative value of historical evidence, and of the true principles of historical philosophy.

And not the Apostles' Creed only; but the whole history and tradition of the universal Church, needing, no doubt, skill and discretion in the application, supply, when applied with the requisite skill and discretion, very valuable and real aid in interpreting Holy Scripture. Sometimes they teach us to discriminate between what is temporary and what is perpetual, as in the case of the Lord's apparent institution of a sacramental washing of the feet, and St. James's apparently universal direction of sacramental unction in sickness; and in so doing, almost seem to overrule the words of Scripture, when in fact they are only interpreting them. Sometimes they supply the practical proof of some apostolic usage which the written Scriptures either very slightly touch, or wholly omit, as in the case of the sanctifying of the Lord's day, and of Infant Baptism.

On this last subject, of Infant Baptism, I may perhaps be permitted to say a few words; for it seems to me to offer a good illustration of the great difference between Mr. Jowett's idea of the mode in which some Christian writers use the Scriptures in proof of doctrine, and that which I believe to be the more true one.

He says, "In the instance of Infant Baptism, the mere mention of a family of a jailor at Philippi who was baptized, (he and all his [s],) has led to the inference that in this family there were probably young children, and hence that Infant Baptism is, first, permissive; secondly, obligatory."

If there be any persons who base the obligation of Infant Baptism thus upon the inference so drawn from Acts xvi. 33, I have nothing to say in their defence; but I do not know of any such.

I believe, on the contrary, that there is not a single passage in the New Testament which directly refers, in its own proper or immediate meaning, to Infant Baptism, much less that there is any which proves its obligatory character.

But upon this fact I base an argument in favour of Infant Baptism which seems to me irrefragable; certainly much stronger than any which could have been founded upon one or two of the plainest texts distinctly commanding it. For such texts never could have been safe from the assaults of "criticism," falsely so called, (that blight which in an unhealthy season is sure to fix itself upon the fairest and divinest blossoms,) while silence may, I hope, escape even from criticism.

[s] Acts xvi. 33.

PREFACE.

The practical question of the due time for baptizing the children of Christian parents must have arisen, in every town and village where the Gospel was preached, within, at the latest, a very few years after the great day of Pentecost; that is, long before a single line of the New Testament was written.

The many thousand adult converts in Jerusalem, whom we read of in the first few chapters of the Acts, must have had children. So must the Christian people in all the towns where St. Paul preached, and in the various countries of the South and East which were visited by the other apostles. The question, I say, must have arisen everywhere, and it must have been settled.

If there had been any difference of opinion or usage concerning it, there must have been argument, dispute, decision. If five years old, or ten, or fifteen, or twenty-one, or any other arbitrarily-fixed age had been the earliest time at which the children of converts could rightly be baptized, such a decision must have been made known. If a council had decreed it for the purpose of avoiding diversity, at least the decree of the council would be heard of: besides that all sorts of questions, collateral to the main one, and necessarily incident to it, must have sprung up and required answers,—as in cases of doubtful age, or desperate sickness, or baptism accidentally administered too soon, or the like; and such questions must inevitably have left traces behind them in the history of the early Churches.

The absolute silence of the sacred writings on all such questions, even though so large a portion of them consists of letters referring to real practical difficulties which had risen up in the Churches, proves beyond the reach of reasonable doubt that the practice of the first or apostolic age, that is, the first century, was uniform, undoubted, and universal.

Being thus uniform and universal, what was it? I answer confidently, that the practice of Christendom for the next 1,500 years, the constant, unquestioned and unquestioning practice of the universal Church, affirmatively testified by ancient Liturgies and Fathers, and negatively proved by the like absence of discussions and decisions as to any other age being the more proper one for receiving baptism, absolutely proves, and with a force to which all these fine-drawn guesses of modern criticism are light as thistle-down, that the Church of Christ has in all ages baptized its infants, and has held that no age is too youthful or immature for admission into the sacred name of the Father, the Son, and the Holy Ghost.

This conclusion is rather confirmed than weakened by the fact that many Christians were desirous to put off baptism until the point of death, in order that the remission of sins therein received might not be endangered by any subsequent falling away from Christ.

For not only is this fact abundantly recorded, though one of partial and occasional occurrence, but also the grounds on which the desire (not an unnatural, though a mistaken one) was founded, were quite unconnected with the idea of any time of life being in itself too early for admission to the Christian family.

When we have proceeded thus far, we may properly turn to the Holy Scriptures; and there we shall find that though, as above stated, there be not a single passage in the New Testament which directly refers to Infant Baptism in its own proper and immediate meaning, yet there are many and various ones which support, strengthen, and confirm it when otherwise established. Such is the narrative of our Lord's acts and words commanding the little children to be brought unto Him, blaming those that would have kept them from Him, exhorting all men to follow their innocency as a model of fitness for entering into the kingdom of heaven, declaring His good-will towards them by embracing them in His arms, laying His hands on them, and blessing them,—a passage replete with inferences indirectly applicable to Infant Baptism, and most fitly chosen to be the Gospel in the Baptismal Office. Such are St. Paul's words, attributing "holiness" in some sense to the children born of one Christian parent,—such is the analogy of the eight-days-old circumcision received by the Lord Himself,—such, even, is the very feeble indication of Acts xvi. 33.

I do not mean to conceal that Mr. Jowett concludes the paragraph from which the foregoing words are quoted, by saying "Infant Baptism has sufficient grounds;" nor do I at all mean to represent him as attacking the practice of baptizing infants. I allege this instance in proof of the power with which Church history and usage ought to be made to bear upon the illustration of Christian doctrine and truth, and by consequence upon the Scriptures of the New Testament. It seems to me to be undeniable that great light is thrown upon such passages as 1 Cor. vii. 14, if it is known and remembered that at that time, and in all the primitive times, it was the universal belief that infants were never too young to receive Holy Baptism; and, by consequence, that if any man cuts off from the illustration of Holy Scripture considerations like these, he commits a heavy offence against real criticism, and the true rules of philosophical interpretation.

It will readily be believed that I do not suppose myself to have *answered* this book. I have not attempted to do so. I have only intended to ask attention to a few considerations which seem to me to be of weight against the general cast of opinions which pervades it. There are a great many other points which I would fain notice, but that I am afraid of extending these scattered remarks too far. I should like, for instance, to observe upon Mr. Jowett's assertion that "there is no foundation in the Gospels or Epistles for any of the higher or supernatural views of inspiration" by drawing out the claim which St. Paul lays to "supernatural" information both of the facts and doctrines of Christianity in Gal. i. 1, 12—16, ii. 2, 7, 8, 9 ; 1 Cor. xv. 1—3 ; 2 Cor. xii. 9 ; Eph. iii. 1—5 ; cf. 1 Cor. vi. 25 ; 2 Cor. viii. 8 ; Acts xxii. 17, 18, &c. Also, I cannot refrain from remarking on some of the same writer's canons of Scriptural interpretation. We have already seen that he disallows everything whatever in the way of historical doctrine,—everything, in short, of every kind except the barest letter of Holy Scripture as throwing light upon its meaning. "The office of the interpreter," he says, "is—to recover the meaning of the words as they first struck on the ears or flashed before the eyes of those who heard and read them. He has to transfer himself to another age, to imagine that he is a disciple of Christ or Paul, to disengage himself from all that follows. The history of Christendom is nothing to him[t]," &c. Will it be believed that the writer who thus excludes all collateral light of historical doctrine, and ignores the traditional knowledge of the Church, "the pillar and ground of the truth," as totally devoid of all connection with the interpretation of Holy Scripture, also objects to what he considers excessive interpretation of the Greek in which it is written; tells us that "there seem to be reasons for doubting whether any considerable light

[t] p. 338.

can be thrown on the New Testament from inquiry into the language^u;" considers that "the discussions respecting the use of the Greek article have gone far beyond the line of utility," and has the hardihood to say that it is an "error to interpret every particle as though it were a link in the argument, instead of being, as is often the case, an excrescence of style [x]?" What, it may be asked, is to be the principle of interpretation, if the discoverable mind of the apostolic Church and the exact examination of language are thus to be both discarded alike? "When the meaning of Greek words is once known, the young student has almost all the real materials which are possessed by the greatest Biblical scholar, in the book itself [y]." Beyond this, "the interpreter needs nothing short of fashioning in himself the image of the mind of Christ. He has to be born again into a new spiritual or intellectual world, from which the thoughts of this world are shut out [z]." Yet let no person suppose that the writer means by these lofty phrases any illumination of the Holy Spirit of God, any divine aid to be won by prayer, or indeed anything whatever of a "supernatural" kind. No: substitute the words "Sophocles or Plato" for the word "Christ" in the last-quoted passage, and you have equally the rule for interpreting Sophocles or Plato. It simply comes to this: a little Greek (not too much) and a strong self-rely-

[u] p. 393.   [x] p. 391.   [y] p. 384.   [z] p. 380.

ing imagination, and you may interpret Holy Scripture as well as—Mr. Jowett! Now, had this writer reminded us that the New Testament Greek is a Greek of a different age from that of the classical writers, had he simply warned us that we must not press our Attic Greek scholarship too far, but study the Alexandrian Greek of the Septuagint, Philo, &c., in order to ascertain the exact meaning of the words and phrases of the writers of the New Testament,—still more, if, as the result of such study on his own part, he had offered us some well-digested observations on the use of tenses, articles, or particles in the sacred writings, he would have done some service, but this talk about "excessive attention to the articles," and "particles being often mere excrescences of style," is of no effect except to expose the writer to ridicule. It sounds as if he had been accustomed to lay down the law to an admiring audience of "clever young men," and had forgotten that there were still "men in Denmark" who understood Greek.

I do not wish it to be supposed that I at all sympathize with those, the especial objects of the hatred and scorn of the Essayists, who would prevent the statement of difficulties or stifle discussion on the subjects of religion. Very far from it. A serious statement of difficulties is a thing to be highly respected, and seriously replied to; and as to discussion, it would shew great want of confidence in what we believe to be the truth of God, if we were afraid of allowing it, or of entering upon it when gravely proposed and conducted. In respect to the present volume, I must repeat that (excepting perhaps the fifth and sixth Essays) it does not seem to me to have any claim to the respect of seriously stated difficulties or grave discussion; nor can I for a moment admit that men in the position of tutors or teachers of youth are justified in writing and printing such things. They are recklessly, as I think, enhancing the evil which is now the chief one under which religion in England suffers,—the spread of infidel, or semi-infidel opinions. Their talk, their views, are all "negative." They offer nothing affirmative,—no belief, no verity, no food for faith or devotion, nothing to be held by in life or death. They will not hear of anything beyond "*nature.*" They would starve all real religion out of the land. They do not seem to reflect that if all the things which they attack in the Christian religion be withdrawn from it, there is absolutely nothing left. If the "supernatural" be denied, as they are bent on denying it, we are merely where the heathens are. Nor do they seem to reflect that if any part of the Christian religion be true, it goes a very long way indeed to guarantee all the rest; so that if a man, holding fast by that of which he is quite certain, from it, as from a point of advantage, addresses himself to consider difficulties or objections, they either disappear, or shrink into insignificant importance, — while if a person begins with his difficulties and negations, and dwells upon them, he can eat the whole heart of his faith out, and find himself after a while possessed of a mere shell, ready to collapse at the first attack of infidelity from without. And there is great danger lest their endeavours should gain a very baneful amount of success. Though I by no means allow the somewhat presumptuous claim which these writers seem to make, of superior intellect, knowledge, love of truth, and power of thought, yet it cannot be denied that at the Universities, views more or less like those maintained in these Essays are welcomed by many young men, especially by such as hold themselves to be most intellectual, and are spreading considerably among them. This is, I believe, a natural re-action from the Romanizing turn which, some fifteen years since, was given to the revival of Church principles among us. The same elements of thought, the same impatience of character, which led some to submit, in voluntary servitude of mind, to the domination of Rome, is now leading others to these opposite yet not unallied conclusions. Alike they crave a *certainty* which they fail to find to their satisfaction in the position of the Church of England; and while some accept, with closed eyes, a so-called certainty, offered by the imposing dogmatism of the Church of Rome, the others hope to find the same by opening their eyes very wide indeed, and eliminating from religion every point of difficulty or question which the most captious criticism can raise, till they leave nothing whatever, in history, doctrine, or rite, unassailed. Moreover, this *liberalizing* of Christianity falls in well with the easy views of religion current in busy secular life, and thus the "negative theologians" find themselves in more accord with the leading men of the active and busy world than has been the case with Christian teachers in any age of the Church.

But the Church of England holds her own, disapproving alike of the Romanizing and the Germanizing impatience, entirely believing and accepting the Word of God as given by inspiration of the Holy Spirit in the Scriptures; holding fast "the objective faith once delivered to the saints" in spite of open enemies or treacherous friends, clinging to her atoning Lord, not afraid to do battle for the truth when assailed from without or from within, content with such amount of light and certainty of evidence as God has been pleased to give; and, believing that in such uncertainty as is left, a brave and manly faith may grow up to be the unfailing root of all that is holiest and most divine in character, she teaches her children not to be wise above what is written, nor to pride themselves upon a pseudo-cleverness which is sure to fall in with and encourage all sorts of evil in those who give way to it, and mar the holy work of sanctification and growing likeness to Christ which God has given her to do in this land.

In the first edition of this preface I added some passages, which I here reprint, from the "Westminster Review" published in October last. I spoke of them as written by "a professed infidel," so designating the writer from the internal evidence of the article. If, as is confidently reported, he is indeed a Fellow of a College in Oxford, I can only express my indignant astonishment at the inconsistency of his language and his position. But his words have their value as shewing, and I think irresistibly, how utterly defenceless, *from the other side*, is the position which the Essayists have taken up, and offering the strongest warning that can be given to those who are not prepared to make a total surrender of their faith, lest they should allow themselves to be seduced from the strong and safe position of the Church by those shallow and half-thought views. Against the views of the Westminster reviewer himself I shall not attempt to argue. For Christian people it is enough that he invites them to a total relinquishment of the faith of Christ, and of everything connected with it. But I wish to quote some passages of the article in order to exhibit what seems to me to be the complete helplessness of our Essayists against the attack on the other side, and to warn those who are caught by the Essays that they are nothing more nor less than mere infidelity very slightly disguised.

On the uniformity of the Essays we read :—

"It cannot escape the most casual reader, first, that there is a virtual unity in the purpose of the whole; secondly, that each writer receives a weight and an authority from all the rest of his associates. It would be equally idle to pretend that each writer is not morally responsible for the general tendency of the whole. What each of the seven writers puts forward comes with increased power when it has the countenance of the other six. They at the very least are guarantees that the views contained in this book have in them nothing dangerous, insidious, or destructive. They at least bear witness that such opinions are an open question, and may be boldly avowed and usefully taught within the very precinct and sanctuary of the Church. Let each of these writers be assured that, as far as moral influence goes, he has said all that each of the others has said, and it is not too hard to remind them that each has implied some things which none of them have said."

Of the compatibility of this teaching with Christian belief, it is said :—

"No fair mind can close this volume without feeling it to be at bottom in direct antagonism to the whole system of popular belief. They profess indeed to come forward as defenders of the creeds against attacks from without; but their hardest blows fall not on the assaulting, but on the resisting force. They throw themselves into the breach; but their principal care is to clear it from its oldest and stoutest defenders. In object, in spirit, and in method, in details, no less than in general design, this book is incompatible with the religious belief of the mass of the Christian public, and the broad principles on which the Protestantism of Englishmen rests. The most elaborate reasoning to prove that they are in harmony can never be anything but futile, and ends in becoming insincere. All attempts to shew that these opinions are in accordance with Scripture, the Articles, the Liturgy, or the Church, have little practical value, and do no small practical harm."

"The men and women around us are told that the whole scheme of salvation has to be entirely re-arranged and altered; divine rewards and punishments; the fall; original sin; the vicarious penalty; and salvation by faith, are all, in the natural sense of the terms, repudiated as immoral delusions. Miracles, inspiration, and prophecy, in their plain and natural sense, are denounced as figments or exploded blunders. The Mosaic history dissolves into a mass of ill-digested legends, the Mosaic ritual into an Oriental system of priestcraft, and the Mosaic origin of the earth and man sinks amid the rubbish of Rabbinical cosmogonies. And yet all this is done in the name of orthodoxy, and for the glory of Christian truth. Nay, unwearied with destroying this great edifice of old belief, our writers enter upon the gigantic and incredible enterprize of rebuilding the whole again from the foundations, upon the same ground-plan, but with stronger walls; and after forcing the simple believer to unlearn his well-conned creed, they sit down to teach it him anew with altered words and remodelled phrases. An expurgated Bible resumes its place. Miracles, inspiration, and prophecy re-appear under the old names with new meanings; the harmonious whole arises anew in loftier and softer outlines with the cardinal features,—with a revised atonement, a transcendental fall, a practical salvation, and an idealized damnation. . . .

"Now in all seriousness we would ask, what is the practical issue of all this? Having made all these deductions from the popular belief, what remains as the residuum? How far is the solvent process to be carried? Are all formulæ whatever discarded, or what materials remain to form new? In their ordinary, if not plain sense, there has been discarded the Word of God, the creation, the fall, the redemption, justification, regeneration and salvation, miracles, inspiration, prophecy, heaven and hell, eternal punishment and a day of judgment, creeds, liturgies, and articles, the truth of Jewish history and of Gospel narrative, a sense of doubt thrown over even the incarnation, the resurrection, and ascension, the divinity of the second Person, and the personality of the Third. It may be that this is a true view of Christianity, but we insist in the name of common sense that it is a new view. Surely it is waste of time to argue that it is agreeable to Scripture, and not contrary to the Canons[a]."

"The Bible is one, and it is too late now to propose to divide it. We shall only point out that even the moral value of the Gospel teaching becomes suspicious when the whole miraculous element is discarded.

[a] p. 305.

"We certainly do think that the Gospels assert a miraculous incarnation, resurrection, and ascension; and that the Epistles teach original sin, and a vicarious sacrifice. If this be doubted by our authors, it is sufficient for us to say that such is the impression they have created on all ages of Christians[b]."

"We desire that if the Bible or any part of it be retained as Holy Writ, it be defended as a miraculous gift to man, and not by distorting the principles of modern science. Let them (the Essayists) be assured that there exists no middle course; that there is no inspiration more than natural, yet not supernatural; no theology which can abandon its doctrines and retain its authority[c]."

I confess that I cannot see how these attacks are to be repelled. The Essayists have thrown themselves into a position which is indefensible. There is no standing-place between the faith of the Church and infidelity. I cannot deny that they have laid themselves open to the invitation to absolute and professsed unbelief, irresistible upon their principles, with which the article concludes:—

"How long shall this last? Until men have the courage to bury their dead convictions out of sight, and the greater courage to form new. All honour to these writers for the boldness with which they have, at great risk, urged their opinions. But what is wanted is strength not merely to face

[b] p. 315.   [c] p. 312.

the world, but to face one's own conclusions. We know the cost. It must be endured. Let each who has thought and felt for himself ask himself first what he *does not* believe, and then, if wise or needful, avow it. Next let him ask himself what he *does* believe, and pursue it to its true and full conclusions. Neither loose accommodation nor sonorous principles will long give them rest. It is of as little use to surrender the more glaring contradictions of science as it is to evaporate a discredited doctrine into a few vague precepts. That end will not be attained by our authors by subliming religion into an emotion, and making an armistice with science. It will not be obtained by any unreal adaptation, nor by this, which is of all recent adaptations at once the most able, the most earnest, and the most suicidal."

Terribly true much of this is: but how will the Essayists receive it? Will they, or any of them, have the courage, the Christian courage, to reflect on the position in which they have placed themselves? to disown, at least, the extreme theories of some of their colleagues? Will they take refuge, at least, in the honest sentiment of St. Peter, when a "difficulty" of no slight magnitude was presented to him, "Lord, to whom shall we go? Thou hast the words of eternal life. And we believe and are sure that Thou art that Christ, the Son of the living God." But whatever be the course to be taken by these writers themselves, will not young men take warning from the sight of the gulf to which these Essays would lead them, and turn back, while they can, to the belief—which is in great degree *moral*, and wholly *spiritual*—in which they have been bred, and which alone is able to give them support, direction, and comfort in life, and peace in death?

CONTENTS.

SERMON I.
(Page 1.)

"Blessed are the poor in spirit."—*St. Matthew* v. 3.

SERMON II.
(Page 24.)

"Blessed are they that mourn."—*St. Matthew* v. 4.

SERMON III.
(Page 51.)

"Blessed are the meek."—*St. Matthew* v. 5.

SERMON IV.
(Page 75.)

"Blessed are they which do hunger and thirst after righteousness."—*St. Matthew* v. 6.

SERMON V.
(Page 100.)

"Blessed are the merciful."—*St. Matthew* v. 7.

SERMON VI.
(Page 115.)

"Blessed are the pure in heart."—*St. Matthew* v. 8.

SERMON VII.
(Page 138.)

"Blessed are the peace-makers."—*St. Matthew* v. 9.

SERMON VIII.

(Page 155.)

"Blessed are they which are persecuted for righteousness sake."—*St. Matthew* v. 10.

SERMON IX.

(Page 171.)

History and Hypocrisy.—*St. Matthew* xxiii. 29—32.

SERMON X.

(Page 192.)

God in the Church.—*Acts* v. 12—14.

SERMON XI.

(Page 219.)

Judas Iscariot.—*St. John* xiii. 18.

SERMON XII.

(Page 244.)

The Convictions of Balaam.—*Revelation* ii. 14.

SERMON XIII.

(Page 265.)

The Power of the Holy Ghost.—*Romans* viii. 9.

SERMONS XIV., XV.

(Pages 285, 302.)

All Saints Kings and Priests.—*Revelation* v. 9, 10.

SERMON I.[a]

St. Matthew v.

3. Blessed are the poor in spirit: for theirs is the kingdom of heaven.

THE Beatitudes, as they are given in the opening of the fifth chapter of St. Matthew's Gospel, may be regarded as the most complete exposition—an exposition which has almost the appearance of being intended to be complete and systematic—which the Gospels furnish of Christian morality.

The Lord, in delivering them, is not, for the time, speaking directly of Christian *doctrine*, either as imparting it at once, or giving anticipation of it in future. He is rather stating, and that in a much more systematic way than is usual in Holy Scripture, the main moral characters or traits which form the complete portraiture of the Christian man; and, with these main characters or traits, the special blessings

[a] Preached at St. Mary's, Oxford, before the University, October 30, 1858.

which, in God's providence and under the Christian system, are attached to each. Christian doctrine, I say, is not directly contained in them; but neither is it to be considered as wholly absent from them. For these traits or characters are those of the man (future at the time at which the Lord actually spoke, but capable of being realized under the Gospel when it should be fully given) who lives in the full and earnest faith of Christ, rests on His death, looks forward to His glory, and is sanctified in body and soul and spirit by the divine illumination of the Holy Ghost. There is also one place, or two, in the Beatitudes where the Christian exposition of the actual words brings doctrine, properly so called, more nearly to the surface than in others.

Therefore the Beatitudes may be truly regarded as an exposition of morality purely *Christian;* and in attempting to make some examination of them, we are to consider ourselves as being under the full light of Christian truth and grace, not dealing with abstract or general morality, but with that which belongs to God's saints in the Church of Christ, and is only possible to them, — and to them possible only by the help and in the strength of that Holy Spirit of whose blessed influences the saints are permitted to drink in the Church.

One of the first points that calls for observation in commenting upon the Beatitudes, is the difference between the two reports of them as contained in the two Gospels of St. Matthew and St. Luke. Of course, in so speaking, I am intending to assume, what I have not at present the opportunity of proving, but what seems to me capable of the most satisfactory proof, that the Sermon on the Mount of St. Matthew's Gospel is the same as that which is recorded in a scattered manner in various parts of St. Luke, and, especially, that the Beatitudes as we read them in the sixth chapter of St. Luke are only a different report of what we read in the fifth chapter of St. Matthew.

I observe, then, that of the eight Beatitudes as given in St. Matthew, four only are recorded by St. Luke; and that those four are in that Gospel accompanied by corresponding denunciations of woe, which are not found in St. Matthew. Blessed are the poor, the hungry, the mourners, and those who are evil spoken of by men; woe to the rich, the full, to those who laugh now, and to those whom men speak well of. Moreover, the blessings promised in St. Luke are fixed— both by the omission of the loftier and more spiritual words which occur in St. Matthew, and by their corresponding denunciations—to more outward, and, so to speak, more superficial cases than those intended in

St. Matthew. Poverty, actual poverty, hunger, sorrow, unpopularity amongst men,—these actual things are (no doubt because of the opportunities which they offer for the exercise of high Christian graces) pronounced to be blessed in St. Luke. Riches, fulness of bread, mirth, popularity amongst men,—these outward things (no doubt because of the manifold and dangerous temptations with which they are accompanied) are the precise things against which in that Gospel woe is denounced.

Purposing as I do, in this and other subsequent sermons, to examine some of the more spiritual Beatitudes as given in St. Matthew, I shall make no further observation upon St. Luke's version of them than this, —that it is plain that they are not to be confined to the inner or spiritual meaning only. Poverty, literal poverty, literal hunger, literal sorrow, literal persecution,—these outward things, literally understood, have their own proper blessedness. They are gifts of God's love, capable of being turned to good in various ways, which it is beside our present purpose to enquire into, but which are nevertheless very real and true.

Turning, then, to the more spiritual Beatitudes, as given by St. Matthew at the opening of the Sermon on the Mount, it is obvious to observe in the first place what an astonishing difference there is between the

Christian character as exhibited in them, and the character of human virtue as pourtrayed by any heathen moralist. Though an occasional glimpse of the superior heroism of the meek and enduring, as compared with the self-exalting and violent forms of goodness, appears to have been attained, as it were for a moment, by one or other of the ancient writers, yet when they come to elaborate their pictures of virtue, they seem to lose themselves altogether in the admiration of those showy and outwardly successful traits of character which have their scope and obtain their reward upon the earth. They have no eyes for anything beyond. They are like men looking, not without some natural powers of sight and discrimination, at a vast and complicated assemblage of objects, seeking in vain for a point of view in which all may be seen together, and in their due relations to one another, and therefore for ever mistaking the comparative greatness, the true relative bearing and real measure of the things that are before them, and sure to be misled in their judgments, in favour of those which are nearest and brightest, and which loom largest to their eyes. Open the Sermon on the Mount, and it is plain at once that the standpoint is gained. Human virtue, on the grandest and truest scale, is seen in its relation to God and eternity, to Christ and judgment; and forthwith the whole confusion is gone. All falls instantly into perfect perspective. The scene is uniform and harmonious, and can be read. For the light of God is on it, and all is seen as it is seen by Him who made it, and is conducting it towards His own great ends.

It can hardly be said that the eight Beatitudes cover the whole ground of human virtue. It is certainly delusive to expect that we are to find completely systematic or exhaustive divisions of things in Holy Scripture. Yet I apprehend that there is often more of such completeness than people think, and that therefore it is useful to trace it as far as we can, and, while we are careful not to introduce our own systematizing into the Bible, to try in each case whether the Holy Spirit has not designed to give full and complete statements where at first sight we may seem to recognise only partial and incomplete ones. So in the Beatitudes. Without supposing that they contain any complete system or code, we may usefully remark that two of them relate to virtues which are purely inward, which belong to a man in his own secret relation to God only, without any reference at all to other men,—purity of heart, and hunger and thirst after righteousness. Two of them are inward virtues, having relation to our position among men,—poverty of spirit and meekness. Two of them rather belong to the passive condition of human virtue, placed in the midst of a sad and unkind world,—sorrow and persecution. One of the remainder, mercy, is the special virtue of the Christian in his active and outward dealings with other men. And in peace-making, the last of the eight, he is regarded as going altogether out from himself, and entering into the transactions which arise between other people, and in which he himself has no share. Thus the Christian character, as drawn in the Beatitudes, is that of the man who in his inner self maintains a heart perfectly pure, by God's grace, from every defilement of the flesh and spirit, and longs for righteousness in Christ with a longing like that of him who hungers and thirsts after food and drink; who in his position in life and among men, has a thorough—yet a strong, not feeble—meekness of mind and poverty of spirit; who accepts the condition of sorrow from God and persecution from men, if it should be the will of God that he be afflicted with them, in thankful submission, and with the single wish to find the blessing in them with which they are charged; who is characterized in the outer dealings wherein he is concerned with other men, by a prevailing and pervading mercy, and who, passing out of himself and entering into the concerns of other men, according to his position in life, is known as ever "seeking peace, and ensuing it," putting men at one with God and with one another, so as to be in the very likeness, the very filial likeness, of God Himself by acting in so God-like a manner among men.

Putting aside, then, further prefatory matter, let us proceed to examine the first of the eight Beatitudes,— "Blessed are the poor in spirit, for theirs is the kingdom of heaven." Who then, first, are to be understood as the poor in spirit?

The word *spirit* cannot, I think, on any ground be interpreted here to mean the Holy Spirit of God; nor indeed has it, so far as I know, been usually so interpreted either in ancient or modern times. No; it rather means, as the absence of the article in the Greek strongly indicates, the *spirit of man*,—that spiritual part of man's nature which is immediately subject to the influences of the Holy Spirit of God, and through which those influences are communicated to the rest of his being.

For, as far as I can trace the psychological language of the New Testament, there seems to be, amid a considerable variety of expression, a prevailing uniformity and harmony in the way in which the various parts or powers of human nature are spoken of. Body, flesh, mind, heart, soul, spirit, and if there be any other such words, all seem to find their place in a consistent and intelligible theory of human nature, common to all the

"BLESSED ARE THE POOR IN SPIRIT." 9

sacred writers. It is not necessary at present to go deeply into this subject, which has been much discussed of late both by English and German theologians. I will only say that the first great and natural division which the sacred writers make, is that of body and soul—the material and the immaterial parts of man; and that this is regarded as an exhaustive division, as it really is, admitting of no third part. This is a real division. The parts of it are really separable: they will be separated in death, and reunited in the resurrection; and in the immaterial part resides the personality, the central being of a man. But the immaterial part, the soul, is occasionally, so to speak, subdivided; not, of course, technically, nor yet so as to signify that these parts are physically separable; but logically only, whensoever, as in a multitude of very important passages, the soul is contra-distinguished from the spirit. When, then, this subdivision takes place, the soul, specifically so called, is to be understood to comprehend all those lower parts of the immaterial man which are more immediately connected with the body, "that assemblage of feelings, movements, and impulses of which the heart is the imaginary tabernacle [b];" while by the

---

[b] Cf. Prof. Ellicott's Sermons, p. 117; Olshausen, Opusc., Berolini, 1834. (Compare also Ellicott on 1 Tim. i. 5.) In referring to my friend Professor Ellicott's works, (not in this instance as altogether agreeing

spirit are meant all those higher and more spiritual portions of the immaterial nature of man, wherein he addresses God with heavenly affections, which is "the medium of our cognizance of the divine, that portion of us which stands in most intimate association with the Holy Spirit[c];" which is capable of receiving directly the influences of the Holy Spirit, and communicating those influences downward, first to our lower soul, and then to our body, whereby our whole being may be sanctified and illuminated with the holy light of God.

Poverty in spirit, then, is not poverty in body; nor is it poverty in the specific soul, but it is poverty in this higher or spiritual part of man. It is not poverty in the body, so as to mean the mere want of money, or the luxuries or comforts which money brings. This sort of poverty may have its blessedness under the Beatitudes of St. Luke, but it is irrelevant to that recorded by St. Matthew. Still less is it poverty in the lower or specific soul and its desires, so as to mean a feeble and ignoble disposition, falling natu-

---

with his views,) I am glad to take the opportunity of expressing my high sense of the very valuable contribution that they have added to the illustration of Holy Scripture. Would that all the commentators on St. Paul of this age were as learned, as modest, as large-minded, as faithful. [c] Ibid., p. 113.

rally below the energy of man's wishes or ambition. This sort of poverty has no blessing in either Gospel; nor is it blessed. It must be a willing poverty, of grace, not of nature, in the higher and spiritual part of man; not an outwardly imposed condition, nor an inward deficiency of force, but a willing and gracious selection and acquiescence by the spirit of a Christian man enlightened and enabled by the Holy Spirit of God, in a place, condition, desires, and the like, analogous to that which belongs to the outwardly and literally poor. It must be a weakness, so to say, that comes of strength; a poverty, so to call it, on the earth, that comes of riches not on the earth. For the word poverty plainly belongs to this world, and the poor in spirit is surely he who, *while he remains here*, is in his spirit as a poor man among men, content to take and occupy the poor man's place, having no personal ambition nor desire of anything greater upon the earth, lowly, and content with lowliness, unaffectedly, simply lowly among men, and in respect of the things which belong to this world.

Blessed, then, is he who thus in his spirit, his higher spiritual nature, informed and illuminated by the Holy Spirit of God, is as a poor man among men upon this earth, not eager for its rewards or honours, nor ambitious of its first places, lowly, and unaffectedly content with lowliness! Blessed, first and generally, because God loveth such; and because such are, in their degree, truly conformed to the likeness of His Son, who though He was rich, yet for our sakes became poor [d], who, though being from the beginning in the form of God, did not deem the being equal with God a thing to be grasped at [e], and retained as a prize, but made Himself of no reputation, and took upon Him the form of a servant, and was made in the likeness of men;—blessed, I say, first and generally, for this; but blessed specially, and as it were paradoxically, for this, that his is the kingdom of heaven. The very thing which he seems to forego, he gains, and gains by foregoing it. He willingly relinquishes the ambition of the high places upon earth, but thereby he wins the high places in heaven. There are high places in heaven. There are seats at the right hand, and left, of Christ the King. And Christ shall give them, for they are His [f] to give to those for whom they are prepared of His Father; and these are none

[d] ἐπτώχευσε . . ἵνα ὑμεῖς τῇ ἐκείνου πτωχείᾳ πλουτήσητε. 2 Cor. viii. 9.   [e] Ellicott, in loco.

[f] St. Matt. xx. 23 is somewhat injuriously translated in the A. V. by the introduction of the words "it shall be given." The Greek, οὐκ ἔστιν ἐμὸν δοῦναι, ἀλλ' οἷς ἡτοίμασται ὑπὸ τοῦ πατρός μου, signifies 'is not Mine to give, save to those for whom,' &c.

"BLESSED ARE THE POOR IN SPIRIT."

other than they who in such poverty of spirit as I have described, humble themselves most truly and unaffectedly on the earth, after the likeness of little children.

But how is all this to be reconciled with the actual state of things upon the earth? A teeming population, a struggling life, a race for distinction, honour, success; competition of the keenest kind pervading every part and portion of our society; in these days directly and professedly introduced into almost every possible corner of our artificial life. Is it not true, that while Christian religion emphatically and repeatedly discourages ambition, and holds up as among the most characteristic Christian virtues the opposite dispositions of humility and lowliness, the current course of human things, particularly in England, stimulates ambition in every possible way, makes life, even more than it is by nature, the keenest and most exciting of races, and urges on the competitors by every worldly motive that can be brought to bear upon them? And does it not also seem to be true that Christian men often lose their bearings in this whirl of ambition, and forget, except perhaps in Christian theory, and on Sunday in church, the calm, lofty, unearthly truth as seen from that high eminence of inspiration whence alone all things are beheld as they are, and in their true and unmistaken relation to one another?

But that truth *may* blend with the things of this earth. It was not given, it is not designed to be, a matter of mere unpractical speculation and admiration. It is by no means the exclusive possession of such as live in the cloister or the hermitage, make vows of voluntary poverty, or in other such mistaken ways "bid their neighbour and their work farewell" in the attempt "to wind themselves," not so much "too high," as in a wrong way, and to the neglect of the real means of elevation, towards heaven.

The hermit is as wrong as the worldling. Both think evangelical holiness and real life things incompatible with each other, though they select differently which of these things, supposed to be incompatible, they will follow. But they are not incompatible; they are very far from being incompatible. On the contrary, if the truth of God be faithfully and deeply digested, if a Christian man have fully taken into his heart the certain blessedness of poverty of spirit, have his spirit's love set altogether upon the high places of the spiritual kingdom, and by consequence is entirely, sacredly, unaffectedly lowly in respect of the successes and distinctions, and other high places of the earth, who is there in all the world so sure as he is to discharge his earthly offices and duties well, loftily, nobly, angelically well? No petty personal objects distract his view; no indirect aims perplex it. For God's sake and in God's service he does that with all his might which God has given him to do, in the earthly place which He has assigned him, and to God he looks for his reward. If he be statesman, if he be soldier, if he be merchant, if he be student, what view of his duties or what motive to discharge them well will lead him on so straight, or keep him so clear of indirectness and perplexity, as this one? It is not impossible, indeed, that the very clearness of his course to his own spiritual sight may make it seem a strange, or an unintelligible, or even an inconsistent one to men around him. Those who have lost their way among the trees of the valley cannot appreciate the directness of the track which he follows who has seen his road from the hill. But he knows whom he serves, and what he seeks, and why he labours; and he serves, and seeks, and labours all the more directly and all the more vigorously because he knows it. Is he successful upon earth? Do the rewards, and honours, and distinctions of the earth attend upon such holy and Christian labours? They may, or they may not. They may—for men do often prize faithful, simple-hearted, lowly labours, when they clearly recognise them, and no personal feeling intrudes to prevent the acknowledgment of them: they may not—for they may be misapprehended by the good, or felt to be a rebuke to the bad, or in many other ways may be unappreciated amongst men. But what then? It was not for the sake of human success that such labours were undertaken. They do not fail of success with God, to whom they were addressed. The high-soaring spirit of the Christian man—yes! and because it soars so high—is unaffectedly poor and lowly upon the earth. And moreover, the Christian man is very conscious of his own sin. None knows, as he knows, his own weakness and personal ill-desert. His high-soaring hopes of the heavenly kingdom are not based upon his own deserts: God forbid! *they* only claim the low places on the earth. Even if, as a man, he feels some disappointment at failure, yet he accepts disappointment as his due. His spirit clings to God the more, and he feels that it is good for him that his position among men is even more poor and lowly than he would have had it. Is such a spirit uncongenial to the world? No doubt to the mere world it is uncongenial: it is unwelcome, and it is unintelligible to the mere world. It sometimes happens that the two sorts of spirit are found side by side in life. They are doing their work laboriously together, and look just alike in the eyes of other people. But they are inwardly and essentially different. One has his eye fixed upon earthly success, and in earthly success, often won, he receives it. He has his reward, and he has none other to look for. The other looks for his reward in the eternal kingdom; and in earthly success, often lost, he loses (or wins, if so it be) what is merely secondary, and unimportant to him.

Imagine, brethren, if an angel of God were allowed to be living among us, as one of us; suppose him undistinguished by any outward mark or sign, so as to be exactly like one of ourselves in appearance, and to be taken for one of us; and how easy it would be to picture the sort of life that he would lead! Would he, think you, shrink into some cloister, or turn monk, or otherwise leave the society and duties in which he was placed? Surely, no; but we can well imagine the cheerful, loyal, devoted, laborious, lowly way in which he would turn himself to discharge all the good works which were given him to do. If his lot lay in public life, how fearless, how simple, how straightforward, how modest, how upright, how unlike the crooked ways of worldly politicians would be his course! If he were a soldier—a sailor—how prompt, how vigorous, how obedient, how pure, how holy, how lofty in its true modesty his noble and, as it were, godlike bearing! A merchant, how would he

> ". . . carry music in his heart
> Through dusky lane and wrangling mart;"

upright, honourable, industrious, trusted, and worthy of all trust! A student, how laborious, how manly, how pure, how far above the debasing pleasures which mislead many, how modest, how zealous of all good knowledge, how devout! How lowly would he be, and yet how lofty in his lowliness! how deserving of all the honours of the world, and yet how indifferent to them!

And as our deserts are lower than those of angels, brethren, so is our calling loftier than theirs. The Son of God took not upon Him the nature of angels. He did not die to redeem angels. The angels neither partake of the corrupt nature of the first Adam, nor are they made members of the body, of the flesh, and of the bones of the second Adam. They have not been made to drink into the Holy Spirit of God. They are not heirs of God, nor joint-heirs with Christ. If an angel might be supposed to live thus among men, how much more doth this lofty poverty of spirit, this high-souled lowliness, become one of us, the natural inheritors of sin and all feebleness, but now by Christ's blood redeemed from sin and everlasting death, planted into His body, therein partaking of the Holy Ghost, and the powers of the world to come, and allowed to look forward to the eternal kingdom—for His sake, and for no merits of our own—as our own sacred inheritance?

Our spirits,—do they not hold continual communion with God in prayer? does not the Holy Spirit, and with Him the Father and the Son, dwell in them? is not the voice of prayer which issues from them the very utterance of the Holy Spirit? And yet, should we not be well contented to be earthly-lowly in these our spirits; we who are so full of weakness and sin, whose consciences should be so full of sorrowful recollections of our sins, whereby we continually, as it were, crucify the Son of God afresh, and put Him to shame? How truly does this lowliness, this lofty lowliness, of the Christian spirit beseem us!

And may we not remember that the poverty of spirit of this Beatitude is, if we pursue the Greek word exactly, rather a beseechingness, a beggingness, if I may coin such a term, of spirit? I do not doubt indeed that it is rightly translated, for in the Greek of the New Testament the word has greatly lost its original meaning and is generally used to signify 'poverty' only. Yet in its true, first force, it signifies that lofty, lowly *begging,* wherewith the spirit of man lays itself in supplication before the Holy Spirit of God, ever begging, ever longing, never satisfied, desiring more and more always of that Divine indwelling wherein is its own strength, and happiness, and peace.

Brethren, young men, you who have, as it were, the world before you, who are entering upon the race of honour and success in life with high hope, and no slight confidence, how important it is for you to lay to heart the very deep and unearthly lesson of this first Christian Beatitude! Blessed, — blessed beyond the worldly-successful,—blessed, far beyond all those who achieve the highest distinctions of this earth,— blessed are the poor, the praying poor, in spirit!

Is your immediate object distinction *here,* and in literary competition? Not one syllable can fall from the preacher's lips to discourage the most earnest and devoted interest in the pursuit of the knowledge,—yes, and of the distinctions with which it has been thought wise to stimulate that pursuit of the knowledge which is given in this place. Give yourselves up to your labour with all that ardour, with all that noble strength of body and soul which belongs to Christian youth; and win, if you can, such honours as the University, in its balanced care for the things of this world and the next, has thought it wise to offer you. But remember throughout all this labour, and all this encouraged emulation,—remember that the kingdom of heaven, and the high places in the kingdom of heaven, are your real prize; and that these things, good in their place, and perhaps wisely set before you quite in your youth, are temporary, earthly, and, if they be pursued for their own sake, deluding and dangerous. Remember that it is the poor in spirit who are the first among the Christian blessed. Remember that these are not mere words, not the mere high-sounding words of the end of a sermon, but the very, solemn truth, the very truth of your Christian life, and of its immortal hopes. Remember this,—that if a young man is labouring for earthly honour, and is not at the same time constant and earnest in his prayers and confessions, so as to keep his heart alive, under the Holy Spirit of God, both to his loftiness and his lowliness, both to the high things which for Christ's sake are before him in heaven, and to the low things which are a sinner's only true deservings on the earth, he must be losing his way, he must be leaving the path which leads through blessing to blessing, and going astray—and, unless he repent, hopelessly astray—after worldly things.

And we, brethren, who are older, on whom the further ambition of the world is apt to tell with not less power, though we may perhaps be skilful to conceal it, than the youthful ambition of academical honours, shall not we, too, lay to heart—and all the more as we draw nearer to the end of life—the blessedness of true Christian poverty of spirit, lofty in its aspirations of the next world, really lowly in its desires of this one? Does not each one of us require to remind himself of this? to check himself, and bring himself, as it were, forcibly back to remember that it is not worldly success or fame that has the blessing and the promise of God, but true Christian poverty of spirit? Do not worldly maxims surround us, and, as it were, penetrate all our life? Do not worldly feelings intrude upon us continually, almost whether we will or no? How many a heart-ache are they spared whose humility is real, whose inner spirit is lowly and spiritually poor in the sight of God! Let us not be misled by deceitful imaginations, as though we desired the high places of the earth, in order, as men say, to be more useful, or the like. This is a very common salve of conscience in the ambitious. But it is a delusive one. We know not where we are most useful. A devoted, Christian man, doing his Christian work with all his might, is of unspeakable use wherever he is. Only let us keep our eyes and our hearts fixed on the eternal kingdom, fixed on the return of the Judge in judgment, and humbling ourselves in daily penitence and confession of sin, and growing stronger daily in holiness and the strength of the Holy Ghost, we shall by His grace realize more and more the lofty lowliness of the blessed poor in spirit, for whom, whatever be the lowness of their place on earth, the high places are surely appointed in the kingdom of heaven.

SERMON II.[a]

ST. MATTHEW v.

4. Blessed are they that mourn ; for they shall be comforted.

SORROW or mourning, according to the arrangement of the Beatitudes which I ventured to give in the preceding discourse, may be said to come as one of the third pair, which apply rather to the passive condition of Christian virtue in the midst of a sad and evil world.

The blessedness of mourning and sorrow is one of the great paradoxes of the Beatitudes. Naturally, and in itself, there does not seem to be happiness or blessing in sorrow. We might rather call mourning 'unhappiness,' and speak of it as the opposite to what is really good and blessed. It is surely in itself one of the sad incidents of the fall of man; and so in itself sad, melancholy, and unhappy. If, then, there be blessedness in mourning and sorrow, it must needs

[a] Preached at St. Mary's, Oxford, Feb. 12, 1860.

be the blessedness of a fallen race; and yet of a race
not wholly and entirely ruined. We cannot conceive
that it should be true of the unfallen angels to say
that it is blessed for them to mourn. For for *what*
should they mourn? How should it be well for them
that the brightness of their exulting innocence should
be dimmed by mourning? Nor can it be true of the
lost angels, who have no hope, that mourning is blessed. Mourning is to them part of the very bitterness of their penalty: it can bring them no blessedness, for it surely promises them no comfort. It is
peculiarly the blessing of men, or rather, of Christian
men; not so peculiarly, I say, of men who are not
Christians, or at least who are not held up by the
faith, more or less explicit, of redemption and restoration. Patriarchs, holy men of old, saints of God,
dying in faith and not looking for transitory promises
only, may be conceived to have been capable, to the
same extent, of apprehending the blessedness of sorrow and mourning. But we can hardly imagine that
heathens could be capable of it. They might accept
sorrow resignedly, or stoically; they might learn to
make the best of it; they might, in a few cases of
sublime virtue,—virtue so sublime as to be almost
unreasonable in one to whom life and immortality
had not been brought to light by the Gospel,—teach

that righteousness in itself, unknown and unappreciated alike by men and gods, and in the midst of any amount of suffering, is good, and unrighteousness evil: but the direct and assured blessedness of sorrow, as such, cannot be known to those who have not been taught by revelation to see through the cloud which, since the Fall, envelopes the natural life of man, and discern the brightness which is beyond it. No; the blessedness of sorrow and mourning, as it does not lie essentially in the sorrow and mourning themselves, so is not to be discovered by all those on whom sorrow and mourning fall. It belongs to men fallen in Adam, and redeemed in Christ; depraved in nature by the fall, and replaced, not in original righteousness, but in a state of hope and promise by Christ,—it belongs to this intermediate condition in which we stand, this state of trial. As it was not the blessedness of the heathen days, so neither will it be the blessedness of the days into which we are to be received into the fulness of our Master's joy. It is the peculiar blessedness of these dim days of offered hope and struggling faith; the peculiar blessedness of men who, depressed by an hereditary sentence of depravation and decay of original righteousness and joy, have the work now set before them, in the Holy Ghost, of making in fear and trembling their sacred calling and election to eternal righteousness and glory sure. And the blessing is to be found by realizing to ourselves the condition in which we really are, not in any way by making it different from what it is; by meekly and cheerfully accepting it as the very means whereby we may rise out of it. To disown it, to shut our eyes to it, to kick against it, to writhe under it, to try to satisfy ourselves with the sparkles of fugitive brightness which we can discover or make in it,—all this is to find in it nothing except its own sad weight and bitterness: whereas, on the contrary, to accept it, to see in it a gracious talent for our use rather than a judgment for our punishment, to see God's goodness, and feel His love in it,—this is to make it what it surely is designed to be, the very instrument of blessing which is capable, if rightly used, of imparting healing and restoration in the very pain it brings.

I speak, first, of outward sorrow; sorrow brought upon us from without — God's dispensation to us. Such sorrow falls, no doubt, with very different degrees of heaviness on different people, allowing some, not in youth only, while the heart is light and the strength unbroken, but almost throughout the whole of life, to know comparatively little of its bitterness;

while on some, even from early days, it lies continually. There are those who have been familiar in all their lives—and they are not the less for that children of God's truest love in Christ—with the sense of pain in its severest and saddest forms; so familiar with it as never to have been without it. And to all in their degree. Sickness, pain, weakness of body, the loss of friends, poverty, disappointment, and as life goes on and strength fails, the blows of sorrow coming thicker and faster, with less elasticity of mind to bear up against them, and the shadow of death gradually closing round and shutting up the onward view,—these things chequer the life of all, and, though they may not always actually befal any one, are all, we well know, possible, likely, perhaps imminent, at every moment of our lives.

I speak now to a congregation which, as little as any that could be gathered together in this land, knows by its own experience the sadness of mourning and sorrow. Any ordinary village or town congregation would supply, it is probable, a larger proportion of people on whom the heavier blows of divinely-sent sorrow had already fallen than this one, composed mainly of young men in their strength, with what seems an unbounded view of life before them—(that view, how boundless and bright as it is looked forward to, how narrow and chequered when we come to look back upon it!)—yet no doubt, even here there are many hearts which have begun to be taught the sacred lesson of mourning, and, I trust, to know the sweet blessedness with which it is charged to a true Christian soul. On this part of the subject, therefore, as less immediately appropriate to the chief part of my audience, I will be brief. But, oh! brethren, ye whom God hath begun to address with the sweet and grave visitations of deep and heart-searching sorrow, learn from the Word of God what these visitations are! They are occasions, opportunities of blessing, of inestimable price. God is nearer to you when sorrow comes upon you: God is laying His grave, loving, fatherly hand upon your heads when He sends you pain, disappointment, bereavement. He is calling you to turn to Him, and see the brightness which He is preparing for you, and which never shines with such pure and winning light as when you see it through the cloud of sorrow. And the very voice and sound of sorrow, what is it else than a voice from the next world,—the world, to the Christian, of joy? Amid the lively, confusing sounds, the busy, bustling noise which surrounds us here when we are well, and our friends are well, when all is going on prosperously round us, and our hearts respond in mirth and comfort to such things, the voice of sorrow, sorrow from without, is nothing else than the very voice of the next world. It is, as it were, set in a different key from all the other notes. It jars among them. But listen to it, disengage your ear from the other din, listen to it, by God's grace, calmly, with prayers, and for some time, and you will find that it has most heavenly music in it. There is no doubt, there can be no doubt of it. If any one, by God's grace, can so lift up his soul under sorrow, as to see and feel the fatherly love of God in sending it to him, as to hear God's voice in it, and in his heart to acknowledge the hand of God in grave mercy laid upon his head, he tastes a sweetness which is unspeakably beyond all the noisy, merry, prosperous joy of the unsorrowing and successful world.

In sorrow, again, we, as it were naturally, put the world by: it is distasteful to us, it is untuneful, it is impertinent to our feeling. We turn naturally—I mean that Christians do so—to God. The utterances that come first and most readily to our lips are utterances of prayer. The ties that bind us so fast at other times to the earth being loosened by the shock of sorrow, a Christian's heart clings all the closer, infinitely the closer, to God and heaven than it had ever known how to cling in the days of earthly joy.

Our sins, again, which at other times had been comparatively regarded lightly, slurred over, perhaps forgotten, shew like sins. Temptations lose much more than half their power. Sacred things gain a flavour which we could never find in them or taste before. In fact, the lower blinding light under which we commonly live, the sunshine, (which, shewing us all the little, lower objects of the earth, conceals from us the view of the heavens,) being under eclipse, we begin as it were to catch sight of the endless depths of else-unseen space, and the mighty procession of the constellations of the heaven, which that which we call day, and think to be brightness, had hidden from our eyes.

Now this is, no doubt, the design of God in every particular case of sorrow or pain with which He is pleased to visit us. Have we any trouble or grief whatever of body or soul upon us, sent to us by God? Are we, in the days of our own strength and well-being, called upon to sympathize in the sorrows and pains of others? Each of such things, be they ever so heavy, or ever so various, is like the voice of an angel from God, a very sweet voice if we will listen to it with a praying heart and a still soul, whispering into our ear that our rest is not here, and, what is more, disposing our ear to welcome and attend to the whisper. I could even add that the very nauseousness of physic, strangely universal as it is, seems to point in the same direction, as if they who were sick were at once removed out of the sphere of common earthly enjoyments, and under God's stern, but sweet and merciful teaching, bidden to frame their disciplined fancy to a different and hitherto unknown world. Sure I am that it is a most gracious provision which ordinarily leads men to their death through pain and weakness, and decay of body,—that dim neutral territory which divides the earthly brightness of the one life from the heavenly brightness of the other. And blessed are they who, when they are strong and well themselves, have been allowed to see that sweetest of all Christian sights, a dear friend passing, perhaps for years, through the gradual descent of hopeless sickness, calm, cheerful, faithful, loving, "content to live yet not afraid to die," and have been permitted to go with them, and to bear them Christian company and sacred communion to the very gate, as it were, of paradise.

In sorrow, again, God seems to visit the soul more personally, more as a friend, as a Father, more as a distinct supporter and upholder, than at any other time. There is danger, when all is bright and cheerful round us, lest God become to our minds rather a doctrine than a being, rather a conviction of our understanding than a near and very merciful Person, whom we may actually address in thoughts and words, and cling to with human affection and real reliance. But in sorrow we instantly crave sympathy, nearness, kind affection, comfort: and I apprehend that the prayers poured forth in sorrow will be found characteristically different from those that are offered when we are in joy, mainly in this, that they are uttered in the much clearer, and, as it were, instinctive consciousness of God as a real Being, a Father,—and we know what a loving and pitying father is,—a merciful and Almighty Person, with whom the soul may hold close and sweet communion, and drink in peace, and soothing, and spiritual strength from that near approach.

Truly it is a sad and deep mistake to look upon sorrow, outward sorrow, in this fallen world of ours, as a judgment, or penalty, or dispensation of the wrath of God. Oh no! it is indeed a blessed talent, an opportunity, a call of God to us which is designed to loosen and detach us from things that are temporary and unreal, and open our eyes to see, and our hearts to love, things that are eternal and true. He who watches us always, watches us, if I may say so, doubly then. He watches us gravely, sweetly, paternally, to see how we will take it. He chasteneth whom He loveth. He cutteth the branches that they may bring forth more fruit. He giveth the sorrow which wringeth His people's hearts as a talent which they may turn to abundant increase, that He may therein be glorified. But remember that it is a talent only, an opportunity only, not in itself anything more at all than an opportunity. God doth not love any man the more for being in sorrow. It is, no doubt, in love that He sendeth sorrow; and with very great and fatherly love He regardeth those who turn to Him in it, and use the sorrow which He sent for the purpose for which He sent it. But let us not confound—and I fear it is not an uncommon confusion—the softness of heart and the temporary alienation from worldly things which are the direct and natural effects of sorrow, with the turning to God, the repentance and amendment, the growth in grace and goodness, which are the divine and spiritual effects of sorrow. Surely it is with sorrow as it is with all other talents; well used, most blessed; wasted, ill-used, it surely operates for evil. What if a person be visited with heavy sickness, or long and afflicting pain, and be *not* turned to God by these things? What if any person be heavily bereaved, and have not learned, permanently learned, to be more detached from the earth, and more devoted to God by it? Is there anything sadder, brethren, than to see sickness or sorrow fail thus to do its work? or to feel that it fails to do its work upon ourselves? Is there a more melancholy sight than to see a nation humble itself before God in prayer and fasting on account of some national calamity or danger on one day, and on the next plunge back again, as if nothing had happened, into all its former recklessness and sin? or to see man or woman receive, so far as we can judge, the talent of sorrow from God in vain, and issue forth from heavy grief or sickness, touched, perhaps, for a time, and then, with the touch gone, the wounds of Heaven healed, and the heart as earthly, and as closely bound to earth, as ever? A heavy sorrow ought to leave its mark for life. Not the miserable, thankless, outward mark of never knowing how to smile again, but the cheerful, gracious, inward mark of deepened devotion, and a heart more habitually set upon the thoughts of God and heaven.

Hitherto, brethren, I have spoken only of outward sorrow, the direct dispensation of God's grave and merciful love to us,—and of this, I well know, very cursorily and slightly,—with the intention of suggesting thoughts on a very deep and solemn subject rather than with any idea of exhausting them. There is another very important part of the Beatitude which must not be omitted; I mean the inward sorrow, the sorrow which a sinner must feel for his own sins,—the self-control, and refusal of various pleasant things,—the mortification, as Holy Scripture calls it, of the members,—to which belongs, no doubt, a large portion of the comfort promised in this Beatitude. This is that godly sorrow which the Apostle so earnestly rejoices to see and acknowledge in his Corinthians [b]; that godly sorrow that worketh repentance unto salvation not to be repented of, which God most surely loveth, at which the blessed angels who surround the throne of God rejoice, and which shall never fail to receive Divine comfort.

Oh brethren! when we recollect that besides that outward cloud of which I have already spoken, which God gathers in love round us all, more or less darkly, we carry, each one of us, our own separate inward darkness, the darkness generated by our own sins, how do we double, nay, much more than double, the vision of sorrow and heaviness which surrounds us ever, though we do not always feel and realize it!

It is very difficult to speak satisfactorily of these things in the abstract. The preacher cannot know anything of the various tales of sin and weakness that your own separate hearts, brethren, know of more or less accurately, and that the Holy Spirit of God knows and reads within you altogether. Yet each one has

[b] 2 Cor. vii. 10.

his secret burthen, the load which he has heaped upon himself by his own fault,—the load of years of imperfect service, and many, many sins. No doubt these burthens are very different in comparative weight and sadness, yet are they sad and weighty, if we would but feel it, to us all; and yet not so sad or weighty to any as that there should not be to every single one among us the fullest and freest offers of blessing and comfort in Christ. No doubt, again, there are many here— many among the young as well as among the old— who are practised in continual repentance and self-denial, who watch their hearts habitually, and pour out before God continually the confession of their sins; but, alas! there are probably many who do not do so, who take life and sin easily; and perhaps some who are even now laying up stores of misery and woe for years of later penitence, if they should be granted to them. What, brethren! can we annihilate sorrow by forgetting it for a season? Are our sins done with because we will not think of them? Is all right with us, because we choose to be so mad as not to remember the reckoning that is to come to us? What is it that gives the sting, the horror, to the prospect of death? What is it that makes the idea so terrible to us of being called upon to leave this life, and pass into God's unseen world? What, but sin? what, but the general dark consciousness of sin unrepented and so unforgiven, and the arrival of the actual time of account, the thought of which we have not chosen to face before? It was sin that first made death penal; and it is we who still make the prospect of death yet more black and terrible than it is in itself when we persist in kindling a fire and compassing ourselves about with sparks; when we will walk in the light of our fire, and the sparks that we have kindled [c]; when we will not consent to shade and reduce these lower, blinding lights of our own kindling, so as to see and know who we are, and where; and *what*—what real light and comfort—is set before us.

But is it, then, the truth that life, Christian life, is to be so sad? Is it the very truth of Christian religion that none can reach the blessedness of Divine comfort except he seek it through this deep and varied experience of sorrow? If this be the actual truth of the Word of God, how does it square with the actual life of Christian people? Do Christians in general seem to feel this, or live like this? Do the older people? do the young? Are there not multitudes of every age, are there not many among yourselves, brethren, who are spending their days, not in sorrow, God knoweth! of any sort, but in the merest

[c] Isa. l. 11.

search for amusement; a search for amusement which throws—I do not say sorrow aside, but sometimes duty, ordinary judgment, and good sense to the winds? Are there not those who, having not long emerged from the pupilage and discipline of boyhood, are tempted—and yield to the temptation—to fool away their youth in wild, wanton recklessness of pleasure, —*fastness*, as they call it,—tampering, it may be, with various kinds of very dangerous and defiling sin, so that momentary enjoyment may be derived from it? Yet what is the truth, the simple, unexaggerated truth, of Holy Scripture? Surely it is this: God doth commend His cup, the cup of which His Son and the holy apostles drank, to the lips of every single Christian, be he who he may. He bids every one who would be His disciple deny himself, and take up his cross daily, and follow in His company. The cost of the tower, the strength of the defending army, must be calculated beforehand. Better not begin to build the tower, better not provoke the war, than fail disgracefully in either. Salt without savour, what is it good for? To put hand to the plough, and look back, to make excuses of pleasure or business in comparison of the Lord's call, to be unready to part with eye or hand, father or mother, lands or goods, to decline to sell all, if so be, and follow Christ, is to be unworthy of

Him. Surely the language of Holy Scripture is everywhere simple, uniform, uncompromising, thorough: and surely no word will be found in any part of it to encourage any person to think that the Christian profession requires less than that he yield himself absolutely up in body and soul to the obedience and imitation of Christ, the Man of sorrows, and seek His blessing, as Christ bids him, in Christian mourning. And let no one think that all these words of Holy Scripture are to be disposed of by an *if*: as though *if* sorrow comes, *if* persecution or mourning comes, *then*, and only then, all these strong and deep words gain their application to ourselves. Alas! what means the daily taking up of the cross? what means the impossibility of being Christ's disciples without entire denial of self? What of the sharing of the sufferings of Christ, that we may also be partakers of His glory?

But, again, is life indeed to be so sad? and can we not be Christ's servants without wearing this continual cloud on our brow and sorrow in our heart? Bear with me, brethren, though I speak things which every Christian knows, while I endeavour to state the truth, as between the extremes on this subject. Consider the metaphor of the cup of God as it is used by the inspired writers in many different parts of

"BLESSED ARE THEY THAT MOURN." 41

Holy Scripture, and see how it supplies the exactness of teaching which we desire. God, as the Master of a feast, is represented as holding in His hand a cup. "In the hand of the Lord there is a cup, and the wine is red [d]." It is full mixed, and He poureth out to the guests of the same. And first to His own Son. To Him He giveth it, full mixed indeed with indescribable bitterness of other men's evil, but un-embittered by any sadness of sin of His own; and His blessed Son drank it deep, drank it dry, in the agony in the garden and upon the cross [e]. And next, to the apostles, represented for the time by the sons of Zebedee, when by themselves or through their mother they asked for the places on the right hand and on the left of the King in His glory: "Ye know not what ye ask. Are ye able to drink of the cup that I shall drink of?" And when they confidently answered, "We are able," He said to them, what no doubt was to be understood of them all, "Ye shall indeed drink of My cup [f]." And they drank it; each his own, each differently mingled,—but all the twelve, *but one*, drank it faithfully, and after their Master's example. And what He said unto them, He said unto all us, for we know that it is as true of us as

[d] Ps. lxxv. 8. [e] St. Matt. xxvi. 39; xxvii. 34.
[f] Ibid. xx. 22, 23.

of them, that "we must suffer with Christ, that we
may also be glorified together [g]." To all the faithful
guests at the feast of God is this cup offered: differently mingled for each, and containing, no doubt,
for every one many bitter ingredients, and unwelcome in itself to the natural taste of those to whom
He offers it. But to those who accept it meekly and
patiently it is "the cup of salvation," "the Lord is
the portion of their cup," "their cup of joy is full
and runneth over [h]:" to them the bitter is overcome
by the sweet, and the flavour that is left upon the
soul is the flavour of life and salvation. But the
Lord of the feast does not stop with His faithful
and godly servants. The blood-red, turbid, full-mixed
wine must be drained to the very dregs by such as are
disobedient and ungodly: "As for the dregs thereof,
all the ungodly of the earth shall drink them and suck
them out." This is that wine-cup of the fury of the
Lord which the Prophet Jeremiah represents himself
as giving by the Lord's command to the nations:
"Then took I the cup at the Lord's hand, and made
all the nations to drink, unto whom the Lord had
sent me;" "And it shall be," the Prophet adds, "if
they refuse to take the cup at thine hand to drink,
then shalt thou say unto them, Thus saith the Lord

[g] Rom. viii. 17.   [h] Ps. cxvi. 13, xvi. 5, xxiii. 5.

of Hosts; Ye shall certainly drink[i]." This, again, is that "wine of the wrath of God which is poured out without mixture into the cup of His indignation," as we read in the Book of the Revelation[k], "the cup of the wine of the fierceness of His wrath" of the same Book[l]. Yet even this cup of unmixed bitterness and judgment may on repentance be made to pass from such as have been condemned to drink it for awhile: for even Jerusalem, which had drunk of the cup of His fury, which had "drunken the dregs of the cup of trembling, and wrung them out," heard these words from the Lord whom she had offended, "Thus saith thy Lord the Lord, and thy God which pleadeth the cause of His people, Behold, I have taken out of thine hand the cup of trembling, even the dregs of the cup of My fury; thou shalt no more drink of it again[m]." See then, brethren, in the remarkable consistency with which this metaphor is maintained in so many and various parts of Holy Scripture, the truth of God in respect of mourning and sorrow. The cup of God, bitter always, but mixed in very different proportions, is offered to the lips of every single man and woman of His people. In it are mingled sorrows outward and sorrows inward;

[i] Jer. xxv. 17, 28. [k] Rev. xiv. 10. [l] Ibid. xvi. 19.
[m] Isa. li. 17, 22.

such as are simply sent to us in love by God Himself, and such as our own sin and evil continually add to the bitter mixture; many things distasteful to our liking, but very profitable to our spiritual health. While it is probable that no two persons living have exactly the same, it is certain that no one, at any period of his life, is devoid of it altogether. It is offered to young children in the form sometimes of pain and sickness and outward affliction, always in discipline, enforced learning, in obedience, duty, and the like; unwelcome things, more or less, to the mere natural taste, but not such as to make the real sweetness and mirth of childhood one whit the less, but rather much the greater, if they be cheerfully and willingly accepted. And is it not offered, constantly and secretly offered, by God to young men? Which of you has not, if he will recognise it, God's most unmistaken cup offered to his lips, that he may secretly and seriously drink of it? Sometimes it comes in the form of sorrow to be borne,—outward sorrow, as of pain or bereavement, very sadly it may be and very heavily, yet to be borne as God's fatherly dispensation, and turned by prayer into sanctification. You have always your own burthen of sin, with all its particulars of aggravation, known to none but you, to be remembered before God in confession and penitence, and that not in word only and profession, but in true inward sorrow of heart; always your work to be done, lust to be curbed, headstrong will to be bent to the will of God, examples to be avoided, temptations to be resisted, which perhaps are the stronger for having been yielded to before; language to be kept under guard, imaginations to be kept holy, prayers to be paid, the heart to be kept straight and whole with God, in inward and real sanctification. If a young man, by the grace of God, thus habitually drinks of God's cup secretly and inwardly; if in his own room, or in company, he remembers that God Himself is offering it to him, and watching him as he drinks it; if he does not refuse it or kick against it because the flavour of it is not in itself or naturally sweet or captivating to his sense,—will his life be really saddened and made unhappy by so doing? Are not all the elements of such sadness and unhappiness already there, whether he will for the present recognise them or no? Does he not, on the contrary, gather a real and deep sweetness from these sadnesses, and by the grace of God learn to turn what otherwise would be mere and incurable unhappiness into divine comfort? Is it not mere madness to refuse it now, so as to have to drain the dregs of it hereafter? And to us, brethren, who are older, does God the less commend His cup to our perpetual drinking? Do not think that these things belong to young men only. Perhaps our own sin and folly in former years may have infused a deeper bitterness into it; probably, as we grow older, external sorrows fall thicker and sadder on our hearts, and certainly the shadow of old age and approaching death deepens naturally round our view. Shall we, too, decline to drink meekly and faithfully? or shall we, by God's grace, learn to find the sweetness, the deep and inexpressible sweetness, which at any time while God spares us to live, and under any circumstances and aggravations of sorrow outward or inward, is to be found by those who will turn to Him in their pain, and penitently lay their griefs before His mercy?

Yes: blessed are they that mourn thus over their sins, whether it be in youth, in manhood, or old age; blessed on the most assured word of Christ, for they shall certainly be comforted. Never did such mourning, never *can* such mourning, fail of Christ's comfort. And what shall be the comfort, and who the Comforter? Can any doubt? Who but the Divine Comforter, the most Holy Spirit of God, knoweth how to comfort? That sacred comfort will conquer every sort of sorrow and bitterness. Pain of body, decay, and the prospect of death,—the utmost bereavements, disappointments, or distresses,—whatever there be of such suffering, the upholding Spirit can fill the soul of man with so deep and divine comfort, that all these things, instead of diminishing his true joy, are felt to be, what they are indeed, helps and aids to reach the happiness of heaven. Sorrow for sin, tears of penitence, deep humbling of the soul in confession and prayer,—in all this, be it as bitter as it may, the Holy Spirit will so support the soul of him who sorrows after a godly sort, as to turn it all into strong faith and holy exultation of pardon and acceptance. But He visits no heart, so far as we know, with comfort but such as have first, at His touch, sorrowed. If our hearts refuse to sorrow, if they will have none of the bitter, then, so far as we know, they must never taste the sweet, but have unmingled bitterness for ever. And as we sorrow more truly and more deeply, the comfort will grow too. They are both the Holy Spirit's work in us; both grow from the same divine stock. For fallen and feeble man godly sorrow and comfort, comfort and godly sorrow, cannot be separated; they are, under the Holy Spirit, the Christian's portion upon earth. Oh, brethren! I would to God that His grace, which even in these feeble words of exhortation moves you, each separate one among you, to think of your own sins and sorrows, and lay them in honest penitence before God, might lead each one of you to that deep and sanctified mourning which brings the inexpressible peace! I speak of the orderly, deep, sober sorrow of Christian men intelligently recognising, by the secret working of the Holy Spirit in their hearts, the exceeding sinfulness of their sins; and of the deep and sober peace which is unfailingly given in the Church of Christ, under His faithful promise, to His sorrowing children. I do not speak of frantic or extraordinary excitements of body or mind, of imaginary visions, direct miraculous assurances, or the like; still less would I be understood as attempting to set limits to the extraordinary workings of the Holy Spirit, or as doubting the power and goodness of God to bring real and perhaps lasting good out of things in themselves imperfect or mistaken. No: it is not of things extraordinary that I am speaking, but of that sober penitence which the Word of God enjoins in every part of Holy Writ, which the Church of God preaches, and has preached in all ages since it was founded, which the Holy Ghost suggests and desires to further and perfect in all Christian people, which you and I, brethren, may surely gain, by His aid, if we will fall on our knees before Him, and examining our hearts and lives, will honestly confess our sins, and sorrowfully ask His forgiveness for Christ's sake,—if we will do so on this very day, and from this day forth. To *that* Christ promises most sure and unfailing comfort: in this life first, while the sorrow and the penitence are still with us, a comfort mingled indeed, but growing, increasing, conquering; and in the next, a comfort unmingled, victorious, and divine, the peace of God, which passeth all understanding, the sweetness of which is beyond all thought.

Would you taste that comfort? Do you wish to have the Holy Spirit of God, the blessed Comforter, really and more and more an inmate in your heart? Do you desire, being God's baptized child, to make that calling and election sure? Are you manly enough, seeing how short time is, and eternity how long, to throw aside the folly and the real childishness which beset the life of many young men, and be what you really are, God's vowed and earnest servant? Oh that man might speak home to the heart of man! Oh that the Holy Spirit of God would wing my words with such power as to pierce the inner soul of such as are thoughtless, and touch them with real seriousness of sorrow, real Christian sorrow, as to make them welcome to their lips God's precious, bitter cup, and drink it so meekly and faithfully here, as not to have to suck out the dregs of it hereafter; that we might all, brethren, gain full taste, both here and hereafter, of that eternal and divine comfort which belongs, on the most certain Word of Christ, to His true and Christian mourners.

SERMON III.[a]

St. Matthew v.

5. Blessed are the meek: for they shall inherit the earth.

THIRD in the order of the Beatitudes, as given by St. Matthew in his report of the Sermon on the Mount, comes the blessedness of meekness. "Blessed are the meek, for they shall inherit the earth."

It may be considered as forming the second of that second pair among the Beatitudes which relate to inward virtues having their scope and exhibiting themselves in the position which a Christian holds among other men. The first of this pair, poverty of spirit, with its peculiar blessing, the possession of the kingdom of heaven, I have before attempted to explain in this place. The latter, meekness, with its still more paradoxical blessing, 'the inheritance of this earth,' I propose to consider this afternoon.

[a] Preached at St. Mary's, Oxford, May 8, 1859.

What then, in the first place, is meekness? and whom are we to understand under the description of the meek?

We have two models of meekness in Holy Scripture. First, the great and divine model of our Lord Himself, who bids us learn of Him, for He is meek and lowly of heart,—apparently in those few words signifying the same two virtues in Himself which in this pair of Beatitudes He pronounces blessed; and secondly, Moses, His great type and predecessor [b],— the man who was very meek above all the men which were upon the face of the earth, whom God sanctified in his faithfulness and meekness, and chose him out of all men [c].

Let us observe, in passing, *who* are these Scriptural models of meekness: the one, the king in Jeshurun [d], the prince, the ruler, the lawgiver, the man of God, the prophet unequalled in Israel [e] till the Antitype appeared; the other, the very Prince of peace, the King to sit for ever on the throne of David, He of whom His father according to the flesh said, by the Holy Spirit of God, "The Lord said unto My Lord, Sit Thou on My right hand, until I make Thine enemies Thy footstool."

[b] Numbers xii. 3.   [c] Ecclus. xlv. 4.
[d] Deut. xxxiii. 5, 1.   [e] Ibid. xxxiv. 10.

What, then, is meekness? and what are the traits by which it is commonly recognised?

I apprehend that they are more or less such as these:—1st, a willingness to take wrong without retaliation. This, I suppose, every person understands to be essential to the character of meekness. Indeed, in the *natural* imitations of Christian meekness,—which are *not* Christian meekness, but are outwardly like it,—this is perhaps the single, certainly the one most characteristic trait of all.

2ndly. A meek man, in a Christian sense, having his place in life, and with it his duties, thinks nothing of himself, his claims, his dignity, his station, but holding under God, and discharging his duty to God, puts himself, and all that relates to himself, out of his sight.

3rdly. A Christianly meek man having duties which affect other people, is gentle in treatment of others, loving and modest, but firm and simple, allowing no provocation to ruffle him, not recognising *himself* or his own claims, but acting as God's minister, and lovingly ruling, teaching, or otherwise directing those whom God has put under his care.

These, and such as these, are, I apprehend, the main characteristics of what men call meekness. It has two sides; its passive side, in which it bears with provocation, controls all feelings of irritation, and refuses to regard personal injury and wrong; and its active side, in which it strongly, bravely, kindly, sweetly,—still and throughout with total absence of the thought of *self*,—discharges towards men the duties which it owes to God.

Let it, however, be remembered that the meekness intended in this Beatitude is surely not meekness of nature, but meekness of grace; and that these, though bearing a considerable external likeness to one another, are really very different from each other, both in themselves and in their history. Natural meekness is very nearly allied with timidity, sometimes with meanness, and sometimes with insensibility. It is the tameness which belongs to a weak, though a placid and amiable nature. But the meekness which is of grace is essentially a brave thing. It is not the natural product of a tasteless tree. It is the Divine product of a strong natural stock. Divine meekness requires strength, self-control, tranquil courage,—and all these in a high degree. Perhaps the natural traits which suit best with the ingrafted element of Divine meekness, are rather such as without grace might have ripened into a character the reverse of meek, than into the soft and yielding disposition which men call meekness. This, I say, it is very important to remember; in this, and in similar cases. For the natural imitations of Divine virtues are often so very unlike them inwardly and really, as in fact to indispose rather than to predispose the person in whom they are found for the exalted and angelic virtues, the strong and noble virtues, which they counterfeit. Such is natural credulity as compared with Divine faith, natural softness of affection as compared with Divine love, natural insensibility to offence as compared with Divine forgiveness, natural tameness of mind as compared with Divine meekness.

Blessed then, no doubt, are the meek. Blessed, for it is of the grace and blessing of God that they have this holy gift of meekness; and the same grace and blessing of God which gave it surely rests upon it when it is given.

Blessed again, assuredly, are the meek; for they have learned of Him who was, above all human-kind, meek and lowly of heart; and in that lesson duly learned they shall find rest—the rest which is from God's blessing, and is a great part of that blessing—unto their souls.

Blessed again are the meek: for that meek and quiet spirit, which is itself the fruit of the Spirit, as we are assured by St. Paul[f], is in the sight of God of great price, as we know on the authority of St. Peter[g].

But all these grounds of blessedness, most real and

[f] Gal. v. 23.   [g] 1 Pet. iii. 4.

true as they are, do not apply to the specific blessing pronounced upon the meek by the Lord in this place, "Blessed are the meek: for they shall *inherit the earth*."

If the general blessedness of meekness, however clear to a well-instructed Christian, is utterly paradoxical in the eyes of worldly men,—for they are apt to think meekness a poor, helpless, pitiful thing, and if they love it at all, love it with a pity which is very near akin to contempt,—if, I say, the general blessedness of meekness is thus utterly paradoxical in the eyes of worldly men, what are we to say of this *reason* for that blessedness? Does meekness, so far as we can see, seem in any intelligible sense to inherit the earth? Do the gentle, the meek, the loving, rule and bear sway in the earth? Did they ever do so? Was there ever a time when violence, and covetousness, and craft did not overpower or circumvent simplicity and gentleness?

So difficult, indeed, is it to understand in what way the meek can be said to inherit the earth, at least in the present state of things, and with the present hearts and tempers of men, that the commentators upon Holy Scripture have commonly set themselves to interpret these hard words in some other way, and by some of the many means of explaining words away, to make them mean something different, something almost opposite to that which at first hearing they seem to say.

Among the ancients, indeed, St. Chrysostom [h] and Theophylact expound the words naturally and simply to signify the possession of this earth. "Some," says Theophylact, "understand by the earth the spiritual earth, τὴν νοητήν, that is, heaven. Nay, but do thou understand this earth also, for inasmuch as the meek are considered to be men despised and deprived of their property, He [the Lord] says that they rather are the possessors of all things [i]." The explanation of St. Augustine [k] is not very different from this.

St. Jerome, with several other ancients, interprets the words to mean 'the land of the living [l],' in opposition to 'the land of the dying,'—that is, a new earth in heaven, in which there is to be no more death.

Modern writers, so far as I have been able to ascertain, generally explain the promise of inheriting the earth to be a mode of speech borrowed from the times of the wandering of the Israelites in the wilderness, and requiring to be explained accordingly. As, they

[h] In loc., vol. vii. 188.   [i] Theophyl. in loc., vol. i. p. 23.
[k] Vol. iii. lib. i. de Serm. in M.
[l] "Nemo enim terram istam per mansuetudinem sed per superbiam possidet."—*St. Hieron. in loc.*

say, in the wilderness the hopes of the Israelites were fed by the constant prospect and promise of obtaining their inheritance in the land which flowed with milk and honey; so, in this wilderness of life, Christians are held up and encouraged by the prospect of obtaining their inheritance in the kingdom of heaven. Heaven is their Canaan. The inheritance which they look for—called of the earth by such reference to the case of the ancient people of God, so often made types of Christian people—is not literally of the earth, but of heaven.

To this prevalent interpretation is to be added an opinion of many, that the words are to be taken as a quotation from the 37th Psalm, and that in the millennial period, or in some future state of things, this actual earth, with all these scenes which we know so well throughout it, may be the abode of God's saints, then, in their meekness, become its true inheriting possessors.

Are these more modern interpretations satisfactory? I cannot think so. I cannot think it satisfactory to explain the word 'earth' to mean 'heaven,' or anything equivalent to 'heaven,' which is, so to speak, the opposite, the constantly contrasted opposite, of the earth. The poor in spirit have the promise of the kingdom of *heaven;* can it be supposed that when

"BLESSED ARE THE MEEK."

the inheritance of the *earth* is immediately promised to the meek, the promise is to be understood exactly in the same sense as that with which it is thus apparently contrasted? Add to which, what is well observed by St. Chrysostom upon this passage, that there are several other passages, besides this one, in the New Testament which speak to the same general effect, some of which are wholly incapable of such a gloss as is thus frequently put upon this verse. Such is the "length of days" promised in the Epistle to the Ephesians [m] to those who obey the fifth Commandment. Such, again, are our Lord's words in the 10th of St. Mark, "Verily I say unto you, There is no man that hath left house, or brethren, or sisters, or father, or mother, or wife, or children, or lands, for My sake, and the Gospel's, but he shall receive an hundred-fold *now in this time*, houses, and brethren, and sisters, and mothers, and children, and lands, *with persecutions;* and in the world to come eternal life [n]:" in which passage there is an undoubted promise of specific blessings in this time or life, in contradistinction from those which shall be given in the next world.

Surely, then, we must needs believe that the meek have in some literal way the promise of inheriting this earth; that besides the blessings stored for them

[m] Eph. vi. 2.   [n] St. Mark x. 29, 30.

in the heavenly kingdom, blessings, no doubt, of the choicest and best,—for who are to hold higher rank in that kingdom than those who are most like the meek humility of little children, those who have learned best to copy the likeness of Him who was meek and lowly of heart?—besides, I say, these blessings, they have the particular and wondrous promise of inheriting this very earth. Strange, wonderful, inexplicable as it may sound, we must face the plain words of revelation, and endeavour to fathom by God's grace the mystery, how it should be that in this scene of violence, of craft, of selfishness, of oppression, of evil passion, and success of evil, yet are the meek— these lowly, loving, self-renouncing, gentle, meek, these lambs among the wolves—the true inheritors, the rightful lords, by divine heirship, of this dark and stormy world in which it is our lot to live.

Nor do I suppose that the words would be adequately interpreted by being understood to refer to the inward peace of mind, the deep, stable, inalienable joy which fills and supports a truly Christian soul even in the midst of the most searching external trials and sufferings. It is surely not in accordance with the simple truthfulness of Holy Scripture to represent *the inheritance of the earth* as meaning not indeed the inheritance of the earth, but a sort of joy

"BLESSED ARE THE MEEK."

which belongs to those who have no earthly inheritance, save in their own inward peace of soul before God. Let it be freely granted that this inward peace forms part of the blessing, yet surely we must look to find something more exactly appropriate to our Lord's words, something more capable of being understood as a real and literal inheritance of the earth.

And I think we may in some degree find what we seek. In the first place, let it be observed that meekness and gentleness, even in such form and degree as we meet with it among men, Christian meekness and gentleness I mean, have really a considerable tendency in themselves to gain power among men. Crossed, opposed, over-ridden, and oppressed as they often are by the opposite qualities, yet in their amiableness which wins upon men, in their truth and honesty which lead men to trust them, in their refusal to be provoked which continually gives them advantage over adversaries, and forces esteem and almost affection even into hatred and opposition, in their consistency which causes them to pursue the same objects, and those good ones, with uniform steadiness and constancy, they have really in them some of the main natural elements of power over mankind. As reason in feebler men against irrational strength in the inferior animals, as virtue in general against vice, have, when a certain necessary proportion of physical power and of union is supposed, a necessary tendency to gain power and to rule, so it is with the particular virtue of meekness as against lawless force and violence. Let meekness be really seen and felt, let its conduct be according to its principles, consistent and regular,—let it be not the meekness and tameness of feeble nature, but the meekness of grace grafted on a most brave and loving nature, or at least making a strong nature thus brave and loving, —and forthwith there is no set or society of men, small or great, in which its power does not begin to shew itself. It gets what men call *moral power*, that is, *essential* power. Violence may assail it; force may achieve a temporary victory over it: but all history and all experience prove that such assaults and victories are really, and in their own nature, accidental and temporary. The inner hearts of men at the sight of true Christian meekness have acknowledged their master. Even while it is temporarily overwhelmed it does not lose its sovereign attributes. None feel its irresistible superiority more strongly than those who for a time overwhelm it. "It is John the Baptist whom I beheaded." The meek man is the master of his tyrant. The true inheritor of the earth has been seen, and conscience, and natural sense, and the inferior souls of the violent, the inconsistent, and the impatient, bow down inwardly before it, and do it an involuntary homage.

Thus, I say, upon a little consideration we may come to see that meekness is really and discoverably a more powerful thing than it seems; that it actually does exercise a much greater control over the affairs and hearts of men than at first sight appears. And, what is more, that besides its actual power, which we should probably find to be greater and greater the more fully we were able to examine it, it is the rightful heir of much more power on the earth than it actually possesses: that it is the real heir of all power on the earth, defrauded and kept out of some part of its inheritance by lawless violence and unfounded claims, but meanwhile the actual and unquestioned possessor of much, and the rightful heir of all.

And then we may remember that it is in the nature of all the promises of God to be capable of richer, or less rich fulfilment, according to the fulness of the obedience and faith of those to whom the promises are given. So meekness the actual possessor of much, the rightful heir of all power upon the earth, may possibly be kept from obtaining its full inheritance, because it is itself imperfect; because the hearts of the meekest Christians are still too full of violent and angry feelings; because they have not attained to that complete mastery of self, that noble, loving, gentle, unresenting courage which is required of those who would frame themselves upon the perfect model of the meekness of their Divine Master.

And thus it may possibly be that the promise, strange as it sounds, is really and fully accomplished: that meekness, perhaps, actually does inherit, in the way of power, guidance and control of mankind and their affairs to the full extent of its own real existence; that there is as much power in meekness *now*, as there is meekness to exercise power; that if there were more meekness there would be more power; that if Christians were as entirely meek, as uniformly gentle, brave, regardless of offence, loving, as they might and should be, the temporary, the accidental, the usurping powers would of themselves, in great measure at least, cease and be no more upon the earth.

Let it be observed also in this connexion how often the promised blessings of the Gospel are stated to have in them this element of *power* over other people. The rulers over ten cities and five cities in the parable of the talents º may perhaps signify persons rewarded in the next life only; but surely the kingdom ap-

º St. Luke xix. 17, 19.

pointed unto them who have continued with the Lord in His temptations, the eating and drinking at the Lord's table in His kingdom, the twelve apostolic thrones of the regeneration, (and is not this the era of the regeneration?) the royalty and priesthood already ours, and the promised "power over the nations" to him that overcometh and keepeth God's works unto the end[p], cannot be wholly confined to the state of the future life, but belong to that which, begun already in the Church of God, begun in right and title, and begun in fact, shall in that future life become entirely and finally perfect. All these powers are inchoate already. Fettered though they may be in their exercise, and imperfect in themselves from the admixture of much that is human, personal, and therefore feeble, much that is as clay combined with the iron, weakness mingled with the essential power of Christian meekness, yet already they tell wherever they are seen, and have undeniable and increasing influence upon the souls of men and the course of things in the world.

But who does not feel that though all this be indeed very true and undoubted, yet it gives a most inadequate account of the power and influence, even in this earth, of divine and Christian meekness?

[p] Matt. xx. 28; Luke xxii. 29; Rev. ii. 26; i. 5.

How blind and senseless should we be if, in thinking of the real powers which move and govern this lower world, we should confine our thoughts only to such influences, and tendencies towards obtaining influence, as our eyes can see and trace, forgetting the great God whose presence is in the midst of all, above all, and through all, and in all; forgetting Christ the Lord who is in His holy temple and body which is the Church; forgetting the Holy Ghost who sanctifieth by His indwelling the heart of every one who has been duly planted into the unity of that sacred and divine body; forgetting the thousands upon thousands of His mighty and glorious angels who camp about His people, serving spirits, ministering to the heirs of salvation, who love and tend with particular affection and interest the little ones, the meek and humble ones of their Master's blessed flock; forgetting the wondrous powers which, according to the very words of that gracious Master, He has bestowed for ever upon the faith, the unwearied prayers of the lowliest, the humblest, the meekest of His people.

If meekness, naturally regarded, seem to have a natural and, in the long run, an irrepressible right of power on the earth, so that the opposite powers, however successful for a time, are seen to be traitorous and usurping rebels against a legitimate and higher-born superior, how wonderfully is this condition of things heightened and illustrated when, lifting for a moment the curtain of the invisible world, fixing our thoughts upon the hosts of God, and the mighty God of hosts Himself, all present, all active, all unspeakably powerful in the world of man, we think of Christian meekness in the unlimited might of its powers of prayer!

Who wields this world? In all the immense and untraceable complication of causes and influences in which we live, who and where is he, who and which are they who direct, who really govern, by whom cities, and nations, and continents, and the whole family of mankind pass through their history, meet with their fortunes, to whom they owe as to men their blessings,—the world's benefactors, the world's real rulers? Who are they who in any generation or series of generations have made one nation happier, greater, more blessed than another? Is it they who in each generation are the highest and most prominent in apparent station and power in a land? Generals, statesmen, princes? they whom blind men think the movers of the world,—and history, well-nigh as blind, alone records for the memory of future ages? Do the effigies of kings and bishops that seem, as corbels, to support the weight of the roofs of our vaulted cathedrals, is it indeed they that bear the roof, or does the roof bear them? Nay, amid the pageantry of earthly powers, and the imaginary effects of much earthly counsel and wisdom, how much we forget how all the course of the world's history, how the successes and the downfalls of nations, the blessings and the judgments, are all within the continual control of the Most High God; and what are those acts, and what those graces in the hearts of His servants, which He is pleased to visit in mercy, and bless with abundant prosperity to themselves, their neighbours, their cities, and their country. We know not where, nor by whom, among the sons of men, this divine sovereignty—for it is verily a part of the sovereignty of God—is wielded most; we cannot tell which and who are they to whom, as to men, nations owe their safety :—

"No,—where th' upholding grace is won,
 We dare not ask, nor Heaven would tell,
 But sure from many a hidden dell,
 From many a rural nook unthought of there,
Rises for that proud world the saints' prevailing prayer."

It is now about a hundred and fifty years since there lived in this country two well-known persons, whose character and history may well illustrate the

"BLESSED ARE THE MEEK."

doctrine and truth of which I speak. The one was one of the greatest men of his time, one whose name occupies one of the principal and brightest pages of common history. A principal agent in the revolution which placed William the Third on the throne of England, he became in the following reign the most powerful and wealthiest of subjects. Through his wife he obtained unlimited power over his sovereign. He was the greatest general of modern history, unequalled until this generation. He repressed the pride and checked the conquests of the Great Monarch, and conquered his most famous leaders. His victories rank among the foremost achievements of the British arms. The result of his wars was a peace, which in the very lowness of the terms on which it was concluded promised to settle upon a new and equitable basis the contending claims of many and mighty nations.

The other had, in earlier years, been lifted from obscurity and made a bishop of the Church of England; but at the time I speak of he was deprived of all position and emolument because he refused the oaths to the new Government. He was poor, evil-spoken of, and watched with jealousy even in his gifts of charity. So little apparent weight had he, or those who acted with him, in the apparent events of English history, that in a recent work of considerable ability and fame, which records that history from the early part of the last century, neither his name nor theirs, neither his conduct nor theirs, neither his existence nor theirs is so much as mentioned.

And yet, if any man should attempt to gauge the influence, the real lasting influence, of these two men upon mankind,—the real essential enduring power,—the true weight on man, on his being, on his heart, on his prospects, on his real self,—which, think you, has most truly inherited this earth in power, the author of the Morning and Evening Hymns, or the conqueror of Blenheim ? he, whose simple words and few, not in themselves either particularly able or particularly beautiful, whose few simple words make, and have made, and no doubt will make sweet Christian music in the hearts of millions who have never heard nor known his name,—or he, whose station, ability, and success blazed before the world's eyes for a few years, and, their effects swept away after a time by other events, then disappeared absolutely and for ever ?

Truly the meek do inherit the earth. In some sort and to some extent they did so naturally and always; much more, and increasingly, they have done so in Christian times. This is the secret of the gradual amelioration of manners, of the gradual growth of candour, courtesy, and gentleness in the dealings of man with man, and nation with nation. This is the secret of the influence of Christian women in families, in parishes, in the hardest and roughest assemblages of men. This is the basis of that discovery of Christian times, that honesty, fairness, kindness, liberality are in the long run influence and power. This is the secret of that strange phenomenon of modern days, that mighty nations, armed to the teeth, in the very moment of their most desperate and lawless aggressions, pause, in the hope that their adversaries may take the first step in violence, and, if not in the eyes of God, yet in the eyes of men, seem to be the first breakers of the sacred law of Christian meekness.

It is true in public life, and it is true in private; it is true in the state, and in every community within the state down to the archetypal community of the single family. Violence and ill-temper, impatience and unkindness may usurp temporary authority: but such authority is essentially unrighteous, and therefore essentially temporary. But meekness, true Christian meekness of mind and heart before God, the meekness that bears, the meekness that does not resent, the meekness that in its place on earth, be it one of obedience only or one of command, patiently, gently, humbly, consistently works on and loves, meekly and humbly towards God, and therefore firmly and lovingly towards man,—the meekness that piously and instantly praying is full of the Holy Spirit of God, and under the continual guard and defence of His good angels, doth in every place and every society, by God's special promise and grace, not fail to inherit the earth.

For it is part—the human part—of the onward growing of the Messiah's kingdom. It is part of that growing onwards to final victory and judgment wherewith the meek and holy Lord, not striving nor crying, nor His voice heard among the loud ones in our streets or in our senates, is gradually putting down, even amid apparent defeat and discouragement of things sacred,—is gradually putting down the high things of the earth that exalt themselves against Him, and preparing the world for the final triumph.

There *is* apparent defeat and discouragement. On many sides it looks as if indifference and worldliness, as if sin and evil were gaining ground against the secret working of the Holy Ghost, against the secret spreading of the kingdom of Christ in this world of His inheritance. But is it so indeed? Can it be so? Can it be true that by lawless force or secret cunning, or by anything whatever except meek and true service of God in our own place, man can gain aught but a fleeting, insecure, ill-founded power?

Brethren, even at this signal moment[q], when the whole civilized world is suddenly aroused by the outbreaking of violence and aggression, which may in all probability lead to universal and long-continued war, — when the flash has passed before our eyes, and we sit counting, as it were, the seconds till the shock of nations thunders around us, it does not seem ill-timed, even now, to speak a few calm and lofty words respecting the divine inheritance of meekness.

If Christ be the Lord of heaven and earth, if the kingdom be already His, if the usurping powers of violence and evil be indeed only rebels against a long-suffering but Almighty Master, destined to speedy and certain overthrow, then assuredly, whatever be the temporary appearances of the world, the meek ones in Christ are, in part already, and at the last to be entirely, the sharers of His triumph. Borne down for awhile, overwhelmed in outward fortune here and there, apparent losers, as they sometimes may be, in the world's conflict, with the meek the

---

[q] This sermon was preached on the 8th of May, 1859. On one of the last days of April war had been declared by Austria, and the Austrian troops had crossed the Ticino. The battle of Montebello was fought on the 20th of May.

victory rests, and will rest; the moral victory, the real victory, the ultimate victory. I know not where, nor how. I know not whether, according to the fanciful thought of some writers, the peaceful inheritance may come in some later and happier age of the perfected Church, when all the well-known places of this very earth of ours—yes, those very plains, those beautiful lakes and rivers which have been so often, and are, alas! to be again the scene of rapine and bloodshed—may be the peaceful inheritance of the untroubled and victorious meek ones,—all this is innocent, perhaps mistaken fancy; but this I know, that not in worldly violence or force, but in the calm, silent strength of that meekness which is of grace, which is not weak or mean, but by the Holy Ghost firm, loving, unresenting, gentle, resides essential power now, and to it shall belong at the last the undisputed, unchallenged, everlasting kingdom of the meek, triumphant Lord.

SERMON IV.[a]

St. Matthew v.

6. Blessed are they which do hunger and thirst after righteousness: for they shall be filled.

IN no other of the Beatitudes does Christian doctrine come so near to the surface of the words as in this one,—the fourth of the series in St. Matthew's order, the second of the first pair, the two purely inward virtues, as I have before ventured to arrange them. It is quite true that doctrine is not really absent from any. All the eight belong to the Christian man alone, and presuppose Christian truth accepted and believed, the aid of the sanctifying Spirit, and the hope of heaven: but the subject of the other seven is more precisely the divine morality of the Christian man,—his hopes, his strength, his belief being presupposed indeed, but not immediately kept in view. In this one the case is otherwise. Christ is Himself

[a] Preached at St. Mary's, Oxford, June 17, 1860.

our righteousness. We have none, nor can have any, save in Him. Blessed is he who hungereth and thirsteth after that righteousness,—for none other,—for righteousness in Christ, for righteousness which is Christ. Righteousness is the very prophetical name of Christ,—"This is the name whereby He shall be called, The Lord our Righteousness [b];" and Righteousness He has been made to us according to the teaching of the Apostle to the Corinthians,—"Of Him are ye in Christ Jesus, who of God is made unto us wisdom, and righteousness, and sanctification, and redemption [c]." Blessed, then, is he who hungereth and thirsteth with a hunger that on earth shall never be finally satisfied, and a thirst that on earth shall never be entirely quenched, but which shall absolutely and for ever be satisfied in heaven, *for Christ our Righteousness.*

Now we understand Christ to be our Righteousness,—

First and chiefly, as He is entirely righteous and unimpeachably holy in Himself, and as He has, in

[b] Jer. xxiii. 6.

[c] 1 Cor. i. 30. I have quoted these words as they stand in the Authorized Version, though I should have been rather disposed to render them thus,—"Of Him are ye in Christ Jesus (who was made unto us wisdom from God) both righteousness, and sanctification, and redemption."

this holiness, offered Himself a sacrifice without spot to God for our sins: whereby God mercifully looks upon us as righteous in Him, imputes His righteousness to us, calls it ours, treats us as if it were ours, pardons us because of it, though it be altogether His, and not ours; we by faith in Him claiming this pardon, coming boldly in the strength of His sacrifice to the throne of grace [d], wrapping ourselves round in faith in the divine mantle of His holiness, and therein being forgiven for His holiness' sake. This is the first, greatest, chiefest way in which Christ is our righteousness. In this His righteousness we trust to be pardoned for the sins which we continually commit, and continually repent of. In this righteousness we trust that, weak and wilful as we are, we are still God's children in Christ, accepted in the Beloved. In this, and in this only, we trust to stand before the judgment-seat of Christ, knowing no righteousness but His, for His sake forgiven finally and for ever, for His sake admitted into the full fruition of His joy, heirs not in title only then and hope, but in actual and full possession, of the heavenly kingdom. This is our great and strong righteousness,—righteousness outward, forensic, imputed,—righteousness which is Christ's, given to man,—righteousness consisting in

[d] Heb. iv. 16.

pardon,—the only righteousness which is real, thorough, trustworthy, which can stand when He appeareth, and endure the severity of His judgment.

Who, then, are they that hunger and thirst for this righteousness? Surely those who have a deep inward conviction of their own sin and weakness, who feel that in themselves they dare not so much as lift up their eyes to heaven; but who, with all this sense of unworthiness, long for pardon from God with the aching pain of hunger and thirst, and are ready to seize upon it, if it be offered them, with the eagerness with which the famished man seizes upon food, and the man that was dying of thirst, on drink.

Observe then, first, that the sacred hunger and thirst contain in them many other elements besides those of mere pain or mere terror. Pangs of pain, fears, or horrors of mind, though they may accompany, or betoken, or precede the gracious hunger of which the Beatitude speaks, are not themselves that hunger, nor anything like it. They may be wholly disjoined from it. It is very possible that they may go no further, or they may go on to become despair or rebellion. They are merely human, not divine. They *may* lead to nothing but a sullen gnawing of the heart, which is rather the token of death than of life. No: it is when, by the grace of the Holy

Spirit of God, the painful sense of deficiency and demerit turns a man's heart to desire earnestly that the deficiency may be supplied and the demerit cancelled,—when the thought of the divine food which may satisfy or alleviate that craving turns pain into longing,—still more when, by the further working of the Holy Spirit in the soul, *hope*, and with hope love, and the complex feelings of filial penitence and loving sorrow are wakened up in the heart, as the divine light of God's love and willingness to give pardon in Christ shines upon it,—that that which is natural becomes spiritual, that which was human divine, that which was but the unsanctified gnawing of remorse and unhappiness of conscious sin becomes the gracious and holy hunger and thirst after righteousness which the Lord pronounces blessed. And observe also, that that is no real hunger which is slow to seize upon the food proper to satisfy it as soon as offered. There are in the body many conditions of inanition and resemblance of hunger, which yet are not real hunger, nor tend at all, like real hunger, to strength, and growth, and invigorated life. We all know what it is when we are ill, to feel as if we were hungry, and yet not be able to eat when the food comes; to feel as if we wanted the food (as indeed we do, as a matter of real need,) and desired it eagerly, and yet when it comes, to have no stomach for it, to turn away from it with disgust, or force ourselves to eat it without benefit. There is a very close parallel to this in the matter of spiritual hunger,—when men, in the deepest and saddest need of God's forgiveness, conscious more or less of the need, and in a sort of way desirous of the supply of it, are yet unable to embrace it when it is offered them, cannot bring themselves to do what is necessary in order to become partakers of it, preferring rather the death of spiritual inanition, or atrophy, to the life of sacred forgiveness in Christ. Spiritual hunger, then, as it requires the grace of the Holy Ghost to make it hopeful, loving, longing, so it requires also the faithful, eager search for that freely offered pardon which is its food. If grace quicken it not into loving faith, if loving faith do not seek eagerly and by all appointed means for the offered food, surely it is no hunger which is blessed or shall be filled, nor can it be more than starvation, famine, death.

Let no person think that this keen longing, this eager hungering and thirsting, belongs only to those who come to Christ for the first time, as converts from heathenism, or to such only as, after years of total neglect and sin, are by the signal working of the Holy Ghost within them enabled to make one great and blessed turn,— a turn well-nigh as great as that of the conversion of a heathen,—from sin to repentance, from Satan to God, within the Church of God. Doubtless in these cases the spiritual hunger is the keenest, the sense of the sweetness of the spiritual food the sweetest. It is like the ravenous hunger that comes on when a person is beginning to get well of some desperate sickness. He may be supposed to have been altogether incapable of eating or drinking, at least with the slightest appetite or relish, for many days or weeks, and all that time may be compared with his many years of unrepented sin and total forgetfulness of God; and then as he begins to get better, and with the improvement of health the appetite begins to spring, we all know with what intense eagerness a person longs for food, never can be satisfied, would be, if he were allowed, always eating, seems to gain, almost visibly, strength from every meal, almost from every mouthful that he eats;—well, that is the sort of hunger and thirst with which a real penitent, one who has many, and heavy, and long-continued sins to be sorry for, for which he has never sorrowed before, longs for God's pardoning righteousness, when by the grace of the Holy Spirit the sacred appetite is wakened up within him, and with it the first symptoms of recovery and restoration from his dire illness begin to shew themselves. And oh, brethren! this very hunger, this keen devouring hunger, this parched and aching thirst, this total conversion of heart from sin and forgetfulness to God, many, *very many*, of us Christian and baptized people must learn to know and feel, if ever we are to be filled with the righteousness of God. I do not preach the abstract and universal necessity of such conversion in baptized people as a *doctrine:* on the contrary, I verily believe that the grace of God first given, and the promise of its continuance given, in Holy Baptism, does in many cases, and may in all, sanctify the hearts of Christian men and women in such sort from the font onwards as that they may maintain—no doubt with occasional lapses of human weakness and infirmity—maintain to the grave, and continually *grow* in the grace of their baptismal conversion. But though I hold it to be most injurious and untrue to preach the universal necessity of such conversion as a doctrine, I do most solemnly declare its very extensive necessity as a fact. Do you doubt, can you doubt, that there are very many indeed among us who require a conversion of heart well-nigh as total as that of a heathen, in some respects more total and more difficult than many heathens, before they can hope to be filled with the sacred food of the righteousness of God? Can you doubt that public life among us, and social life, to say nothing of the ignorance and debasement of many in the lower ranks of society; that political life, that commercial life, that sporting life, that military life, that academical life, in spite of all the bright and holy examples which no doubt are afforded in many of them, are yet full in many, many instances of the deepest need of this gracious hunger of divine righteousness? We baptize, brethren, freely and without stint, and we surely obey the Lord's will and words in so doing, we baptize, as it were, broadcast over the land; and, in a Christian country, and to the children of baptized parents, we surely do that which is right and just in so doing. I cannot now stay to ask whether we discharge the corresponding duty of training and educating all whom we baptize, though it is a grave and serious question, brethren,—as though we gave birth to countless multitudes of helpless infants, and then left them to starve, or grow up to be the pests and plagues of society;—but I would ask whether the freeness with which we baptize, joined with the loose and careless ways of living prevalent all around us, do not make the necessity of a true and real conversion of heart very plain, and fearfully strong. Is it not most clear that, coupling this universality of baptism with this laxity of life, conversion of heart, conversion of the baptized to Christ, the late turning of those who should have been turned early, who should have been turned in all their lives, should be a great, and earnest, and pressing topic with every Christian preacher? And not only does the need of this strong hunger of pardoning righteousness belong to such as I have spoken of, such as have never yet turned seriously to God in all their lives, such as have never yet known what it is to pour one hearty confession, one earnest spiritual prayer to God in Christ: but we, brethren, each and all of us who are here present, do we not need,—more and less no doubt,—but do we not need, does not each one of us need, if we will seriously think of ourselves and our lives before God, an earnest, a more earnest turning to God in repentance than ever we have turned before, that we may learn more truly to feel that aching hunger and thirst, that gracious hunger and thirst after righteousness, which shall never be unsatisfied? Indeed it is so. Day by day and hour by hour the cleansing, pardoning, atoning grace is necessary—oh! how necessary!—to do away the continual sin, the continual stain which that continual sin spreads and keeps up in our hearts. If we did not constantly ask pardon in Christ, if we did not constantly feel assured of pardon in Christ in answer to our asking, what would become of us? This is a topic on which I cannot dwell with any fulness now. Perhaps it might seem to be a topic more suitable to the season of Lent, than to this time of joy and mirthfulness. I do not ask that a Christian's heart should always be keeping Lent: but if it know no Christian Lent, how can it know a Christian Easter? If it maintain not a real hungering and thirsting after God's pardoning righteousness within, how can it know real peace? If grave thoughts, and grave actions too, confessions, humbling of ourselves before God, prayers, be not with us always, how can we taste any true joy? It is a truism, I know, brethren, — all practical preaching is to Christians truism, yet not on that account less useful or necessary, — yet accept it as a blessed Christian truism: None can be freely, nor innocently, nor unreservedly, nor really happy, but those whose happiness is based upon penitence, based upon the rock of the consciousness that they are at peace with God, through the atoning sacrifice of Christ.

And I have yet one or two practical words to say, brethren, on this part of my subject. By learning to feel the true hunger in ourselves, we shall best help to waken it up in our neighbours. As there is no sham so contemptible as that of mourning over the wickedness of other men while we are not mourning over and mending our own, so there is no means of doing other men good so deep, so true, or so effectual as becoming really good ourselves. True Christian hunger of righteousness is infectious. A good Christian man, one honestly and with all his heart striving to be a good Christian man, is a preacher of righteousness without opening his lips, a missionary to his brethren without stirring a foot from his own door. One who truly hungers and thirsts for the forgiveness of God, has helped to win others to the like holy longing by the secret radiation of his own spirit-lighted heart, before he knows or suspects that he has been noticed or observed at all.

And yet one more very practical word, brethren. I said that in this Beatitude sacred doctrine came nearer to the surface than in any of the others, for that Christ Himself is the righteousness which it is thus blessed to hunger and thirst for; Christ who died and gave Himself for our sins[e], who gave His life a ransom for many[f]; Christ who was once offered to bear the sins of many; Christ the propitiation for our sins[g]. The great doctrine of the atonement of Christ is the very heart of this Beatitude. Then believe me, brethren, that if you let your mind admit cavil or doubt about the doctrine of the atonement and

[e] Gal. i. 4.   [f] Heb. ix. 28.   [g] 1 John ii. 2.

propitiation of Christ, you do to the same extent incapacitate yourself for the gracious hunger which the Lord pronounces blessed. You *cannot* hunger faithfully and lovingly for Christ your Saviour when you have let in and digested the poison of doubting of the validity of vicarious sacrifice, and the other particulars that go to make up the doctrine of the Atonement. The famished, empty soul which would fain feel the honest aching of hunger for its divine food, which would willingly give up life itself for one genuine pang of the faithful hunger after Christ which, perhaps, it used to feel in simpler days, is apt to be slain outright by the miserable intellectual doubts which it has admitted once, and cannot for its life shake off and get rid of. I will not say that he who thus lets his mind in its self-styled strength grow weak in faith and learn to doubt of the atonement of Christ, is a worse man than he who sins against the laws of God morally and breaks the commandments; I will not say it, for I do not mean it; but I will say that there is more hope of reviving the gracious hunger after righteousness in the immoral sinner, than there is in the fair-living intellectual doubter. The one is as a man suffering under dangerous sickness, who may yet by the mercy of God not improbably get well, and getting well, recover the full tone of natural and healthful appetite, and resume even more than his original strength; the other is as one who has early impaired his digestive powers, who has made natural and healthful hunger impossible to him, who can never know the sweet taste of food, the delicious quenching of painful thirst again.

Tell me not that those who would weaken your belief, your trustful, Christian, lifelong belief in the atoning Blood of your Lord, are amiable, kindly, pious. It may be so; the danger may not improbably be not the less because it is so. I judge them not: but if you listen to such things, if you let such doubts get hold of your minds, if you allow your faith in the atoning Blood of your Lord to be intellectually shaken, you will go near to lose the most precious joy and peace which is given to weak and sinful man upon this earth, the joy and peace in believing[h]. Imagine not that such have discovered a deeper knowledge, are men of profounder mind, are able to lead you into loftier intellectual fields than those which the saints of God have trodden in every age from the apostles. "Knowledge puffeth up: charity edifieth[i]." It is not Christian charity which helps to unsettle,—and that in days when every cavil is welcomed, and a pious-seeming man who gives up ever so many points of

[h] Rom. xv. 13. [i] 1 Cor. viii. 1.

the sacred inherited truth is hailed as a godsend by all the scoffers and unbelievers in the land,—which helps, I say, to unsettle the simple honest faith of those who have been bred up in the love and fear of God. Nor is it knowledge. It is no knowledge which puts out of sight the consenting witness of the Church of God, the very pillar and ground of the truth, the witness of eighteen hundred years, and claims to interpret by the wretched guesswork of modern philosophy the sacred Scriptures. Oh! my young brethren, among whom there are many who are to me as sons, I do not lament that you should hear and know of such things, for it is your inevitable trial—nay, more, it is the very price you pay for freedom of thought, and in freedom of thought your ultimate faith finds and recognises its strongest and most unassailable foundations; we do not wish your faith, the faith of educated men, to rest on blindness, or deafness, or dulness, or shrinking, or flight; —no; I do not lament that you should hear of such things, but I do most earnestly pray you to cling to your Saviour, ("Lord: to whom shall we go? Thou hast the words of eternal life,") to cling to your prayers, to let no canker of impureness or wilful sin undermine the faith which these false views would attack in the superstructure. Half your strength in the intellectual struggle is *moral;* all of it is *spiritual.* If you forget your prayers, if you are negligent of Holy Communion, if you allow sin, of any of the defiling kinds in which it most solicits young men, to get a hold upon your habits, you are already half won to unbelief. The conclusions of the new philosophy are too welcome to a sinner's soul not to find ready access to his reason, when his heart is already gained. I have not now the duty of arguing against this philosophy; suffice it for the present, and in connexion with my present subject, to warn you emphatically that as you learn to throw discredit on the doctrine of the Atonement of Christ, so do you inevitably, and in the same proportion, disable yourself from ever feeling again, except by a miracle of mercy, that sacred, gracious hunger and thirst after Christ, your pardoning righteousness, which is blessed, because it shall surely and eternally be filled.

I have spoken thus far of outward righteousness, the righteousness of pardon, Christ's righteousness imputed to us, wherein alone we can stand upright before God, and hope to endure the severity of His judgment in the last day. Yet it is plain that the hunger and thirst of this Beatitude are not limited to this sort of righteousness. Most surely the Lord's words refer also to the eager, earnest inward desire of personal, real goodness and holiness; the burning gracious wish, the constant persevering effort to win higher and higher attainments of righteousness in Christ under the sanctifying Spirit. As David in the Psalms gives abundant utterance to the feelings of the former sort of spiritual hunger, "Be merciful unto me of Thy great goodness, O Lord: according to the multitude of Thy tender mercies blot out my transgressions," "blessed is he whose unrighteousness is forgiven, and whose sin is covered;" so not less often and not less fervently does he give expression to that other sense of spiritual hunger of which I now speak: "O that my ways were made so direct that I might keep Thy statutes. Like as the hart desireth the waterbrooks, so longeth my soul after Thee, O God. My soul is athirst for God, yea, even for the living God. Create in me a clean heart, O God, and renew a right spirit within me. O God, Thou art my God, early will I seek Thee. My soul thirsteth for Thee in a barren and dry land where no water is. My soul breaketh out for the very fervent desire that it hath alway unto Thy judgments. Teach me, O Lord, the way of Thy statutes, and I shall keep it unto the end. O Lord, what love have I unto Thy law: all the day long is my study in it. I have longed for Thy salvation, O Lord, and Thy law is my delight." No doubt the two sorts of spiritual hunger are closely connected together, in themselves and in men; so closely that they cannot be found asunder. As the food of reparation and the food of growth are distinguishable, though not separate, in respect of the body, so in discoursing of spiritual hunger should we limit the subject injuriously if we spoke only of the eager grasping for pardon, and the outward covering of the blessed mantle of Christ's righteousness, and forgot to speak of that which is no less characteristic of a Christian, the intense and loving longing after inward goodness, the desire, and with the desire the real and persevering effort, of growing more and more like to Christian personal attainments of holiness. If the one hunger is like the keen and, as it were, furious hunger of one that is recovering from terrible sickness, the other is like the regular appetite of growing health in youth, regularly returning for each healthful meal, making each meal healthful, and so continually leading to the strengthening and growth of the body, and to the full and healthful development of all its proper powers. If we imagine a person who from the beginning of his Christian life has been as completely holy as man's imperfect nature admits,—even he needing, deeply, absolutely needing, and well knowing his need of the mantle of his Lord's righteousness, in which alone he can stand upright before God in the judgment of the last day,—but if we think of such an one, in his true, inward, continual sanctification, we can readily understand the regular and recurring delight with which every office of prayer and praise, every stated and orderly means of grace, every returning meal, so to speak, of divine righteousness, will inspire him. Continually satisfied, and continually hungering again, strengthened and refreshed in his soul by the sacred food of grace with which all these meals are supplied abundantly, all the sacred faculties of his soul are developed, and he grows continually in that divine life which, begun on earth, shall pass through death uninjured, and be his for ever and ever in heaven. Is not this, think you, the blessed hunger and thirst after righteousness which God will surely satisfy? And ought not such hunger and thirst, if not in such sweet and orderly continuity and increase in holiness as I have supposed, yet at least in some onwardness of spiritual growing, be in us all? in us all, brethren, baptized into Christ, living on in the midst of dangers from within and from without, surrounded by the means of grace and holy growing, having before us we know not how many years, or weeks, or days in which to make our calling and election sure?

Brethren, let me find an illustration—hardly, indeed, an illustration, so closely is it connected with the subject on which I am speaking—in the manna given to be food to the Israelites in the wilderness. That "small round thing" which, "when the dew was gone up," lay "as small as the hoar frost upon the ground," was, remember, not only the wondrous food of the children of Israel in those forty years, but was also the type of the bread of God which cometh down from heaven, and of the hidden manna to be given to him that finally overcometh [k], the sweetness whereof none knoweth saving he that receiveth it; that is to say, the manna of the peninsula of Mount Sinai did actually typify the spiritual food, the spiritual fulness and satisfaction which God gives to His saints, both now, while they are fighting their upward battle in the militant Church, and hereafter, when they shall have attained their final victory, in the Church triumphant. It was tasteless, insipid, like the taste of fresh oil. "The children of Israel wept again, and said, Who shall give us flesh to eat? our soul is dried away, there is nothing at all but this manna before our eyes. There is no bread, neither any water, and our soul loatheth this light bread [l]."

And so is the food of God, at this day, tasteless

[k] St. John vi. 31, 32, 58; 1 Cor. x. 3; Rev. ii. 17.
[l] Numb. xi. 4, 6; xxi. 5.

and insipid to us, brethren, till by God's grace we have learned to hunger and thirst for it. Prayers are dull, reading the Word of God is dull, the Holy Communion, the direct antitype of the manna, is unwelcome. Hardly a quarter of the population go to church; hardly a tenth of those who go to church stay to partake of the Lord's Supper. How like is all this to the manna in the wilderness?

The manna must be gathered every day. There is no such thing as storing up the food of God. We cannot afford to lose one gathering, for we cannot keep one. Sufficient for the day the food thereof. The morrow must take thought for the things of itself. The Christian who does not daily hunger for his daily bread, and daily ask for it, is in the way to starve. Yesterday's prayer will not do for to-day, nor to-day's for to-morrow. Every day, night and day, day and night, must he who is in earnest in hungering and thirsting for the sacred food of righteousness, seek it, gather it, — it lies about his path and about his tent, it is in his Bible, it is in his chapel, if he will kneel down and ask for it, it is everywhere,—and feed upon it to his soul's health.

Each must gather it for himself. You cannot delegate to any other, be he who he may, the work of feeding your soul with the food of God. As the children of Israel could not send one to gather for many, nor employ those that were younger, or poorer, or less noble to gather instead of them, so is the work of feeding on the sacred food of God, now and for ever, a strictly personal one. None can do it for another. Not father, nor mother, not pastor, not companion, not the soul's own closest and nearest brother. It is a lonely, inward work. We may advise one another, we may pray for one another; but to act for one another, to hunger spiritually, or feed for one another, to reach or touch each other's soul, we are totally powerless. The work is to be done in the solitude and depth of each separate soul by itself and for itself. There, where none penetrates, save the Holy Spirit of God,—there where none can affect or work upon our secret spirits save the Holy Spirit of God,—there we must yield ourselves up to Him, without reserve of earthly liking, and learn under His discipline to hunger and thirst after the inexpressible sweetness of that sacred food in which our natural taste takes no pleasure.

Then blessed are they which do hunger and thirst after righteousness, for surely they shall be filled. Blessed are they which do hunger and thirst for the pardoning righteousness of Christ, who cling to their atoning Lord, and put their whole trust in the merit of that propitiation which, offered for the sins of the whole world upon the Cross of Calvary, and more than sufficient to win pardon for all, is the only deserving righteousness, the only thing which for its own worth and value God will reward and love. And blessed are they, too, which do hunger and thirst after the sanctifying righteousness of Christ in the Holy Spirit, earnestly, perseveringly, and faithfully striving to win towards His holy likeness, and bear fruit in which the Father may be glorified. For they shall be filled. Every yearning of their souls towards God shall be fully and absolutely satisfied. More than we can know or think of now shall be theirs at once, and no doubt an eternal growing of new capacity of bliss, and higher bliss to fill it. On earth, we *had* the type, and we *have* the image; the type, the manna of Sinai, the image, the spiritual food of the Holy Eucharist. Then we shall have that which far transcends both the type and the image, the divine reality itself, that which is spoken of in the Book of the Revelation as the hidden manna, the actual joy of the Lord, the actual presence of God.

There is an earnest of this in every good gift of the Holy Spirit now. The comfort which belongs to hearty confession, the glow of assured pardon which is the gift attached to true Christian prayers, the inexpressible sweetness of the spiritual feeding on the Body and Blood of Christ in the Holy Eucharist, the consciousness of putting ourselves in body and soul under the discipline of the Holy Spirit, and resigning, without reserve, every thought, word, and work to His guidance and His approval,—all this, and all like this, is the present, earthly earnest of the things of infinite price that are to be ours hereafter, if we are faithful to the end.

Have a care, brethren, that you train your tastes to like and love these things of gentle and sacred flavour. There are many keener, higher, more tempting flavours; and your bodies and your souls, your sense and your intellect love them naturally, and when indulged, crave for them painfully. Be on your guard. If you yield yourselves to them, they will kill the divine flavour to your sense, and the hunger for it will become impossible. The heavenly hunger and the heavenly taste are to be kept alive on earth by heavenly lives. They are not natural. They do not spring up in us of ourselves. They come of the Holy Spirit of God, and under the culture of the Holy Spirit of God alone they grow.

Brethren, bear with me, if I seem to linger on my last words, and on this the last occasion of addressing you, to feel reluctant to hold my peace. But *here*, in this place, which should be and is the stronghold of the Church of England, speaking among those who are to be the teachers of the Church of England in the next generation, conscious of the extreme and terrible laxity of faith and manners which prevails in the land around us, conscious, deeply conscious of the poison which seems to be spreading here, and to be attracting many of the most gifted minds of the young to listen and imbibe it, I would fain leave the ringing of one clear and unmistaken note upon your ears. Christ is our righteousness, our atoning, propitiatory, sanctifying righteousness. To hunger and thirst for Him, as it is the Holy Spirit's work within us, so is it blessed with the further gift of the Holy Spirit, who alone is fulness and satisfaction to our souls. Immoral living, neglected prayers, overlay, stifle, oppress that divine hunger: intellectual doubts kill it. May God give us grace so to watch our hearts, and cling to Him who is our righteousness, that we may keep it alive and growing within us, and so at last by His mercy taste the blessed fulness which Christ has promised to such as faithfully and to the end hunger and thirst for Him.

SERMON V.[a]

St. Matthew v.

7. Blessed are the merciful: for they shall obtain mercy.

THIS Beatitude forms, according to the arrangement of the preceding sermons, the first of the last pair. In it the Christian man is not so properly regarded as he is in himself alone, as in the first of the eight; nor as he is in the sight of God, as in the second of the first pair; nor as he is inwardly, in regard to other men, as in the second pair; nor as he is passively in regard to outer circumstances of sorrow and suffering, divine or human, as in the third pair. He is now regarded in his outward and active dealings with other men, standing forward in his position of life, and from the eminence of his own Christian estate, exhibiting to them the fruit of the Christian spirit and character within him. Let it be

[a] Preached in Winchester College Chapel.

observed, then, in this, as in the other later Beatitudes, that the Christian character and spirit in general, and many of the specific virtues which in these verses are pronounced to be blessed, are assumed to belong to the man who in any true sense can be called 'merciful.' He must be pure in heart, and hungering and thirsting after righteousness,—he must have a Christian poverty of spirit, and true meekness,—he must know how to win the spiritual blessing which belongs to sorrow and persecution,—he must have these in some considerable degree, and be earnestly seeking to have them more completely, before he can go forth out of himself, and be the merciful man whom the Lord in this Beatitude pronounces blessed.

Perhaps the word here translated by 'merciful,' might with greater propriety have been rendered into English by the word 'pitiful.' Mercy seems, at least in modern English, to involve the idea of a person in a higher position shewing leniency or kindness to an inferior. A prince to a subject, a judge to a criminal, a superior in any position in life may shew mercy to an inferior. But the Greek word does not carry this idea in it of necessity: it is equally applicable to all people who pity,—who pity those below them, those on their own level, or those above them. And again, 'mercy' involves the further idea of *pardon;* of guilt incurred, and forgiveness given; which is not in the Greek adjective. Pity, then, which more nearly represents the original word, may be felt alike for persons above us or below us; or for sufferings deserved or undeserved; for those who are guilty and justly liable to suffering, or those who are altogether guiltless. It is, I think, plain that we enlarge the scope of this Beatitude very much by thus regarding it. For while all occasions of mercy, properly so called, fall under it still, (for mercy is one considerable province, if I may so speak, of pity,) a vast number of other cases, in which mercy has no place, are seen to be included under it. Wherever there is sorrow or suffering, wherever there is pain of mind or body, wherever there is ignorance, wherever there is sin, wherever there is anything of the nature of evil or unhappiness, there is room for pity, and call for pity; and there Christian pity, pity for Christ's sake, pity for Christ's people desiring pity itself from Christ, may win blessing, the precious blessing of Christ's pity. And yet one more observation I may make on the Greek word. It is not 'blessed are those that shew pity,' but 'blessed are the pitiful.' It is the quality, the matured Christian quality, of Christian pity or compassion, rather than the separate acts in which it exhibits itself, that the Lord pronounces blessed. And this, again, enlarges the sphere of the Beatitude still further: for while the acts of pity cannot but wait for the occasions of sorrow, the Christian quality of pity is ever present, and ever capable of being recognised,—softening the glance of the eye, sweetening the look of the face, making gentle and sympathetic the tone, the manner, the mirth,—assuring all with whom a man has dealing or conversation that his heart is one of ready pity, of wide and unaffected sympathy, that he is, not now and then, but always, and deeply, and Christianly pitiful.

No doubt, men are by nature very differently constituted in this respect. There are many whose temper is naturally harsh, or reserved, who do not readily blend themselves with the feelings of others, either because they really do not enter into them easily, or are engrossed with their own, or because they have a natural difficulty or shyness which keeps them from passing in feeling, or at least in expression of feeling, over the limit between themselves and their neighbours. We all know such. Perhaps they are naturally the majority; or, at least, it may perhaps be said that, what with natural harshness and reserve, and what with a harshness and reserve engendered by familiarity with mankind and the necessity of caution and coldness, most men in life look as if such harshness and reserve were natural to them. And in the same way, there are many who plainly have a sympathizing and pitiful nature, who readily pass out of themselves to understand and blend with the feelings of others, whose ear is easily won, and whose heart is soon touched, by tales of sorrow and the like,—men who in this hard world are not unfrequently the prey of designing knaves, and objects of pity, not unmixed with contempt, to their colder-hearted neighbours. But neither the prudent and calculating pity of the colder-hearted, nor the instinctive warmth and sympathy of the naturally compassionate, is the pitifulness meant in this Beatitude; nor has it, consequently, any claim to this blessing. This pitifulness is altogether a Christian one; based on Christian reasons, proceeding on Christian rules, done for Christ's sake, and looking for Christian rewards. Indeed, I hardly know whether a large natural pitifulness may not be regarded as less than helpful towards the high Christian pitifulness of this Beatitude. For Christian pitifulness is a strong thing. It has its own sure grounds, and it has its own clear scope. But the large natural pitifulness of which I spoke is rather a weak thing, which is apt to yield to instinctive impulses, rather than to be based on what is sure and strong, and to see its objects clearly and forcibly, and to confine itself to them.

Christian pitifulness, then, is based upon the consciousness of sin as upon its ultimate foundation. Whatever divine or angelic pitifulness we might feel if we were unfallen creatures, or creatures of a higher race or stock than human, the pitifulness of Christian men rests on this, that they desire pity for themselves, that blessed pity from God which is truly called 'mercy.' The Christian man knows himself to be deeply, and in himself hopelessly, sinful. He has in himself neither the conscience of past innocence, nor the confidence of future goodness. If he had this, he might perhaps pity, as an angel pities, with a loftier, holier, more heavenly pity. But he, on the contrary, knows, and the more truly Christian he is the more thoroughly he knows, that in himself there dwelleth, and hath dwelt, no good thing: so that if he were left to himself, to be such as his own nature would make him, or if he were left to receive such treatment at the hands of God as his own deeds would deserve, nothing but unspeakable sin and unspeakable wretchedness would be his portion. But he knows also—in the bottom of his heart he knows—that God has been pleased to send His Son upon earth to save sinners, and that that blessed Son has given His life upon the Cross as a ransom for human sin,—a ransom altogether sufficient, more than sufficient, to redeem the sins of the whole world. This he knows in general; but he also knows that he himself has been made God's beloved child in Christ, and that for those that be in Christ there is no condemnation. So he relies, and the more Christian he is the more confidently and cheerfully he relies, upon Christ his Saviour. Sinful though he knows himself, and sinning too continually, yet continually and ever repenting, laying his sins before God in Christ, and in Christ assured of pardon, he counts on the firm promise of the mercy of God with full, unhesitating faith: he knows that whatever uncertainty there may be of his own perseverance or steadiness in repentance and faithful holiness, in God's mercy there is no uncertainty or shadow of doubtfulness.

And this certainty and this uncertainty alike fit him to go forth and be pitiful to his brethren in all the transactions in which he is engaged with them. As he is certain of God's mercy, there is cheerfulness, brightness, buoyancy in the pitifulness that he shews to others. As he is deeply uncertain of himself, so there mingles with this bright cheerfulness an earnest and deeply felt self-distrust, which gives tenderness, and sympathy, and earnestness to the feeling of piti-

"BLESSED ARE THE MERCIFUL."

fulness for others. He pities, not from above, not as a higher, holier being than they, but from their own level; as one who knows by his own sad experience the weight of temptation and the bitterness of sin, and now cheerfully hopes that he has obtained mercy of God to be faithful. And thus the Christian assurance of mercy already received, and the firm Christian hope of the consummation of mercy yet to come, become the real Christian basis of that divine pitifulness which the Lord in this precious verse pronounces blessed.

Rich, then, in the sense of divine mercy to himself, the man of Christian pitifulness looks forth upon the various people by whom he finds himself surrounded in life, and reflects upon them the radiance of that divine pity in which he has his own peace. Does any wrong or offend him? We live in the midst of a world full of wrongs and offences, and few indeed are they, especially if they live at all in the eyes of men, who are so fortunate as to escape them. And very hard these often are to bear; so that it becomes a great struggle, and one that often wants the strongest exertion of Christian charity and love to bear them, when ingratitude, or unworthiness, or scorn, or many other such things, aggravate almost beyond endurance some undeserved wrong. Besides that, people are very fond of talking about their neighbours, and it seldom happens that such talk is very charitable and kind, while often it abounds with all sorts of causeless and baseless evil-speaking, and spreading of injurious reports and stories. Subject then, as he is, to at least his share of all this injury and reviling, how does the man of Christian pitifulness, when it comes to his ears, as sooner or later it usually does, meet and repel it? First, he forgives; with all his heart and soul he forgives. He forces himself, he conquers himself to forgive: knowing for how much, for how much more than any one but himself knows or suspects, he needs the forgiveness of God. He will allow himself no peace till he has won by prayers the grace to forgive with all his heart. Then, and this is another struggle for the resentful temper of the natural man, he tries to look upon his injurer, not with a feeling of anger, but of Christian pity; and surely, of the two, the man who does the wrong is the more real object of pity than the man who suffers it. Then, pitying, (and that not in that scornful, insulting tone of pity which we sometimes hear of, which aggravates wrong, and retorts it, under the false disguise of Christian pity,) he tries to *win* the injurer to a better and more Christian mind. This may often be done. There is that amount of generosity in many minds that leads them, when they see the injuries that they have done by deed or word kindly taken, and love rather than hatred returned to them for their evil, to turn round with a strong admiring affection towards persons so much their superiors in the school of Christian pitifulness. Any way, whether the pitiful bearing of wrong wins or fails to win the man that does the injury, it wins to itself the blessing of God, assured in this Beatitude. The peculiar *power* of meekness and its cognate virtues in winning and subduing men, belongs rather to another of the Beatitudes. The one which we are considering to-night confines our view rather to the blessing which comes, and is to come hereafter, upon the head of him who pities as he would himself be pitied.

Then, consider how the man of Christian pitifulness treats such as come in any way before him as guilty persons; not now of wrongs and offences done against himself, but generally guilty or sinful persons, with whom he is brought in contact. How tenderly, how soothingly, how Christianly he will deal with them! With his own mind full of his own sin and guilt, and the blessed pardon of Christ warm in his heart, with what gentle, sympathizing, manly, faithful conduct he will behave to them! And observe, there will be no weakness, no foolish, nor unwise softness in this conduct. The same Christian pitifulness which makes him tender, makes him firm too. It is a most bastard and untrue pity which pities sin and guilt in such a manner as not to discourage and repress them with the utmost and most unmistaken force. The Christian, pitying such people, pities them as hating their sin, while he loves themselves for Christ's sake, to whom they still belong. Suppose him a magistrate, or a judge,—suppose him one in whom resides the ultimate power of deciding whether a person convicted of capital crime is to be executed or no, can you not readily feel how the Christian pitifulness will blend with the Christian firmness, and how the man who cherishes in his own heart his deep secret of God's mercy to himself, will, so to say, overflow with that firm and manly pity for his guilty brother which, whatever be its effect upon that brother, is to himself one token more, one assured and blessed token more, of God's mercy and acceptance? And in common life, when those who are in any position of authority, as fathers, or masters of families, or in any way have others under them, or when we have to deal merely as neighbours with erring and sinful people, whom we only know as erring and sinful, can we not readily judge how we, who have the precious inward sense of God's mercy assuredly hoped for towards ourselves, should treat such persons? Must we not feel, Are we not very sinful too? Do not our own hearts warn us that if we had our deserts, not they only, but we too must be the objects of stern and just condemnation? Shall not we pity, and if we may, by pitying, by active, zealous, affectionate, yet firm and manly pitying, *win*—win to repentance and from sin those whom possibly it is our duty to punish,—anyway, to discourage and repress by every means in our power?

And, lastly, consider with what deep and gentle tenderness the man of Christian pitifulness treats those who are in sorrow,—mental sorrow, or bodily sorrow; who are in sickness and pain, or in the sadness of bereavement, or in the still greater sadness of religious distress,—all the numerous cases of deep and various affliction which crave, which sometimes almost shrink from the touch of human pity. No doubt common natural pity is sweet in such cases,—just the ordinary tenderness of natural compassion which naturally bleeds at the sight of suffering; but, oh! what is this at its best and warmest, in comparison of that deep and true Christian pity which, strong in the sense of its own assured mercy, seeing Christ in His suffering people, looking on to the consummated mercy of the coming world in Christ, comes to the sufferer's side, with something of Christ's own loving tenderness, and cheers, and helps, and comforts him in all temporal ways that are possible; and, better than all temporal ways, by lifting his heart up to God in Christ, and teaching him how to win the blessing, the precious blessing, which God gives to those who mourn aright in Christ? The faithful clergyman among his sick or his afflicted people, the Christian nurse in the wards of the hospital, the well-known Christian friend of the afflicted in every rank of life, man and woman, oftener woman,—whom every sufferer knows of, and goes to first, or who herself seeks out suffering and is the first to know of it,—do not these bring a deep and priceless comfort to many a poor soul whom God is trying with sorrow? There are many such: not only the greater and more heroic cases of such Christian pitifulness which the whole nation knows, but true and real ones which each little parish and village knows for itself,—God's pitiful ones, Christ's pitiful ones,—who in the mercy and pity which they shew shall surely themselves find mercy,—blessed, eternal, loving mercy in Christ for ever and ever in glory.

And do not suppose, brethren, that this Christian pitifulness of which I have been speaking is a thing confined to the great sorrows of later life, or to the more difficult sorts of sympathy which are often shewn by older people. No, as *you* too, boys as you are, are learning to feel in your hearts the sense of God's mercy in Christ to yourselves, so should you be learning to radiate, if I may so speak, the warmth of the like pity outwards upon others. I hardly see how anybody can hope that he really appreciates God's mercy to himself, unless he is shewing something of the like to others. And you have indeed a great multitude of ways in which you may shew it. Even in boys' lives there is, as you well know, a very great difference between those that are harsh, unkind, and unpitying, and those whose eye is kindly, whose touch is gentle, whose conduct is helpful and encouraging. How much more when that kindly gentleness and pity is *Christian;* exercised not merely from the softness of a naturally tender heart, but the firm, trustworthy pitifulness of one who cherishes inwardly God's most undeserved mercy to himself? And I think that a half-year like the present, when probably some sixty or seventy of you will be thinking carefully of your own sins, and coming more expressly before God in Confirmation and Communion, is surely the time in which such mutual Christian pitifulness should have a great renewing. By the mercy, then, which you will be asking, be Christianly merciful to one another; to one another, and to all men; shewing forth, so far as you have the means and opportunity, the earnestness with which you embrace your own mercy, in the true heartiness with which you extend it to others.

To your own companions, particularly to such as are younger and more helpless than yourselves, to others with whom you come in contact, to tradespeople, to servants, to all these, by the truest Christian goodwill, civility, and courtesy, and, where they need it, by some express pity,—to the poor, and to all whom you come near who are in any suffering or evil case, —to the ignorant and sinful,—to the heathen,—by helping, as far as you can, all Christian efforts to win them to the knowledge and love of Christ,—shewing to all these and such as these how deeply you prize your own mercy by shewing the like to them; remembering that while there is no mercy for such as shew no mercy, no forgiveness for such as do not forgive, no pity for those who will not pity their brethren, the present peace of God, and His eternal kingdom, mercy now and mercy for ever, are in this Beatitude assured to such as are truly pitiful for Christ's sake.

SERMON VI.[a]

St. Matthew v.

8. Blessed are the pure in heart: for they shall see God.

THIS Beatitude, sixth in the order as given by St. Matthew, may in some sort be regarded as the first of the series. For if we divide the eight virtues which all Christian generations are to call 'blessed,' into four pairs, and regard as the first pair the two purely inward virtues,—purity of heart, and hunger and thirst after righteousness,—we shall naturally put this one, purity of heart, as being the simplest and most absolutely inward, the first of all. It is, as it were, a basis of the Christian moral character, on which the others may all be said to rest, according to the words of St. James, who tells us that the wisdom that is from above is first pure, then peaceable, gentle, and the rest[b]. Not, of course,

[a] Preached at St. Mary's, Oxford, Nov. 20, 1859.
[b] St. James iii. 17.

as though it could be perfectly possessed alone, or separately from the rest, or as though in order of time it were to be wholly won before all the others, —though it has in this way, too, a real priority over the rest, being in great measure a virtue of youth;— but that when the entire moral character of a faithful and true Christian man is divinely pourtrayed in eight particulars, this one may be regarded as the first in arrangement, the one out of which the others, more complicated in point of circumstance and description, naturally seem to flow.

The terms in which the Beatitude is stated are entirely simple. There is not in them, as in several of the others, the least sound of paradox. There is no difficulty, such as we meet in several of the others, where we have to understand how sorrow or persecution, things naturally painful and sad, can be called 'blessed,' or how meekness can have the promise of inheriting this earth. All here is perfectly simple and plain. Neither in the first part, "Blessed are the pure in heart," is there difficulty, for man can naturally see that pureness is a blessed and sweet thing; nor yet in the second, "for they shall see God." Yet we may truly say that in these last words there is something greater than paradox: there is revelation. For these words surely open to

"BLESSED ARE THE PURE IN HEART."

us a truth, which naturally we could not know, of the invisible world; a very sacred and precious truth, respecting what we may call, without impropriety, *the senses of the soul*, that those who are pure in heart, and no doubt those only, shall hereafter be admitted and able to see God.

Who, then, are the pure in heart? By the heart we must, I suppose, understand the feelings and desires, the likings and affections of a man, as these are distinguished from his more purely mental faculties and operations on the one hand, and from his spiritual capacities on the other: so that, as we have in a previous sermon [c] distinguished the soul, specifically so called, from the spirit of a man, so we may subdivide, so to speak, the specific soul into the mind, the seat of thought, reflection, and memory, and the heart, the imaginary receptacle of the love and desire, the affections and impulses, of the soul.

Purity in the heart, then, means no doubt the absence of all manner of defilement, whether it be of one sort or another, in it. Corrupt and corrupting desires,—some absolutely and in themselves corrupt, some corrupt in their excess, and faulty direction,—all such, of whatever particular kind they be, are destructive of perfect purity in the heart. Bodily

[c] Vid. Serm. I. p. 9.

desires of all sorts, desires of ambition, of covetousness, of dislike, of indignation,—all these, and such as these, as soon as they pass the limit of entire innocence in degree and direction, begin to be destructive of that perfect purity of heart which is surely meant in this Beatitude. Purity is the freedom from all these. It is a clear brightness of the soul in respect of things moral: a transparent clearness, not arising from stillness, or original feebleness in the natural desires, but from the perfectly ordered activity of naturally vigorous desire towards its legitimate objects, whereby, in respect of all things moral, the soul of a man is clear before God of everything that defiles,—the lively springs of feeling and desire welling continually up with nothing but the bright and crystal waters of a pure and holy activity. I need not say that such purity is not of nature. No; in this Beatitude, as in the others, we are reading of men as they are under the grace of the Holy Spirit, not as they are by nature. The natural activities of desire and feeling, corrupt from the first, when left to themselves grow more and more corrupt continually, so that real purity of heart is to the natural man impossible. Nothing but the divine strength and sweetness of the Holy Spirit of God given in the Body of Christ, given to prayer,

"BLESSED ARE THE PURE IN HEART."

can so purify these naturally foul and turbid springs, as to make it possible that fallen man should in any way reach towards that true purity of heart which the Lord pronounces blessed.

But though this purity of heart belongs, no doubt, to the whole subject of human desires, so as to require the absence of all defilement, of whatsoever kind it be, it can yet hardly be doubted that there is one sort of defilement, which from its spreading, secret poison, from its universally diffused danger, growing, as it is too apt to do, with the growth of the body, and, alas! too often re-acting upon the body in all sorts of terrible evil; from the hold which it gains upon the imagination; from the way in which it is capable of being transmitted and caught from one impure mind to another, and fed secretly by all kinds of apparently innocent objects; from the difficulty of dealing with it, and the natural (and sometimes the morbid) unwillingness which there is in men even to have it alluded to, though it may notoriously be eating out the very heart of faith in a Christian land,—there is one sort of defilement, I say, which is surely most prominent in the thought of every one who reads that only "the pure in heart shall see God." Blessed pure in heart! Verily blessed, if there be such, those who by the grace of the Holy Spirit have been kept clean and pure in boyhood, youth, manhood; whose life has been undefiled in the midst of a contaminated and contaminating world, like a bright river, never mingling with the stagnant waters of some muddy lake through which it flows, and issuing thence at last not less clear and bright than when it entered them! And blessed too those who, having known somewhat of the opposite stain and evil, have purified themselves by repentance and confession, and have received that divine forgiveness and restoration which are never refused to such within the Christian covenant as with true, sound, and earnest intention of heart ask for it. Blessed are the pure, and the purified, those who have been kept from such stain, and those in whom the stain has been washed away by timely tears, while the day of probation, the day of grace, has lasted!

" Blessed are the pure in heart: *for they shall see God.*"

What, then, is the promise of seeing God? For, no doubt, in some way all shall see Him. Every eye, we know, shall see Christ when He cometh in judgment, even they also which pierced Him; but that sight shall be with a wailing of all the kindreds of the earth because of Him. Those who do not see

Him in love, shall surely see Him in His terrible anger when all the nations shall be gathered before the throne of His glory. And how inconceivably dreadful will the sight be to one who has gone on wilfully offending God throughout his life, without repentance; who has trampled under foot the grace of his baptism; steeped himself in impurity of heart, and died so! How inconceivably dreadful it will be for such an one to stand face to face with the Redeemer whom he has despised! now sitting on His awful throne of judgment, His countenance no longer merciful and loving, but most terrible in its almighty vengeance!

But His own, His pure ones, shall in that awful day be enabled to lift up their eyes in a faith sustained by His own most Holy Spirit, and see Him as He is! They shall see Him looking down upon them with that unspeakable love which infuseth divine life. The quickening aspect of His gracious, pardoning love shall support their souls, which else would faint and perish at His presence. They shall see Him loving and gracious, and they shall see Him so for ever. They shall surround His throne with endless praise and endless joy, always and altogether blest in the beatific vision of the most high God, who has become their portion for ever.

For their purity of heart shall have become to them as a sacred, immortal sense, a holy faculty of vision, a divine gift of spiritual sight, whereby they shall see, and know, and feel, and be eternally upheld by the presence of God and His immortal love, while the impure are utterly blind to Him, except in His terrors, as they already are blind to all that is divine.

It is hardly a mere imagination that even here, on this dark earth, visions of beings spiritual, altogether unseen and unthought-of by the worldly and sensual, may sometimes be seen by the purer eyes of innocent children. But be this as it may, certainly in many ways in which the presence and power of God are capable of being recognised and known upon earth,—as in conscience, in the events and occurrences of the world, in people, in places,—none have so purged and clear a sight as such as keep themselves from all defilement of the flesh and spirit, and by God's grace live among spiritual things by chastity and purity of heart, even while they remain in the flesh. This upon earth, and during life. But most surely after death, when the things of the earth shall have passed away, this text plainly teaches us that there shall be a great difference between the souls of men, a difference analogous to that which there is now in their bodies, a difference which may at least be understood by calling it a difference of *sense*, whereby one soul shall have some blessed gift of divine sight, and another be utterly blind and devoid of it. And not this text only, for St. Paul teaches us that "without holiness no man shall see the Lord [d];" and St. John further shews us that the sight of the Lord, won by purity, shall have a transforming power upon those who gain it, bringing them at once to their perfection, in likeness to Him; for he says in his first general Epistle, "Beloved, now are we the sons of God, and it doth not yet appear what we shall be; but we know that when He shall appear, we shall be like Him, for we shall see Him as He is. And every man that hath this hope in Him, purifieth himself, even as He is pure [e]." See how this text of St. John falls in minutely with the doctrine which I have been urging, and supports it throughout. The sons of God purify themselves, while they remain in this life, after the likeness of the purity of Christ, because they know assuredly that when Christ comes back again upon the earth, they shall thus be enabled to see Him, as He is, in His love and grace, and so seeing Him, they shall at once be transformed—their remaining weaknesses removed, and their perfection suddenly achieved—into His like-

[d] Heb. xii. 14.   [e] 1 St. John iii. 2.

ness. Their purity of heart, won on earth by His grace, shall give them that divine power of sight, which shall bring them, on their last waking, to His immortal and sacred likeness, in which every holy craving of their souls shall be fully and for ever satisfied.

These passages, I say, confirm the doctrine that the souls of the pure win a kind of heavenly sense, necessary for the seeing of God as He is,—the God, that is, of mercy and love,—in His eternal kingdom of glory and joy. And remember, too, that striking passage of St. Luke's Gospel, in which the Lord, after explaining to His disciples "*when* the kingdom of God should come," and likening it to the suddenness and brightness of the lightning, goes on to answer their further question, "*Where*, Lord?" by the remarkable image of the birds of prey flocking to the carcase [f]. As though He said, Do you then ask further *where* the Lord shall come? where you must go to meet Him? where, on all this round globe, shall the place of His appearing be, so that you may go there and be ready to meet Him if you be alive, or be buried there if you die, so as any way to be as ready as you can to fly to Him at the first news of His return? Do you ask, I say, *where?* See how the birds of prey flock to

[f] St. Luke xvii. 37.

the dead body! See how, when camel or horse falls down in the midst of the wildest and most arid desert, where, as far as the eye of man can strain, no sign of animal or vegetable life is to be discovered on any side, see how instantly the dark speck of some vulture, or other bird that feeds on carrion, is to be seen on the distant horizon, sailing up from the east or west, from the north or south, to reach its far-discovered food! What sense warns that distant bird? what sight, what smell, what unknown faculty informs it that what it seeks is here? Something, like to that sense, whatever it be,—something, at least, which from that sense we may conceive and understand, will bring the just, will bring the people of God, from every quarter under heaven, to meet their risen Lord. Something, like to that wonderful and unexplored faculty which leads the bird with unerring direction to its nest, and the bee to its hive, which has been known, over and over again, to guide a poor dog to its well-known home over many miles of country wholly untraversed and unknown before, shall surely gather together the people of God from all the lands under heaven, to meet in good time their own dear Lord—whom they have believed, loved, imitated— when He returns in judgment upon the earth.

Shall we ask what the nature of this sense shall be,

and how far Holy Scripture will aid us in discovering it? Surely one of these passages may be made to throw light upon the other, and we may confidently say, that whatever other elements may enter into it, yet it is in purity of heart, faithful, lifelong purity of heart, that it is promised to Christian man that he shall see God. Not by any new discoveries in devotion, not by extravagances of feeling, not by ascetic or solitary living, not by monastic vows or hard obligations of will-worship, not by any of the various indirect ways which men have devised for winding themselves up so high, as to be above the real life and duty of their station in the world, but by simple, unpretending purity of heart in the Holy Ghost,—by purity of heart which *may* be won in the Holy Ghost in any position or condition of a Christian's life,—shall man in Christ see God. Purity of heart, sweet and innocent in childhood, strong, self-controlling, and victorious in youth, established, settled, entirely won and possessed in manhood! Purity of heart, which, as it is the fairest and most beautiful of all the graces which the Holy Spirit worketh in the soul of man, the inward basis and foundation of all the rest, without which they cannot be, so is that which brings him nearest to the angelic nature, and fits him most for the presence and the sight of God!

But O! brethren, while we thus exalt the blessedness (as how can it be too high exalted?) of purity, true, life-long purity of heart, how shall we speak of those whose conscience tells them, loudly and unmistakeably, that it is not *they* to whom this sweet grace, this lofty blessedness belongs? What of those who in a greater or less degree have let their hearts know of and love that which is opposite to pureness; on whose soul there is a secret stain, unknown and unsuspected perhaps by others, but to themselves, alas! sometimes the source of the deepest and most corroding inward distress, and too often the profound secret of more real alienation from God than other men imagine, or perhaps they at all adequately realize to themselves? O! brethren, what is the real state in respect of this most anxious and most important subject, of the social life which is all around us, and which, from the mere necessity of its contiguity to ourselves, and its extremely contagious nature, can hardly fail to have affected, with more or less of evil, many even of our own hearts? Is it not notorious, is it not beyond doubt or denial, that in this land, and in this age, the creeping plague of impurity is very near at the heart of our national life, of our faith, and of our holiness? eating it away, more or less secretly; undermining and counteracting the true and genuine efforts of holiness and restoration which are really making on many sides of us, and threatening the utmost evil to our Church and country? While the extreme freedom of our institutions offers, almost without the slightest legal check, openly and notoriously in the streets of our cities, free-trade in sin; while voluptuous and seductive literature, so to call it, and the continual reports of the public journals, supply constant food to the diseased and foul imagination; while the legitimate efforts to probe, or in any real way to reach the sore, are discouraged as dangerous to faith and morals, and so the sore is left to itself to fester and grow corrupt in many a heart that might be turned to repentance, because men persist in shutting their eyes to the truth, and resolving to believe the real inner state of hearts as good and pure as the outward manners of the world and society seem to shew them,—who, I say, can doubt or deny that the blessedness of purity, and the extreme danger of impurity, are among the chief subjects which in faithful simplicity and truth the preacher is called upon to bring before the people? Trace the life of a man, bred up as we are, brethren, in this country; follow him from the day when he first emerges from the innocence of the nursery; trace him through the companionship of school, public or private; through the temptations of the university, of the garrison, of the city ; consider how he becomes familiarized in all his life with the realities of impureness, which are only too notorious and visible on every side, and think how many a soul of man among us must be conscious of that bitter secret plague, the inward misery of the too-defiling knowledge—alas! too often more than the mere exterior knowledge—of impure sin.

O! brethren, let us not deceive ourselves! Only the pure in heart shall see God. Let no man deceive you by undervaluing or extenuating the guilt of impure sin! Let no man deceive you, as some try to deceive you, by representing that men are very much alike to one another; that there are no such great differences among them; that it cannot be believed that the amiable, kind-hearted, hospitable, fair-seeming people among whom we live, should be lost in the next world; that there is no such distinction between the lives of men as that it should be credible that so mighty a difference should be made between them, as we believe there will be, in the day of judgment. So men do teach sometimes, and so many think; but it is a terrible deceit. The chasm will surely open in the midst of us, and will separate us from one another. It will divide us into two, and only two, companies On the one side will be found the pure, the faithful, the penitent; and surely the rest will be on the other. But shall, then, all those amiable qualities, shall all that kindness, and family affection, and generosity, and honesty, and justice, and all those other traits which made men seem so much alike, even though they be altogether and finally dissevered from faith and repentance,—shall these things go down into condemnation, to sweeten and alleviate, if it be possible, the society of the lost? No, surely. Remember, brethren, that stern, but certain and oft-repeated word of Christ, "From him that hath not, shall be taken even that which he hath [g]." From him that hath not the evangelical graces of faith in God and repentance of sin, all his exterior sweetness which was not of grace, and his justice, and all those other qualities which attracted the love which they did not deserve, shall be taken away. They were not his own; they were lent him. He may not keep them longer. They shall be taken away from him, and given to some happier brother, in whom, perhaps, these qualities had been wanting on earth, but who now is made perfect in Christ. Nothing that is lovely and sweet can go down into hell. Nothing that is lovely and sweet can be wanting in heaven. No,—to die impure, to die with the heart still hankering after things im-

[g] St. Matt. xxv. 29.

"BLESSED ARE THE PURE IN HEART." 131

pure, the imagination stained and foul, the man unrepentant,—what is it but to be lost? By no express sentence, it may be, but by the divinely-lighted conscience turned into fire in the soul, those who have died impure, and impenitent in their impurity, will know at once their own wretched lot, away from the sight of God, and far from all possible joy. "In nowise shall anything enter into that kingdom that defiles [h];" "the highway into that kingdom shall be called The Way of Holiness: the unclean shall not pass over it [i]."

And remember, brethren, the words of the Prophet Daniel, how "those that sleep in the dust of the earth shall awake, some to everlasting life, and some to shame and everlasting contempt [j]." What, may we suppose, is this eternal shame? We know that, as the Lord carried with Himself into heaven His own glorious wounds, never to be obliterated, so the just, the martyrs of God, shall wear for ever the tokens and marks of their holy sufferings, whereby they fill up that which is behind of the afflictions of Christ in their flesh [k],—marks and tokens, base and dishonouring in the sight of dim-eyed men, but become not less glorious than immortal in the world of glory:—how

[h] Rev. xxi. 27; xxii. 15. [i] Isa. xxxv. 8.
[j] Dan. xii. 2. [k] Col. i. 24.

may not these lost souls, lost for their unrepented impurity, carry on their foul bodies the eternal tokens of their filthy shame, the badges of everlasting contempt, even in the regions of the lost?

O! young men, baptized into Christ, and looking forward in Him to glory, whose hearts are even now solicited by the Holy Spirit of God to devote yourselves altogether to His service in your various stations of life, O! guard yourselves now, guard yourselves *here* against this creeping plague, this secret poison and well of misery, an impure heart! Having such promises as you have, brethren, such great and precious promises, cleanse yourselves from all filthiness of the flesh and spirit, perfecting holiness in the fear of God[1]! Guard your secret imaginations under the Holy Spirit! It is in the imagination that the main fuel of this sin is found,—the imagination quickened and made lively by education, and then allowed to run riot in loose talking, loose reading, luxurious living,—let not such words be once named among you, as becometh saints; neither filthiness nor foolish talking, nor jesting, which are not convenient[m]. Words lightly spoken and lightly heard in youth, and deeds little thought of when done or seen, often fix themselves so deeply in the memory,

[1] 2 Cor. vii. 1. [m] Eph. v. 4.

as to recur, uninvited and unwelcome, all through life; even in holy times, and when the soul, into the very substance of which they seem, as it were, to be burned, loathes and abhors them. Believe me, it is by the polluting of the imagination principally, that the trial becomes to so many a fiery and fatal one; and so, the imagination which is allowed to be lax, and idle, and feed itself on all the chance, and stray, and mischievous food that may be presented to it, keeps sin alive in the soul which else might let it go, and get well of it.

But do not think that it is by any flying away from life, and station, and duty that safety is to be won. The imagination that is content to be polluted can find its food everywhere. In solitude alike, and in society; from nature, from art, from books, from newspapers; nay, from the very Word of God itself it can draw the poison it loves. In intercourse and conversation with other people such a man turns everything into evil. All that he hears, turns, as it were, sour upon his soul. Every bad word and thought clings. The good ones all fly away. Every bad neighbour attaches him; every good one holds aloof, or is distasteful to him.

O! miserable taint of an unclean heart! of which I would not speak, but that I fear there may, too probably, be a secret echo to my words in the depth of the conscience of not a few, perhaps, who hear me!

But what says St. John, the loving and beloved disciple? "I write unto you, young men, because ye have overcome the wicked one;" "I have written unto you, young men, because ye are strong, and the Word of God abideth in you, and ye have overcome the wicked one [n]." Ye are in your strength,—strength of body, strength of mind, strength of labour, strength of resistance, strength of will. There is no attack of the wicked one so strong, or so subtle, or so universal as that with which he assails young men on the side of impurity. And so there is no victory greater, no innocence more gracious, no self-conquest more blessed than that of high-minded, heroic, Christian purity in youth. If there is one thing more angelic than another to be seen in ordinary human life, it is a young man having the Word of God abiding in him, not unconscious of temptation, nor different in constitution and natural desire from his neighbours; who in his clear, lofty pureness of Christian grace throws aside the temptations of uncleanness of all kinds, as things with which he will have no parley nor concern; on whom such words and thoughts fall harmless;

[n] 1 St. John ii. 13, 14.

whose chastity of imagination, filled with all that is innocent, and busy with what is useful, does not admit the ideas or visions of sin, till evil spirits and evil men cease to present them. And such, I verily believe, there are among you, brethren, and by God's grace not a few; retiring it may be, and unknown sometimes, perhaps not unknown and unprized by their neighbours, but surely beloved of God and good angels, and more or less secretly the sources of blessing to all around them.

And do not suppose, brethren, that this lofty condition is of nature. Ask yourselves whether it be so, or no. No: it is neither of nature, nor yet so contrary to nature as that it may not be won by any Christian soul of man under God's almighty and most blessed grace. It is the gift of God to such as have used the early measures of grace well, who have kept themselves from sin in their young days, who have been pious, and full of prayers, feeding on the Word of God, keeping their hearts ever as in the sight of God, habitually feeling themselves in His presence, realizing in youth and manhood the sweet promise of early piety and goodness.

To them, first, and most: and next, to such as, having known taint, as having felt something of the bitter distress of such stain of mind, will turn round,

—at any time while they are spared to live and hear of the gracious promises of God,—and, repenting of their sin, will strive with earnest and persevering intention of purpose (for nothing less than a very earnest and persevering intention will do) to purify their hearts by true confession, by hearty prayer, and lifelong repentance. It is possible that they may not regain altogether, while they remain on earth, that fair brightness of soul which belongs to those who have never known of such evil. The guilt of such sin may, no doubt, be washed out by divine forgiveness for Christ's sake while man lives, but I fear that its stains, at least when they have been deep in youth, and have dwelt some time upon the mind, are wellnigh indelible as regards the memory they leave and the distress they bring.

But by God's mercy to the penitent in Christ, they will be washed out finally and for ever in the Resurrection. Those who are at last accepted in the Beloved, shall awake up from the dead in the likeness of the Redeemer, (and how should that be otherwise than altogether pure and holy?) and in it be perfectly and for ever satisfied. And then the pure and the purified together, the innocent and the repentant, shall find that in this cleanness of heart, this hard-won, it may be, and graciously kept cleanness of heart, they have

"BLESSED ARE THE PURE IN HEART."

gained that wondrous sense of the soul which, while the sensual and the impenitent can see nothing but the wrath and terrors of the Judge, will enable them to lift up their eyes, redeemed, sanctified, *saved*, to see, and see for ever, the eternal love and mercy of God in Christ to those who are made like Him at His coming.

SERMON VII.[a]

St. Matthew v.

9. Blessed are the peace-makers: for they shall be called the children of God.

WE all remember well what are called the Beatitudes; that is, those sentences of divine blessing with which the Lord begins His Sermon on the Mount, as recorded in the 5th chapter of St. Matthew's Gospel.

There are eight of them.

These eight sentences do not describe eight different classes of people, who all, for different reasons or in different degrees, are blessed; but they describe eight different traits or points of character in the same man. They form, united, the moral portrait of the perfect Christian man. None but a Christian man can have them perfectly; for they require the onward, faithful looking forward to glory in Christ, through His aton-

---

[a] Preached for the Charitable Society of Aliens, Winchester Cathedral, Dec. 15, 1859.

ing blood; and they require the indwelling aid of the Holy Ghost, which, richly offered to Christian men in the Church of Christ, is not, so far as we know, given, save in that Church. None but a Christian man can have them perfectly; and he who has them not at all, can hardly be called a Christian man at all. He may have the position, the opportunities, the offered hopes, the responsibilities of a Christian man, but in all the character, in all the moral acceptableness, in all that should adorn and justify his profession, he is surely no Christian man at all.

Now I observe of these eight Beatitudes, that two of them relate to virtues which are purely inward, absolutely confined to the interior depths of a Christian man's spirit,—purity of heart, and hunger and thirst after righteousness. Two of them are virtues inward indeed, but having relation to our position among men,—poverty of spirit and meekness. Two of them rather belong to the passive condition of human virtue, placed in the midst of a sad and unkind world,— sorrow and persecution. The seventh, mercy, is the special virtue of the Christian in his active and outward dealings with other men; and in peace-making, the last of the eight, he is regarded as going altogether out from himself, and entering into the transactions which arise between other people, and in which he himself has, personally, no share. Thus the Christian character, as drawn in the Beatitudes, is that of the man who in his inner and secret self maintains a perfect purity of heart, and longs for righteousness, true, irreproachable righteousness in Christ, with a longing like that with which the hungry man longs for food, or the thirsty for drink; who in his position of life, and his claims for himself among men, has a real, deep meekness of mind, and gracious poverty of spirit; who accepts the lot of sorrow, and the distress of persecution, if it be the will of God that he be afflicted with them, in thankful submission, only desirous to find in them the blessing with which they are most surely charged; who is characterized in his outer dealings by a prevailing and pervading mercy; and who, passing out of himself and his own private affairs, and entering into the concerns of other men,—regarded now as the neighbour, the townsman, the citizen,—is known as ever seeking peace and ensuing it, putting men at one with God and with one another, so as to be in the very filial likeness of God, by acting in so God-like a manner amongst men.

Now before I go on to speak in more detail of the Christian peace-maker,—a subject which I have chosen, brethren, as not ill-suited for our sacred meeting of this day, when we are come together as Christian fellow-townsmen, desiring to do Christian good to the bodies and souls of our brethren, and in peaceful and brotherly union to spread thus Christ's peace among ourselves and our neighbours,—before I go on to speak in more detail of the character of the Christian peace-maker, I wish to make one observation, and a very important one too, as arising out of what I have already said about the eight Beatitudes. Understand, then, that no man can be really a Christian peace-maker, unless he be also a man striving after true purity of heart, and longing very ardently after righteousness in Christ; unless he be truly meek, and in the sight of God poor in spirit; unless he take sorrow and persecution, as far as he is visited with them, as good gifts of God, and strive to find in them the blessing which they are meant to convey; unless he be a man of Christian mercy in all his dealings with those with whom his position brings him in contact. This first; and further, he can be none of these things, unless he be a faithful Christian man, resting on the Redeemer who has bought him with His own blood, strong only in the grace of the blessed Spirit of God, for which he ever prays, and always looking forward in cheerful and faithful hope to the blessed coming of the Lord Jesus in glory upon the earth, and to the eternal inheritance prepared for those who shall be His,—whether alive in the flesh upon the earth, or waiting in his tranquil paradise after death,—who shall be His at His coming. I do not say that he must be all these things *perfectly*, before he can be a Christian peace-maker *at all;* but I say that unless he be these things in some degree, unless he be endeavouring to be these things, unless he be growing in them, and doing his best, under the Holy Spirit of God, to grow in them more and more, he is no Christian peace-maker at all, nor one of those who can hope to receive the Christian peace-maker's blessing. He may be a good-natured man, he may be one who likes to see other people comfortable and peaceable, rather than uncomfortable or quarrelling, he may be liberal, or careless of his money, and free in giving, or a lover of quiet,—but all this is hollow, uncertain, and undiscriminating. A man who is only this may change his mind, or he may take offence, or he may become soured by troubles or disappointments, or by ingratitude, so as to become harsh in his judgments, and unkind in his words. Any way he is no Christian peace-maker; nor can he be called —for a softness which is of nature and not of grace, which comes rather of human weakness than of divine strength—the child of God, doing, like his Father, God-like work in the world.

But let us endeavour to describe the Christian peace-maker more exactly.

We shall do this best by ascertaining what peace is; what that is which he proposes and desires to make.

Now, first, it is obvious that there is such a thing as a very spurious kind of peace, and consequently that there is such a thing as a very spurious kind of peace-making.

This sort of spurious peace-making consists simply in 'letting things alone,' 'not meddling,' 'being sure that all will come right,' 'taking things easily,' 'minding one's own business, and letting one's neighbours mind theirs.'

Now this 'let alone' sort of peace-making makes—if it can be said to *make* anything—a very shabby sort of peace. It leaves vice unchecked, it leaves ungodliness rampant, it leaves ignorance untaught, it leaves secret grudges to fester in people's hearts: I know not whether selfishness or cowardice have the greater part in it; for selfishness and cowardice are both very largely present in it, and selfishness and cowardice are the very opposites of Christian peace-making. And such miserable peace is no peace at all; for though it may be quiet for a time, yet there is no security whatever that it may not blaze out at any moment into the wildest excesses of strife or evil.

No: this is not the peace which the Christian peace-maker designs to make. He wishes, as far as he may, to set men at one together really, not in a hollow, temporary, deceitful way: he would lead them to Christian forbearance and forgiveness, to Christian liberality and gratitude, to Christian kindness; to think as well of one another, and interpret as favourably one another's words and deeds as possible; to have, that is, a Christian peace with one another, based upon a true Christian peace within themselves: for the man who is at peace with God in Christ, that is, who is humble, faithful, and pious inwardly, is alone able to be at real peace with his neighbours.

How, then, shall the citizen,—I do not now speak of the clergyman, whose express and professional duty it is to remind his people of God, and His truth and will,—how is the ordinary citizen to set to work to make this sort of peace among his fellow-citizens and neighbours?

First, brethren, and chiefly, by having it himself. Believe me, of all the things that he can say or do, by far the most effective is that he should be truly, faithfully, and in unsuspected earnest, Christian and peaceful in Christ himself. We may talk till Doomsday without effect, if talk is all. More eyes are on us, more judgments are forming of us, more particulars of our conduct, look, manner, words, and silence, and I know not what besides, are noted and observed in us than any one of us at all suspects. Men and women round us are forming judgments of us perpetually,—censoriously, no doubt, often, and unkindly, sometimes unjustly; but, on the whole, with a sort of severe fairness, verging generally to the worse side, which would sometimes be painfully wholesome to our self-love, if we could be perfectly aware of it. And a Christian man, unsuspected of hollowness, and above such suspicion, setting forth an example of personal religion in his family, among his dependents, in his daily habits, in his controlled and earnest words, in his honest, industrious ways, in his cheerful resignation and patience under sorrow, in his words and looks of Christian sympathy, is a Christian peacemaker in the truest sense, before ever he has set his foot beyond his own threshold. His light radiates far and wide, farther and wider than we commonly think, before *he* has discovered that he has any light in him at all. And observe, that some people, even within their own houses and daily business, have so large a sphere of Christian peace-making opened to them, that, without stepping beyond their own door, they may exercise it very extensively indeed. I mean such people as have large establishments, as of workpeople, pupils, soldiers, or servants, under their own especial care. Some, I say, have a *very large* sphere of such Christian peace-making at home: and I beg you to observe that every single member of every single family has really a more considerable opportunity of such peace-making than we sometimes think. Fathers and mothers of families many of you are, and brothers and sisters of families: do you not know well the difference between the cross, misinterpreting, aggravating, unkind one in your home, —the one with whom every one must be on their guard lest they continually give unnecessary offence, and meet dark looks and harsh words,—and the dear, sunny, Christian child, the sweet peace-making brother or sister, whose presence is an ensuring of happy, kindly, loving deeds and words? Think of it, brethren; for you will find that you know, as well as I do, the sweet mission of unsuspected peace-making that each single one of us bears in his own home.

However, our Christian peace-maker does go forth. He lives in a town, we will suppose, where, as is, alas! too usual in this generation, there is, with a good deal of true religion and earnestness among many, a great deal of careless and worldly living, involving all sorts of party-feeling and estrangement among

"BLESSED ARE THE PEACE-MAKERS." 147

very many, a great deal of secret ill-will, hard words, and spiteful, injurious conduct, and a fearful amount of notorious and soul-destroying sin, not always confined to the most ignorant of the people.

See, at once and from the first, how brave our Christian peace-maker must be! how simply and innocently brave! It is not a brave thing to let men and things alone; it is not a brave thing to be a noisy partisan: but it is a very brave thing to risk the displeasure of all sides, to see the good points of both parties in a quarrel, to speak one's mind firmly and gently, neither willingly provoking, and resolved not to be provoked to unnecessary displeasure; to tell, it may be, an angry and unreasonable man that he is in the wrong, without mingling the slightest bitterness in the rebuke, to defend the right when it is unpopular, and to take part with the innocent man when he is unduly vilified or oppressed.

Such bravery, such gentle, quiet, but indomitable courage, is essentially necessary to the character of the Christian peace-maker. Timidity, which sometimes looks like peace-making, and still oftener tries to look like it, absolutely and always fails of producing real peace. Mere timidity, which is mere weakness, expressly foments the evils which are contrary to peace. Timidity in combination with audacity (a very common mixture) produces a kind of noisy, hectoring bravery, which also directly stimulates the same evils. True, calm, patient Christian courage alone can take and keep its own clear line, and is found to impart, not unfrequently, of its own calm and peaceful strength to the jarring and disquieted hearts by which it is surrounded.

Yes; our Christian peace-maker must be perfectly brave. But bravery, the simplest, most indomitable, and gentle bravery, will not do alone. Who does not see how essential it is that he must be very wise, Christianly wise, in every step he takes, and every word he speaks? The questions in dispute among people are sometimes, it is true, quite simple; when all the wrong is on one side and all the right on the other: but much more often they are very complicated and difficult, and there are faults on every side, and it needs a very great deal of care and skill to come to the rights, as they say, of a case. And then, again, men's feelings and women's feelings are apt to be irritated, or irritable, and take fire at an indiscreet word or hasty phrase, and set themselves strongly against the attempt at peace-making which any way they can interpret into an offence. Bravery, I own, is most necessary; but what a wreck, what endless mischief would bravery do alone! No, our peace-maker must be as wise as a serpent, watching his times,—often holding his hand and his tongue, where deed or word would aggravate the sore,—ready to drop in the healing and softening word, or the considerate act, just at the moment when it will do good, wording even his rebuke with the utmost caution, warning a man who is provoked that *it is he who returns the blow that begins the quarrel*, suggesting some kind word or conciliatory step at a moment when it will sink deeply into an adversary's heart. In public questions as in private ones, he will watch his opportunities to bring men together,—discouraging strong words and needless declamations, (for eloquence, as a good old writer says, never was a vulnerary herb, and never will be,)—not afraid of holding his own opinions, or stating them,—not adopting the spurious liberality of modern days, which, bidding him remember that others are as likely to be right as he is, wishes him to pitch his conduct half-way between their convictions and his own,—not doing those foolish things, which *are* weak while they think they are strong, but with firm, gentle wisdom giving others credit for the same honesty which he claims for himself, and softening by his careful and prudent course the asperities of inevitable division.

He must be most brave, and entirely wise: but

what are both of these if he be not *loving*? unless
the forward courage with which he ventures to interfere with things not altogether his own, and the discretion with which he handles them, be not sweetened,
recommended, made lovely by a true and unmistakeable love of souls, and the peace of souls, in him? Do
men *like* to find others interfering in their quarrels?
Does it make them like such interference better that
it is perfectly *brave*? No doubt, if it be *wise*, it will
avoid all unnecessary causes of offence, and do an unwelcome thing in the least unwelcome way; but what
is to make this unwelcome thing welcome? What
is to make men accept the interference, and follow
heartily the lead and guidance, of him who thus interferes? What but that such bravery and such wisdom be altogether mingled and made sweet by unmistaken and unmistakeable love? Love, pure and
disinterested, love perfectly clear of indirect objects,
and unspoiled by weakness or silliness of manner, love,
strong, simple, hearty, Christian love, is irresistible.
A perverse man may fret awhile at it, an obstinate
man may, so to say, set his teeth against being influenced by it, a bad man may try to find out some
round-about reason for throwing suspicion upon it,—
some idea of inconsistency, or partiality, or deep design, or I know not what,—but sooner or later, love

is irresistible, such brave, wise, Christian love as I speak of. Even if *one* determinately wrong-headed man, here or there, sets himself against it permanently, as he sets himself against everything that is good, yet is he overborne by the general consent of his neighbours. The Christian peace-maker, if he be truly there, cannot fail to be known: if he be known he cannot fail to be loved, and being loved, he is sure to be a blessing and a spring of blessing to all those who are so happy as to come within the sphere of his good influence. Wherever he be seen, good men welcome him, and that spark or element of good which there is in most men's hearts welcomes him. If they meet him in the street,—if he comes into their company,—if there be meeting, argument, discussion, they rejoice to see *him*. No asperity will fall from his lips, no secret sarcasm need be feared there, he has no indirect objects, he will interpret everything and every man as kindly as is possible, he is not afraid nor ashamed to have and to own his own opinions, and to act upon them, yet will his endeavours be (every one knows it) earnest for Christian peace,—not sham nor hollow peace which is no peace, but Christian peace; peace, manly and above-board, peace that is altogether true, honest, and Christian. He may not be rich nor able in worldly riches and ability, but by the grace of God which is with him, he is very rich and very able to do greater, deeper, and more lasting good than any which can come of worldly riches or worldly ability.

"Blessed are the peace-makers, for they shall be called the children of God." Men will bless them; many a secret word and wish of those whom they have done good to will bless them unawares. Men will see and own that they are God's sons, doing their Father's work as sons, being about their Father's business, proving themselves His sons by the likeness of their good Christian peace-making. But the words of Christ, brethren, in this Beatitude are not limited to men's blessings, or to their recognition of the filial resemblance which the Christian peace-maker bears to God his Father in Christ.

No; the special blessing which is theirs is the blessing of God; and the particular nature of it is that they shall be called, that is, that they shall be, God's sons—God's sons in Christ—God's sons in Christ for ever, made free indeed in Christ, sons for ever in their heavenly Father's immortal mansions.

Brethren, I have endeavoured thus to sketch out the main features of the Christian peace-maker, whom the Lord calls, and by that call makes, blessed.

Are you and I, brethren, such as he? Are you

and I, each of us in our place of life, so possessed of Christian peace in our own hearts, as that we are, to the extent of our powers and influence, centres and spreaders of Christian peace to the people that are round us? We all can be, in Christ; we all must be, if we are to remain and abide in Christ.

Here is Christmas coming upon us,—the very season of the advent of peace,—" on earth peace, and good-will towards men;" the time, as even men who are careless of Christian peace can feel, for mutual acts of kindness, charity, and family affection. And we are met to-day to celebrate, as for near two hundred years past, this good work of Christian benevolence and peace towards our poorer neighbours.

Well; may God bless the work to us who do it, to those for whose benefit it is done, and to His own glory.

Well; but remember that, beyond these outward and public works, more precious than visible and recognized acts of charity is the inward peace, leading to the general outer peace-making, the inward communion with God in the spirit, leading to the general outer bravery, wisdom, and lovingness of peace-making of which I have been speaking.

And this lesson may God commend to our separate hearts, brethren, this day. Be at peace with God in

Christ, bending your will to His will, confessing and abandoning your sins, putting your whole trust and confidence in His abundant and unfailing mercy,— and then shall you become blessed peace-makers in your generation; true, free sons of God for ever and ever in Christ.

SERMON VIII.[a]

St. Matthew v.

10. *Blessed are they which are persecuted for righteousness' sake : for theirs is the kingdom of heaven.*

THIS is the eighth and last of the Beatitudes in the order in which they are recorded by St. Matthew. It may otherwise be regarded as the second of the third pair; the pair which speaks of the sufferings to which the Christian man is exposed in this sad and unkind world.

Unlike the other Beatitudes, which are completed each in a single verse, Christian maxims or apophthegms uttered without further explanation or addition, this one is followed by two verses which are to be regarded as the application of the Beatitude to the special case of the disciples to whom the Lord was speaking : "Blessed are ye when men shall revile you, and persecute you, and shall say all manner of evil against

[a] Preached in Winchester College Chapel.

you falsely, for My sake. Rejoice, and be exceeding glad; for great is your reward in heaven: for so persecuted they the prophets which were before you." These verses also add explanatory particulars which enable us to understand the Beatitude itself with greater fulness and certainty.

Blessed are they which are persecuted: we learn from the verses which I have just read that we may add to actual persecution in deeds, that they too are blessed which are reviled, and spoken all manner of evil of,—falsely, however,—for true words of reviling and evil carry no blessing with them. Blessed are they which are thus persecuted for righteousness' sake: we learn again from the next verse that 'for righteousness' sake' may be interpreted 'for My sake,' that is, 'for Christ's sake.' Blessed are they which are thus persecuted for righteousness' or Christ's sake: for theirs is the kingdom of heaven, great is their reward in heaven; they may rejoice and be exceeding glad on earth, even in the midst of all such persecution, however immediately sad or painful, for they are lifted thereby to the rank of God's prophets of old time, persecuted for the like cause, faithfulness to Christ, and with them they shall inherit the kingdom of heaven.

There is little that needs detailed explanation in

the words of this Beatitude. We know well what is the meaning of being persecuted. The primitive Christians were persecuted,—chiefly in the ten great historical persecutions, by the heathen emperors of Rome. The Protestants were persecuted in this country, as in many of the countries of Europe, in the days of the Reformation and before it. They, too, have not unfrequently retorted upon the Roman Catholics by persecuting them when they have had the power. There have been fearful persecutions of Christians occasionally in later years in heathen countries,—as in Japan and Madagascar. All such cases of distinct, overt persecution, where loss of life, or goods, or other painful sufferings have been inflicted, for religion's sake, upon Christian people, are plain and intelligible at once without further explanation. Then there are all sorts of more secret persecution, without actual violence; as when men, or women, or even children, have been ill thought of or evil spoken of, harshly or unkindly treated, looked upon with jealousy and dislike, because they were bent on serving God in Christ. Cases of this sort are obviously very various, and have, no doubt, in all times been extremely numerous, as when irreligious parents, or neighbours, or irreligious companions have made the outward profession of religion, if not actually dangerous to life, or limb, or property, yet difficult and painful; when people have thrown all sorts of indirect but very deeply-felt obstacles in the way of others' religion, and the world round about has looked coldly upon such as have been trying to please God, and circulated all manner of evil stories against them. I suppose that the persecution which has been inflicted, and goes on being inflicted, in this way, has been in the whole amount very much more considerable, as it is very much more lasting, than the outward and violent persecutions which we more commonly think of under this name. And I cannot but think that it has been, on the whole, not less trying than those outward and violent persecutions. For persons assailed by it have to bear their troubles mostly in secret. They have little sympathy from others; nor any of the rising of the spirit of passive (passing into active) heroism which, when men's eyes are on it, is naturally roused into energetic resistance. For indeed there are several things which tend to hold a man up in his visible endurance of visible persecution. He is as a champion of a cause; his personal bravery and earnestness, as well as his conscience, are on trial. He knows that even among those who hound on the cry of persecution against him, there are those who admire his firmness in bearing it. He believes that though overpowered himself, and put to death perhaps, yet suffering and death bravely borne leave a seed behind them, which germinates and grows in spite of persecution, and is wont to outlive it. All these things and such as these mingle themselves up with the convictions of conscience, and strengthen it, when the persecution for righteousness' sake takes place in the sight of men. But it is otherwise with all the secret, and, if I may so call it, unpicturesque suffering of social or domestic life,—the chill, and the estrangement, and the unkindness, and the evil report, and the misrepresentation, the thwarting and jealousy, all the details of inward and unseen misery which go to make up the real persecution which has visited, and no doubt visits still, thousands of people whose hearts' desire it is to serve God faithfully, and are content to bear with evil for Christ's sake. And so I can hardly doubt that "when that last account 'twixt heaven and earth shall be made up," it will be found that the persecution of private and social life has been in total amount greater, and maybe its actual bitterness not less, and so its ultimate title of blessedness in Christ under this Beatitude as great, as that of those who have been the well-known and admired sufferers, the "persecuted unto blood" for Christ's sake.

But all cases of persecution, in order to come under

the scope of this Beatitude, must be for righteousness' sake. There may be all sorts of cruelty, injustice, and hard-heartedness,—destined, no doubt, if it be not repented of on the part of those who inflict it, to suffer God's heavy judgment hereafter, and sure to be set to rights and, so to say, made up for to the sufferers,—which yet is far away from the peculiar promise made in this verse. Again, I can hardly think that even moral goodness, such as truth, honesty, soberness, purity, or the like, are the precise meaning of righteousness in this verse,—as though the Lord offered the kingdom of heaven to such as bear with ill-treatment or persecution on earth rather than tell lies, or cheat, or become drunken, or impure, precious as such moral martyrdom is,—unless this 'righteousness' be a religious righteousness, that is, unless it be maintained for Christ's sake, and with a view to the blessed kingdom of Christ. And here I think we see the value of that further verse, which, as I said, contains the *application* of this Beatitude to the disciples,—" Blessed are ye when men shall revile you, and persecute you, and shall say all manner of evil against you falsely, *for My sake*." To be honest and truthful for Christ's sake, to let no amount of ill-treatment or persecution force us into telling lies, or doing dishonesty, because by so doing we should break the law of Christ, and risk the

"BLESSED ARE THEY WHICH ARE PERSECUTED."

forfeiture of our inheritance in Him, to keep from intemperance or impurity on the Christian grounds,—how can I do so great wickedness, and sin against Christ,—this it is which alone brings a sufferer from man's persecution fairly and fully under the scope of this precious Beatitude.

Blessed, then, are they which thus outwardly and visibly in the eyes of men, or thus secretly and unknown in their home or society, are persecuted, by act, or word, or feeling, for the sake of Christ, for the sake of maintaining their estate of forgiveness and holiness in Christ. Blessed are they, even in their suffering, for theirs is the kingdom of heaven. They may rejoice and be exceeding glad, for it is a great reward indeed that awaits them in Christ's kingdom, where they will rank amid the holy prophets of old, —the men who were stoned, were sawn asunder, were tempted, were slain with the sword, who wandered about in sheepskins and goatskins, being destitute, afflicted, tormented, of whom the world was not worthy, —and be made perfect with God's faithful confessors of every age.

Indeed, the language of Holy Scripture in several places teaches us that all the suffering endured for Christ's sake, and inflicted on earth, is to be regarded as giving so many declarations or tokens of what is to

M

be the case in the other or heavenly kingdom. Read the history, so to speak, backwards, put those who are lowest in such transactions upon earth highest, and the highest lowest, and you see how the persecutors and the persecuted will stand in relation to one another hereafter. So St. Paul encourages the Philippians [b] in their sufferings. 'Be not at all terrified,' he says, 'by your adversaries, for their persecution of you is *to them* an evident token of perdition, but *to you* of salvation, and that of God;' that is to say, when you suffer persecution thus for Christ's sake, God bids you read the whole transaction as His declaration of what is to be hereafter. To the persecutors He says, 'See in the persecution which you inflict an evident token of the loss of your souls, unless ye repent.' To the people persecuted, 'See,' he says, 'in what you suffer, a manifest token of your salvation [c]. If you bear it patiently, bear it for Christ's sake, bear it well, you may be quite sure that it means nothing less than that God loves you dearly for Christ's sake; allows you, in His love, to suffer for Christ's sake, and be partakers of Christ's sufferings, and assures you a share in the glory of Christ, as having been sharers in His sufferings [d].' We are, it has been well said, in this life busy weaving, as it were, a beautiful piece of heavenly tapestry from

[b] Chap. i. 28. [c] 2 Thess. i. 5. [d] Rom. viii. 17.

the back. We do not see the pattern which we are making. We do not know which are to be the bright parts and which are the dark ones. It all looks like confusion; there is little beauty, little order. But wait awhile—the work is growing under our hands even now; though we cannot see it, God sees it even now. When the times of restitution come it will be finished, and all men and angels shall see it, and we shall wonder to find how all the dark parts, as they seemed, in working, are indeed the bright ones in the glorious completeness, and those that seemed bright and glowing behind are in fact, and are to be for ever, the dark and gloomy foils of the brightness which shall never fade.

But those who would find the blessedness of this Beatitude to their own souls must carry with them one or two most important cautions, lest unawares they lose the very thing they are in search of, and find that their heavy sufferings have all been borne in vain.

First, and chiefly. The Christian endurance of which I have spoken must be entirely full, entirely penetrated, within and without, with Christian charity. If we do not forgive every one his brother their trespasses, we know well that we have no right to expect any forgiveness of our trespasses at God's hand. If, therefore, a person suffering under any sort or degree of persecution, even persecution for Christ's sake, at the hand of tyrants, or unkind parents, or neighbours, or companions, cherishes in his trouble a bitter spirit, longs for revenge, nurses a secret spite, or, indeed, comes short of a true Christian forgiveness,— a forgiveness as total as that which he looks to receive from God for Christ's sake for his own sins,—I do not see how he can look to find his sufferings a source of Christian blessing, or a title to a divine inheritance. Alas, then, for him who poisons the blessing in the very cup, by uncharitableness and an unforgiving spirit! Surely even in fighting, in enduring, in dying for Christ, he is none of His.

This, you will readily see, is one most important caution for those to remember who hope that they are suffering for Christ's sake. And I do not know whether the second that I have to mention is not a more important one still,—both in itself, and because it is more likely to be overlooked and forgotten by people who are in earnest in endeavouring to please God. Remember, then, that no man has any right whatever to court, or bring about, or wilfully incur any persecution or ill-treatment whatever which he might with good conscience avoid, for the sake of winning the blessing pronounced by our Lord in this

Beatitude. Remember that the blessing won by the persecuted is all won away from the persecutors. The 'token of salvation' which God gives to the sufferer, in a case of ill-treatment, is correlative with 'the token of perdition' which He gives, in the same case, to him who inflicts the suffering. Would you, then, make another man sin? Would you cause a brother to commit the great offence of injuring Christ in His people? Would *you* willingly be the cause of a 'memorial' going up to heaven against *his* soul, as an unchristian persecutor, because you are ambitious of a 'memorial' going up in favour of yours as a Christian sufferer? Is it not, when properly understood, the height of uncharitableness in any person, then, to court or invite ill-treatment, or by any conduct of his own to aggravate it, or put himself in the way of it, or otherwise to bring it about, of himself, and because he would fain have the blessing of a Christian sufferer? I hardly know whether that ought to be called by so high a name as Christian suffering, which a person might have avoided with a safe conscience if he had chosen. Christian suffering in Holy Scripture is called a gift of God[e]. But that is no gift which is asked for, usurped, taken ungiven: besides that, it is plain that it is terribly vitiated by the want

[e] Phil. i. 29.

of charity which thus wins it at the expense of another's sin.

No: the persecution which carries the blessing must be absolutely and wholly free from any taint of this kind. It must come, when it comes, altogether from other people's evil. No wilful indiscretions, no want of charity in us, must mar it. It must be the doing of evil men against our most careful, most charitable *righteousness*. Then, and then only, is it God's gift to us, and then, and then only, does it carry a blessing.

And observe, that thus it is, I suppose, possible for many a case of ill-usage, apparently of Christian suffering, to take place, and yet no token of salvation to issue from it. Persecution on one side, want of charity or wilfulness on the other; and no blessing won by either. And perhaps it may be said that cases of ill-usage may possibly arise where no 'token of perdition' either really results from them: as where the persecution is done in honest though mistaken zeal to do God service, and is borne with all charity and Christian submission.

Any way, you will easily see that this Beatitude, and the peculiar blessedness of which it speaks, belong to a turbid and agitated, and at the same time transitory and passing state of the world. If all were good, this Beatitude would have no place; none would

"BLESSED ARE THEY WHICH ARE PERSECUTED."

persecute, and none could win the blessing of being persecuted. There can be no such blessing won in heaven, where all is love and goodness. And, no doubt, the blessing will be greater when this blessing can be won no more. In the days when Christian love and brotherhood are rifer, and men cease from troubling the righteous, the righteous will be the first to rejoice that that particular blessedness which was to be won away from their neighbour's loss is to be won no longer.

I have spoken to you, brethren, on this subject this evening, more as a matter of general Christian instruction and interpretation of Holy Scripture, than as thinking that it refers with any special fitness to yourselves. There may have been days in which in schools the maintenance of Christian usages, as of saying prayers, and perhaps the refraining from unchristian things, such as profane swearing or the like, may have subjected boys to cruel usage, amounting to persecution; and there may have been boys who, not giving way to such unholy compliances, like Christian sufferers endured in all charity and submission the consequent ill-usage. The more common case, I fear, was that the wish of righteousness was easily stifled, and direct ill-usage was neither inflicted nor endured. But however it may have been in former

days, surely it is not so now. Do your best to
maintain a Christian righteousness: clinging closely
to your Lord in faith and prayers, and maintaining
a pure and innocent behaviour, do your duty diligently and faithfully, and I feel entirely assured that,
on the whole and in general, you will find not opposition but encouragement, not persecution but help
and aid, from at least the majority and the most influential of your neighbours. But I will not say that
it will be always so, even here. The unquestionable
duty of *one* not unfrequently runs across the convenience of many others, and nothing is more easy than
to raise up a storm of unpopularity against inconvenient conscientiousness on the part of a school-fellow.
There may be times when the faithful search after
Christian righteousness is not unpopular: but he that
searches after Christian righteousness must not reckon
upon this in his own case; he must be prepared to
find himself unpopular; and with the first breath of
unpopularity all that delicacy of Christian wisdom and
charity, all that brave and careful treading of which
I have spoken, which wins the blessing without aggravating the sore, which gains the grace of the sufferer
without enhancing the guilt of the inflictor, becomes
immediately necessary.

But in the after days, the days of actual life, the

right understanding of this Beatitude becomes extremely necessary to every Christian man. In the conflict of opinions, in the abundance of offences, in the fierceness of opposition, and the obstinate holding fast of various notions and usages among us, the wise and charitable search after Christian righteousness becomes a matter of no slight difficulty sometimes,—as, for instance, when we should speak, or when we should forbear; when our words should, in faithfulness, be strong and uncompromising; when our acts should be firm and unyielding, and when words or acts may, without loss of faithfulness or conscience, be softer and more full of consideration. The difficulties in such cases are very great and very various; nor can they be settled in the abstract. Each case must be dealt with as it rises. Only let these points be quite clear in our minds:—

1st. That we must be holding fast by Christ's righteousness, and not confounding with it our own selves, or our wishes, or our likings, or any such thing.

2ndly. That if people oppose us, the opposition, or ill-treatment if it should so be, must be wholly their doing, and in no degree courted, provoked, or desired by us.

3rdly. That we are utterly and completely charitable to them; both in the way of forgiving their wrong, and in endeavouring to win them from it; not aggravating it by needless resistance, not embittering it by hard words, but doing our best to make their sin as small as possible, and to gain them to repentance.

And lastly, that though in this mixed and evil world it is most true that to be persecuted for righteousness' sake is blessed, and they who bear it Christianly win the kingdom by Christian sharing in their Master's sufferings, yet is the kingdom not made dependent on our being ill-treated. Even more blessed were it if, by God's grace upon our wary Christian walking, we might change persecution into mutual Christian help, and instead of winning our salvation out of our brother's perdition, might all with one heart press towards the same mark in Christ, and reach the kingdom together that is set before us all.

SERMON IX.[a]

St. Matthew xxiii.

29. *Woe unto you, Scribes and Pharisees, hypocrites! because ye build the tombs of the prophets, and garnish the sepulchres of the righteous,*

30. *And say, If we had been in the days of our fathers, we would not have been partakers with them in the blood of the prophets.*

31. *Wherefore ye be witnesses unto yourselves, that ye are the children of them which killed the prophets.*

32. *Fill ye up then the measure of your fathers.*

THE particular ground of the woe denounced in these verses against the hypocrisy of the Scribes and Pharisees lies, if I mistake not, in this, that they, looking back upon the bad acts of their fathers, seeing plainly how bad they were, and condemning them freely, did yet proceed not only to copy and imitate them, but to be guilty of far worse in the same kind. The guilt which their fathers incurred in some degree, they incurred in the highest and most terrible

[a] Preached at St. Mary's, Oxford, King Charles the Martyr, Jan. 30, 1857.

degree that was possible. They acknowledged themselves the children of those who killed the prophets. They did not object to bear the light responsibility of confessing their descent from them. They made a sort of merit of declaring, perhaps of exaggerating, their fathers' sins. They published, by their handsome tombs and well-garnished sepulchres, their fathers' guilt, and, by a sort of tacit consequence, their own comparative goodness; and while they were doing all this unreservedly, immodestly, even ostentatiously, they were also following practically the very track and footprints of their fathers' conduct, persecuting and killing Him whom all those prophets had foretold, the very Son Himself, of whom they had only been the warning servants.

Let me remark in passing, that men still do sometimes find a comfort, and perhaps some encouragement, in imperfect living, from such candid condemnation of others with whom they are themselves connected. We are apt to be very candid about the faults of our country, for instance, or our Church, or other people to whom in various ways we belong. Phrases such as these, good in themselves, 'It is a humbling thought,' 'We ought to humble ourselves,' and the like, used in reference to some act or delinquency on the part of those with whom we are connected, have

HISTORY AND HYPOCRISY.

their danger, lest we should not be humbled, but rather encouraged and comforted by the sense of our own candour, and perhaps superiority, in using them.

To return, however, to the case of the Jews. Their conduct in this instance seems to have been partly a blindness, and partly what we more commonly call an hypocrisy; that is, according to the large usage of the word 'hypocrisy' in the New Testament, partly an hypocrisy incurred unawares, and partly a deliberate and intentional hypocrisy. For if we examine the passages of the New Testament in which the word hypocrite and its related words occur, we shall find that the meaning which it bears is one more close to its etymology than that in which we commonly use it. It means an actor—a man of two characters; a man who is one thing in the sight of God, and another thing in the sight of men, or in his own sight; and that it is by no means to be concluded that in every case such a person is distinctly aware of his own duplicity, or puts it on with particular and deliberate design. For example, the hypocrisy of the man who desires to pull the mote out of his brother's eye, is quite compatible with an unconsciousness or inconsideration of the beam that is in his own eye, and hardly amounts to that broad, coarse sin which we usually call by that name. So, again, the hypocrisy of not discerning the signs of the times (mentioned by St. Matthew and St. Luke—it is remarkable that no word of this family occurs in any part of St. John) is surely a *doubleness*, not directly wilful, and deliberately assumed for a base end, but more like what we should call a sinful inconsistency, —an hypocrisy, that is to say, in the larger sense. So, too, in this 23rd chapter of St. Matthew, where the hypocrisy of the Scribes and Pharisees is denounced on several grounds, there are some among them which hardly suggest the idea of the coarse, base, deliberate sin which we usually call by that name,—such, for instance, as the compassing sea and land to make one proselyte; and the addition of "Ye fools and blind" twice made to the allegation, and "Thou blind Pharisee," seem in like manner to shew an extent of meaning in the word hypocrisy far greater than we now commonly assign to it,—a meaning in which it is compatible not with folly only, but with blindness also.

Indeed, when we consider that the word ὑποκριτής, used in a moral sense, and standing alone, is altogether derived from our Lord's use of it in the New Testament, it becomes curious, and it is curiously indicative of the tendency of human nature, to observe how we have by usage narrowed its meaning, and confined its application to those coarse, broad, odious cases, in which the appearance of sanctity is deliberately assumed to cover intentional and determined unholiness. And then we compound for the narrow limits within which we confine the sin, by being doubly severe in our denunciations of it when it occurs in that unmistakeable and detestable form. Alas! when we thus narrow the scope of sins and duties, when hypocrisy is thus shut up into the close limits of such vile sin, when charity is shrunk into giving of money, taking up the cross daily into willingness to submit to external persecution if it comes, and the like, how broad and easy becomes the neutral road of things indifferent, in which we may walk in peace, and do as we like best!

Thus the Scribes and Pharisees in the particular case before us seem to come more properly under the second and larger sense of hypocrisy. Though their acts, of building the tombs of the murdered prophets, and seeking at the same time to kill the Lord, may not have been done without some suspicion on their parts of double-facedness or wilful hypocrisy, yet it is more probable that they are to be regarded as running, more or less blindly, into the very sin of their fathers, more or less unawares traversing the very same line of conduct which in their fathers they did so freely and ostentatiously condemn. For men do not readily foresee the ulterior things which they shall be led to do, by doing this or that. Nor have they their whole ways of acting before them, when some pressure or sudden temptation is upon them, so as to be careful or able to maintain a consistency in all that they do. Judgments are cool, actions are passionate: no interests are involved in the judgments, all interests seem to depend on the actions; the judgments are not hurried nor carry consequences, great and immediate pressure seems to necessitate the action. God forbid that I should seem to underrate the *sin* of the Scribes and Pharisees in this case; but it seems to me the fairest and truest view to think that their hypocrisy in this particular instance of duplicity, or double-facedness, was rather of the blind than of the deliberate species.

And it is this view of their conduct which suggests the thoughts that I desire to propose to you on this day; for the danger of this *hypocrisy unawares*, this actually being of two characters at once without clearly knowing it or intending to be so, is probably a far greater and more common one than we think. Indeed, who can suppose that he is wholly free from it? Who can suppose that he is in constant outward act that which he is in inward conviction, knowledge, and profession? that that which he seems to be to others, and thinks to be himself, is identical with that which he is in the eyes of God? The beginnings of evil lie so close and near round our path, the temptations to it are so various and so disguised, the influences which tell upon our conduct are so many, so unseen, and often so unsuspected, that our actual life continually diverges from our inner selves—that we find ourselves involved we know not how, separating ourselves from ourselves, incurring the danger of that habitual diversity which the Holy Scriptures know under the stern name of hypocrisy.

Where, then, are men, engaged in the midst of the turmoil of active life, surrounded by all these complexities of influence and difficulty, these various forces and pitfalls,—where, I say, are they to find the *standing-place*, the point of view, from which they may regard themselves as they really are, and judge themselves, even as they walk on and take their separate steps of life, with something of a true and undeceived judgment?

Is there any means whereby we may look, as it were, back upon ourselves, even as we live and act? whereby we may gain something like a retrospective view of ourselves, something of that clear and accurate judgment which men so freely pronounce when they look backward upon past events? Can we anyhow gain a position in which we may anticipate the verdict of history, and see ourselves as we shall be seen when the perplexities which beset us in acting are past and gone?

No doubt there is: one means, and one only: and that means is to live in the present with our eye and our heart fixed, steadily and immoveably fixed, upon the future, the sacred future, the judgment-future: to let no present interests, no present difficulties, dim or intercept our constant, invariable sight of that great and solemn account which we must render one day at the judgment-seat of Christ. For we are not mere creatures of time. We are not beings to whom this duration which we call time is essential. We belong to eternity. Though now it is our lot to pass through a succession, and to have all, or well-nigh all our thoughts and words so framed upon the ideas of succession, as if such were all that our minds *could* frame; yet in memory, which grasps all the past together, and keeps it fresh and clear for ever, and in faith, which anticipates, and anticipating possesses, the future, we can in some sort occupy the whole succession at once, and be, even in the midst of time, the immortal creatures that we are. *Memory* and *faith!* They are the links by which we are bound to immortality; they are our witnesses of immortality; they are our remembrancers of righteousness and judgment; they surround us with the thought of God. There are those who so live in the past, that to them the present is a mere trouble, and the future nothing. There are those who so live in the present, that the past is a mere armoury of weapons for their immediate encounters, and the future an idle speculation. Happy those who so live in the sacred future as to feel in the present the road, the trial-ground, the place of preparation—stored indeed with lessons and warnings from the unforgotten past—whereby that sacred future is to be gained!

We are met together this day to recal the remembrance of one of the most stirring and important periods of our history,—a time in which the ancient landmarks of authority and order were violently displaced, and men's passions and principles thrown into the most intense and eager opposition. In those tumultuous years which preceded the breaking out of actual war, still more amidst the alarms and changes of the Civil War itself, who was there who acted throughout as he *would?* Who was not driven to and fro by various and well-nigh irresistible forces which pressed upon him on every side? who took and kept,—who *could possibly* take and keep, as new occasions and complications arose, one uniform self-chosen line of action and conduct? If, then, there were any who, in the midst of that terrible overthrow, did strive to keep his heart humbly and trustfully anchored upon God,—if there were any, whether Cavalier or Roundhead, who, having all his soul fixed on the solemn thought of judgment to come, was content to be, to do, and to suffer whatever present hardness or evil the providence of God might put upon him; who, holding fast and sacredly the faith wherein he was bred, and simply maintaining the station in which God placed him, did keep the thought of the holy judgment-seat of Christ ever clear before his eyes, and by *that* guided his difficult and necessarily devious course,—if there were any who did so in any considerable degree, whether on this side or on that,—and we may well believe that there were many,—then those men, to the extent that they did so, stand forth in the midst of their tumultuous times, not, indeed, the heroes of human history, but the true great men, the immortal men,—in the sight of God the good men, in the sight of men and angels assembled at the Judgment the one-hearted men, the men of far-sighted and holy wisdom, the men who, living, bound up the sacred future into their present, for whom retrospective judgment is but the blessed confirmation and realization of their brave and holy prospective faith.

Human history ought to be, and is designed to be,

a great help to men in thus uniting the retrospective view of actions with their present onward acting. History is memory on a large scale. It recovers so many traces of the past from such various sources; it sees so clearly the real magnitude of difficulties which pressed upon men's conduct, and which they themselves had no means of appreciating justly; it can estimate so much more accurately than the actual agents the real motives and designs of their contemporaries; it gains so much light from the onward and after-course of events; it can detach so clearly the movements of passion from the deliberate acts of judgment; it can, as it were, put its finger so precisely on the point at which a man went wrong, and took the step which involved him, perhaps, in hopeless ruin, that, if it be faithfully written and honestly studied, it does form a sacred mirror, in which, gaining the retrospective view of the earthly life of other men of like passions and weaknesses as ourselves, who were tried, and whose trial is over, in signal positions of eminence and difficulty, we may be helped to use our own present, our own fleeting but most important present, in the sacred light of the judgment-future.

But human history sometimes deserts its vocation, and ministers to the very evil against which it is designed to be a help. It is easy and interesting to select some striking recollections, and by the aid of shaping imagination to supply, *à posteriori*, as we do in dreams, a colouring which is not real, and, taking advantage of casual traits, to give untrue expression to the picture. And men love this sort of history. It is vivid and interesting, and impresses the outline of facts that are past clearly on the memory: but the true, faithful mirroring of the immortal dead, the sacred picturing of the past, out of which we are to learn to live for the future,—all this is neglected and forgotten. Still worse and more dangerous is partisan history, which, using the memorials of the undying past only for the convenience of the conflicts of the present, distorts the record, makes the present *all*, foully wrongs the dead, and perverts in every way the legitimate object and scope of true history.

For history should be the very remembrancer of immortality and judgment. In so far as it *can* clearly see, and *does* truly judge, it does act as a faithful witness of that which is to be hereafter; warning us that all our actions will be so looked back upon in judgment, and that the character and aspect that they will then wear is already on them, capable of being seen and recognised, and exhibited to the approving or condemning judgment of men even now, and in this world. And observe how, in its very imperfection, history seems to give a still more striking and emphatic witness of judgment to come. How little does it really know of past times! How little does it know of the inner life and true inward heart even of those on whom it most dwells, and seems to know best! What countless multitudes of those who have lived, who have had their full trial of life, their anxious struggles and various fortunes, who have not been without great influence, more or less secret, on the fortunes and trials of their neighbours and their country, has it wholly and absolutely forgotten! How different might we suppose the aspect of the civil wars, for instance, and their history to be, in the sight of one of God's good angels camped round about His people then as now, from the not unfaithful record of some impartial and laborious human historian! Surely I am not wrong in saying that the very imperfection of human history makes its warnings, its judgment-warnings, more solemn. It is like a stammering witness, pointing to one which can speak aloud: it is like a half-informed witness, warning us of one which knoweth all. It keeps the sound of the past round our ears now, in order that we may never forget that the past doth not really pass away, but that it all *lives*, and will live; that the agents in these past things live, and their deeds live; and that the day will come when all, from the beginning to the end, will be seen together, even as they are together, and men be judged according to the very truth of their works.

For we believe that though they be passed out of the flesh, and are no more seen upon the earth, the souls of men do wait even now in the unseen place, living, truly and really living, in no uncertain anticipation of the judgment of the great day. Two places only we know of: the 'paradise' of the penitent thief; and the 'own place' of Judas. In one or other of these do the souls of men await the consummation of their happiness or woe. In one or other of these do the souls of those who were busy on the earth in the great events which belong to this day's mournful solemnity, now live and wait. Who shall say in which? who shall venture to pronounce, for any one on either side, in which? Though we know of many a trait of apparently most real faith and devotion, though we confidently believe that many were true servants of God,—and one portraiture be in our hands which seems to depict a faithful follower of his Lord in solitude and suffering,—yet can we not pronounce of any, without presumption, where his soul rests in the secret places of God. Nor need we wish to do so. Canonization, as practised in the

Church of Rome, is not less a mistake than a miserable presumption. It substitutes a baseless assumption for a precious and well-grounded hope; a sight, which is no sight, for a heart-consoling and very sacred *faith*. The due lesson to be learned from the dead is not only one which does *not* depend upon our *certain* knowledge of their ultimate doom, but it rests in great degree upon our very uncertainty. The imitation of their virtues as far as we know them, the confident trust in their sincerity of faith and holiness, mingled with a deep consciousness that we cannot know to the bottom what is in the heart of man,—this, and the faithful belief that the souls of the dead, the just alike and the unjust, are in the hands of God, who alone knoweth all that those souls are, and have done and thought, all their secret sins, struggles, and repentances,—this is the true lesson to be learned from thinking of the state of the dead. They have merely passed from among us. We could not see to the bottom of their heart while they were among us. They have passed into what seems to us the dark chamber of God's house, which to the just is assuredly brighter, calmer, happier far than this which we call life. The darkness and the light to God are both alike; but that which we call darkness is the real light. The love of God on which they rested amid the scenes of trial here, and the hope of heaven which animated them, are brought nearer, and are sweeter and more assured to their souls.

This is truth; real, most certain, most heart-consoling, most heart-awakening truth. It is not more sure that we are met now and here in this house of God to speak and hear of these things, than it is that the spirits of those who are gone hence, the spirits of those who took part in that great struggle of which we speak to-day, are as truly alive as ourselves.

Ere long we shall join them. They are in their respective places, according as in their own time they lived for the future, for God, for eternity, or forgot these things, and lived only for their miserable present. That present has now descended to us; and we, in like complications of life, in the midst of like temptations, with like helps and hopes, are threading our way—God and our own consciences only know how carefully and religiously—towards that meeting; that meeting, which is going on now day by day, and hour by hour, as those who were our contemporaries, with whom we have lived, and worked, it may be, and walked in love and friendship, slip out of this trial-present, and take their place in this one or that one of God's secret waiting-chambers among the living-dead.

And when the appointed time comes, when the appointed number of souls of men have been born, tried, and had their trial finished, then shall we and they, and the countless multitudes of those who have lived before us, and used their own respective present as in the sight of God they have used it,—we and our children, and our children's children, stand before the judgment-seat of the Son of Man to receive our doom for all things done in the body. Then shall the past stand up in its eternal, unforgotten being. Then shall the whole course and track that each one of us has followed, his true inner self in all his history, be seen and shewn, more brightly than in the noon-day sun, by the unerring light of the Divine retrospect: nothing forgotten, nothing unappreciated; the life of those who lived in Christ, who walked in faith, whose hearts were in heaven, and their eyes fixed on the eternal judgment of God, whatever may have been their own distresses, or the mistaken judgments of their contemporaries or successors, seen and shewn to be the life which leads to peace and joy unspeakable; the life of those who lived only for the present, the miserable, fugitive present, and did not repent, seen and shewn to be the downward track that leads to outer exile and unutterable darkness.

The portion of the *hypocrites!* the portion of those who have in life been *actors*, who have had two characters,—who have been one thing as God has seen them, another as they have thought themselves, or have been thought by men,—who have been one thing in their judgments, and another in their deeds. O! my brethren, if hypocrisy be thus in Scriptural language the very formula of sin, the very description which includes the guilt of all those who shall be lost at the last, reflect, I pray you, how much the danger of hypocrisy is increased for those whose lot in life it is to study the records of past times, and to judge of the characters and actions of the dead! How lightly we look back! how freely we judge! how clearly and readily do we condemn! how naturally do we identify ourselves with the good and great of past times, taking part with them and against their adversaries, taking it, as it were, for granted that if we had been in the days of our fathers, we should have been on the side of the good, and not have been partakers of the deeds of the evil. And all this is good and useful in itself, for it is a universal and unsuspicious evidence, borne even by the thoughtless and the sinful, to the goodness and holiness of virtue, and to the deformity of vice, so plainly seen and recognised in retrospect. And most good and most useful to us, if we read all these lessons and form these judgments with continual reference to our own life, and learn from them to see ourselves in the light of that dreadful judgment-future which is surely before us. But what if we read history, and form all these current and easy judgments with no such practical consequence? what if we read of the dead, and judge thus of them, for all sorts of present purposes only, for party warfare, for immediate distinction, for any sort of present triumph or success, and meanwhile live carelessly? if we practically tread over again the very same track along which others whom we judge lost the way to heaven, and thus partake unawares of the very same kinds of guilt and sin? Was not this the very case of the Pharisees, hypocrites? who condemned and imitated their fathers all at once? who put themselves to ostentatious shame by building the tombs of those whom their fathers slew, while they filled up the measure of their fathers' guilt by slaying Him whom all these prophets had foretold? They who sin, who sin in any kind, and do not repent, crucify to themselves, we know, the Son of God afresh, and put Him to an open shame. How, then, do they escape the very hypocrisy of the Pharisees whom they condemn? They condemn them for the very act which practically they repeat. If we read history, and judge the dead, and yet live for the present,—sin, and repent not,—are we not hypocrites? Hypocrites, perhaps, more or less unawares, but still really hypocrites? *Actors?* Actors before God, and in danger of the *actor's* portion?

And is this not, brethren, a real danger? real in itself, and especially real to many in this place, to whom the history of past times and of the dead—the Christian dead—is a matter of ordinary study, pursued constantly for collateral and indirect objects? Are we not liable to forget in the pursuit of these things the sacredness of the subject,—*the living souls of the waiting dead*—and the purpose for which this power of retrospect was given us? They have left behind them their names upon the earth, and many material records of themselves are round about us, and their bodies lie in dust in our graveyards, and we theorize about them, and examine, and judge in all freeness, and much justice, from what we know of them,—but the very living souls themselves are in their own place, waiting for that last dread, unerring retrospect which they and we must meet together.

Brethren, receive the warning. To read of past times, and to judge of the dead, and yet to live in disobedience to the law and will of God, in the language of Holy Scripture is hypocrisy. He that judgeth of the past must live in God's holy truth,—that single, simple, undivided obedience, which is called in Scripture *doing* the truth,—if he desires that his knowledge of the past, and his free and clear retrospective judging of the dead, may not place him among the *actors* in the dread day of his own judgment.

SERMON X.[a]

ACTS v.

12. *And they were all with one accord in Solomon's porch.*
13. *And of the rest durst no man join himself to them: but the people magnified them.*
14. *And believers were the more added to the Lord, multitudes both of men and women.*

THESE few words, placed, not without good cause, in a parenthesis in our version of the Acts of the Apostles, contain a short account of the state of things in the Church at a very important and interesting moment. They come almost immediately after the narrative of the judgment and death of Ananias and Sapphira, and express the feelings of the Church and the surrounding Jews which arose out of that transaction in chief, and other miracles unspecified in detail, which were wrought by the hand of the apostles.

The judgment of Ananias and Sapphira is one of

[a] Preached at St. Mary's, Oxford, on Whit-Sunday, 1849.

the first passages of Holy Scripture, as it appears to me, which strikes upon young hearts: carrying to them a chilling and awful lesson on the subject of the first great sin of early youth,—falsehood. The slight apparent deceit, the stern enquiry of the Apostle, the instant and awful doom executed by divine power as soon as pronounced,—and then the repetition of the same punishment on the wife, who would not be warned by the Apostle's considerate and merciful question,—all this forms so striking a scene, that none who hears it ever forgets it, and it sinks, as I said, with tenfold weight upon the hearts of young people. I would not willingly say a word which should diminish the force of this great lesson, or take off from the sense of awe with which any person, young or old, has learned from it to regard the wrath of God on lies.

But it is obvious that the sin of Ananias and Sapphira was really a much deeper one than mere falsehood.

It arose out of the state of things mentioned at the close of the two former chapters:—"The multitude of them that believed were of one heart and of one soul; neither said any of them that aught of the things which he possessed was his own, but they had all things common." "Neither was there any among them that lacked: for as many as were possessors of land or houses, sold them, and brought the prices of the things that were sold, and laid them down at the apostles' feet; and distribution was made unto every man according as he had need."

This was the general condition of things. It was no community of goods in the ordinary sense of the expression, as a law or institution of the Church. It was no precedent or ruling instance against property of individuals. The very narrative on which we are occupied absolutely disproves any such idea.

There was a great flocking into the Church of thousands, rich and poor, one with another; and there was a large, general, and most free disposition of the rich to give—much or all, as they thought best—of their own, for the benefit of all, to the disposal of the Twelve.

No doubt the rich gave largely; and received thanks and honour for their gifts. Joses, for instance, the rich Levite of the Isle of Cyprus, the brother of the Mary who still retained as her own a house in the city of Jerusalem in which she could receive the apostles, possessing some property in land, sold it, and presenting the price of it to the apostles, received the name of the Son of Consolation from them; by which good name he is known in all the Church to the present day, as the Apostle St. Barnabas.

GOD IN THE CHURCH.

In emulation perhaps of this devotion, and desirous of such honour as had attended it, two Christians, newly baptized, determined that they also would sell some property which they possessed, and give it to the Church.

They did not give the land, if land it were, to the apostles in order that they might sell it, and apply the produce to the common stock; but they sold it themselves, and out of the purchase-money reserved, or withheld a portion.

Short as this narrative is, it is sufficient, as it seems, to explain the state of the case, and to exclude various opinions and hypotheses which have been formed about it.

There is, for instance, no reason at all to suppose that these people were mere hypocrites, who had received baptism in entire unbelief. There was nothing in the condition or fortunes of the Church to tempt hypocrites into it, and the only fact which we know of these persons, namely, their gift, seems to be quite inconsistent with such an idea.

Equally unfounded seems the notion that they did their deed for simple covetousness. Indeed, if it were not that this explanation of their act has been sometimes suggested, it would seem hardly worthy of notice. Who ever heard of people selling their property, in order to be able to claim, as paupers, their share in a common stock? The *small* sum abstracted from the 'price of the land, for small it must needs have been, gives no additional credibility to this theory.

No, the case seems to be a clear one[b], and to need no resort to any explanation of this kind. Ananias and Sapphira do not seem to have acted otherwise than many probably do, and many more are tempted to do in many cases. Recently baptized, and that without express hypocrisy or double dealing, they were induced by the fashion or the credit, mingling up in some undiscoverable proportion with the genuine devotion from which such gifts ought to proceed, to sell some land in order to give it, perhaps in some public and ostentatious way, to the common stock under the control of the apostles.

At some period in the transaction they must, in some manner, have made a promise or profession,—possibly even a vow; though there is nothing in the narrative to enforce that view,—yet certainly a promise

---

[b] "Miser ille homo, cujus animum gloriæ cupido et avaritia distrahebant, unà cum aliis, κοινωνίαν suam demonstraturus, ad legatos Jesu Christi accedebat, atque pretii ex agro vendito capti partem ad pedes eorum collocabat, additâ oratione, se pauperum fratrum amore tactum, patrimonium vendidisse," &c.—*Mosheim, de Rebus, &c.*, p. 115.

or profession, either in word or deed, that they would give the price of that land to the Church [c].

The land was accordingly sold; and obtained, we must suppose, rather a larger price than they had expected, or than others might expect, for otherwise they could not have hoped to be undiscovered in their act.

In this *balance* then, this margin, this difference between the reasonable and the actual sale-money, lay the temptation. Why should they give *this?* They had promised the price of the land; why should they not give the *fair* price, the price which none could except against, the price they had expected, and keep the difference? All kinds of plausible defences might be made for such an appropriation, even if it were known;—but how should it be known? who could discover it?

Accordingly, Ananias tendered a sum of money to the apostles, as the price of the land, which in fact was not the whole of that which he had actually received for it. And I think it important to remark that not one single word is stated to have been spoken by Ananias in the whole proceeding. It is perfectly possible that, after his profession of his intention to

[c] The ancients seem all to have supposed a vow. Vide Mede, pp. 118 and 116, and the Fathers there quoted; Corn. à Lap., 115 (a).

give the price of the land, which itself may not have been made in words, he may not have uttered with his lips a single word in relation to it.

Where, then, lay the sin in all this? Did it lie simply in this, that they tendered a sum of money as the price of the land, and that it was somewhat less than the actual price of the land? Did it lie simply in this, that their words (if words there were) fell somewhat short of exactness of truth, and their actual devotion in a gift somewhat below their expressed intention? Was it precisely the sin of falsehood, as modern writers generally say, or precisely that of sacrilege, as is the general opinion of medieval writers?

Nay, it lay here,—that it was to the Holy Ghost that they used a miserable deceit, not to St. Peter, not to the apostles, to whom, as I said, they perhaps never uttered one word respecting it. To the Holy Ghost they lied in heart. The Holy Spirit of God was within that Church of which they had so lately been made members, and they believed it so little as to dream of doing a lie in His presence. The eternal, omniscient God dwelt, as in a temple, amid those frail, imperfect, yet earnest men who had been made by sacred baptism to drink into one Spirit, and they, though built therein, and by position partaking of that divine gift, did not realize, nor in faith believe, nor in their inner heart of hearts reverence and bow down before that Presence! *That* was their sin. A petty, miserable cheat was the way in which their deep sin shewed itself. It was not so properly the sin, as it shewed, brought out, betrayed the deep lurking inner sin. But the sin itself lay deeper far than that petty, miserable act. The sin was not in the *money*, the sin was not in the *words;* the sin was in the heart; deep and latent, till some such wretched temptation should elicit and exhibit it; in the heart which, though baptized, believed not that *God, omniscient and Almighty, was in His Church.*

They designed to be Christians in a manner, and to a degree,—wishing for the hope, not declining the unpopularity, willing to undergo the danger, able to rise to some height of devotion in giving, which belonged to the true profession of the Church. They had all this: but the heart was cankered, the root was corrupt. They could think of deceiving God; they could dream of lying to the Holy Ghost. The sense of God in the Church,—God to whom all thoughts, as well as words and works, are open, God dwelling as in a tent among His baptized, the holy, searching, fiery Spirit trying them one by one with that sword of flame which destroys what it does not purify,—this they had not. They had some; they had much; but what they wanted was the root, the ground, the strength of all,—the true faith of *God dwelling in the Church.*

But He was in the Church then as ever. And He had His visible and immediate agents of inspiration to prove and avenge His presence. "Ananias, why hath Satan filled thine heart to lie to the Holy Ghost? ... Thou hast not lied unto men, but unto God. ... How is it that ye have agreed together to tempt the Spirit of the Lord?" This was the solemn remonstrance of the inspired Apostle; and the instant death of the miserable culprits vindicated the Almighty presence of the Most High God in the Church.

And this, brethren, seems to be the particular lesson to be derived from this awful tale,—*God is in His Church.* As He dwelleth in His people, one by one,—from the birth of water and the Holy Ghost making them separately to be temples, in such sort, of His presence, that if any man defile that temple, him shall God destroy [d],—so doth He also dwell among them collectively, making all the separate members to be the Body of His Christ. One by one, they are born of water and the Holy Ghost [e]; one by one, as they love God more and keep His words better [f],

[d] 1 Cor. iii. 17.   [e] John iii. 5.   [f] Ibid. xiv. 23.

GOD IN THE CHURCH.

the Father and the Son love them more, come unto them, and abide with them more; one by one, Christ is more and more formed in them [g], according to their diligent use of the means of grace and earnest devotion; one by one, they are stones [h], lively with the Spirit, wrought into the temple of God. But beyond and above this separate estate of each, He is specially with them, and in them as a body. They are "the temple of the living God, as God hath said, I will dwell in them, and walk in them, and I will be their God, and they shall be My people [i]." Assembling even in twos or threes to worship Him, He is in the midst of them [k]. He is with them even unto the end of the world [l]; the Giver of their new life, the Baptizer with the Holy Ghost [m] in the one Sacrament, the actual food of life and spiritual strengthening [n] when (no longer one by one, but in necessary communion) they partake of the other Sacrament; the Imparter of grace in their confirmations [o]; the Giver of the sacred commission [p] and its requisite strength in their ordinations [q]; the Solemnizer of their sacred marriages [r]; the ever-present and only Forgiver in

---

[g] Gal. iv. 19. [h] 1 Pet. ii. 5. [i] 2 Cor. vi. 16.
[k] Matt. xviii. 20. [l] Ibid. xxviii. 20. [m] John i. 33.
[n] Ibid. vi. 51. [o] Acts viii. 17. [p] 2 Tim. i. 6.
[q] 1 Tim. iv. 14. [r] Eph. v. 31; Matt. xix. 6.

their solemn absolutions[s]; present in His poor[t], present in His persecuted[u], present in His ministers[x], present in His gatherings together of prayer[y], present in His soul-searching prophesyings[z].

It hath pleased Him, in His infinite wisdom, to withdraw the ordinary manifestation of outward works of wonder from His Church. No inspired Apostle can now vindicate with immediate and visible judgment the sentence of God's wrath upon those who believe not in this sacred Presence. The absence of such power completes the dispensation of faith in that which is spiritual, begun by the departure of the Lord in the flesh from the Church. All is invisible now; all except the outer means, and the history, the divine testimony of the past. The great Emmanuel is here still; but even the visible shape of the lowly Son of Mary is gone to heaven; and His power, His presence, and His divine indwelling, — which His people see and know, for He dwelleth with them, and in them they live,—the world seeth not, neither knoweth.

And the Body of Christ, that temple of God on earth,—the Church, that ark of souls,—looks in the world as if it were of the world. It, too, has its history, often a melancholy and debasing history. It

---

[s] Matt. xviii. 18; John xx. 23.   [t] Matt. xxv. 40.   [u] Acts ix. 5.
[x] Matt. x. 20, 40.   [y] Ibid. xviii. 20.   [z] 1 Cor. xiv. 24, 25.

is mixed up, of necessity, with the evil lives, the mixed motives, the various fortunes of men. The powers of the world encircle it—often fetter it. The neighbourhood of the world betrays it; the spurious liberality of the world infects it.

Oh! if the sin of Ananias and Sapphira was possible in those early days,—in those days of vivid faith and universal devotion, those days which still retained as a recent memory the recollection of the gracious words and deeds of the ascended Lord, all too many to be recorded in books, which still possessed the visible society of the faithful Twelve, and the others who had companied with Him in all the time that the Lord Jesus went out and in among them,—how liable must we be to commit it in days like these, when no external signs, no plain and undoubted vindications of the divine Presence are given to us, when the Lord who is among us, allows for the trial of our faith the scorn, the coldness, the unbelief of the world to make this very central doctrine of the Church sound like a paradox, an enthusiasm, a priestcraft in the ears of men! when, as in His life, He striveth not, nor crieth, nor is His voice heard in the streets; when He withdraweth, replieth not, resisteth not, until the awful day when He shall send forth judgment unto victory!

Alas! when we think of the religious and irreligious notions of these latter days, of the easy, contemptuous way in which the so-called Christian world thinks and speaks of spiritual claims, of the way in which all sorts of strange societies and alien forms of belief crowd round God's Church, and in the eyes of mankind pass for as good, as sacred, as divine as itself,—how can we help fearing lest the deep inner sin of Ananias and Sapphira be the corroding, deep-seated fatal root of sin in this cold and unbelieving generation?

The world is bent on thinking *Christianity*, as it calls it, to be nothing more than a good form and way of thinking and living.

According to the Bible, *the Church* is the temple in all the world, of God's peculiar and saving presence.

The world is bent on discouraging high pretensions, bigotry, exclusiveness; on comparing different religions, as it speaks, together; on choosing what it will believe, scorning what sounds supernatural; referring all that is taught to itself as to a living centre and test of truth; living peaceably with *Christianity*, as it calls the Church, if *Christianity* will be neighbourly and accommodating with it upon these easy terms.

According to the Bible, *the Church* is the single ar

of safety amid a deluge; the little boat on the lake of Gennesareth, whose strength and safety was in the Lord who lieth, as it were, asleep in it; the body of Christ composed of members instinct with the Holy Spirit; the temple of Christ built of stones alive with the Holy Spirit; the vine of Christ, the sap which circulates in the remotest branches of which is the Holy Spirit.

What is there in common between these two views —the view of the world and the view of the Bible? Nothing. They are the very opposites to one another. And who cannot see that the view of the world is none other than the sin of Ananias and Sapphira? the sin of not believing the divine Presence in the Church of Christ? A sin, venial it may be, and slight in such as have never been admitted into that Church, but heavy indeed in such as have been received therein in Holy Baptism, and made members of the sacred spiritual body?

Such then, brethren, being the sin of these miserable unbelievers, and such its application to all ages of the Church, observe, next, how the sacred narrative proceeds to describe the effects produced on all, both within and without the Church, who witnessed their awful punishment.

"Great fear fell upon all the Church, and upon as

many as heard these things," and then a verse later comes the passage of the text, "and of the rest durst no man join himself to them, but the people magnified them. And believers were the more added to the Lord, multitudes both of men and women."

These, first, were the effects on those who were outside of the Church. Great fear, great shrinking away of all who did not belong, or did not choose to belong, to the sacred body inhabited by the fiery, omniscient Spirit: great thronging of multitudes both of men and women, anxious to be received into that body in the authorized and legitimate way.

Effects apparently inconsistent, and yet how truly consistent! The presence of God within the Church is vindicated by an astonishing miracle, and away retire in awe and confusion all those patronizing, philosophical, political people who desired to be on good terms with it, but were not really of it. The presence of God within the Church is vindicated by an astonishing miracle, and there crowd in multitudes the honest-hearted, simple throngs of men and women who desire to be saved. The vindicated presence of God frightens away the crowd of copyists and pretenders, but it multiplies by thousands the catechumens. Those who would lay low its walls, confound its limits, be mistaken for its members, do not shrink away more suddenly, or in greater numbers, than humble converts flock round the gate of Holy Baptism, and try to press with holy violence into the kingdom by the appointed way.

Surely, brethren, this is a serious and striking reflection; and, believe me, the truth of it is not confined only to the early days of the Church and the circumstances of the awful narrative of which I have been speaking.

Whensoever the great doctrine of the presence of God in His Church is obscured, or doubtfully held, or kept in the back-ground, or anyway disowned or neglected, then the world feels little enmity against the so-called Church. Then it crowds round, admires its morality, ranks it among philosophies and religions, sees it as it were in profile, lives neighbourly with it, tolerates first, and then betrays its remaining sternnesses of faith or practice. Then the sacred entrance of the Church, the single sacred entrance of the Church, I mean Holy Baptism, is lightly esteemed. There seems to be so little difference, there *is* so little difference, between the lives and doctrines of many who have received it, and who have not received it, that it sinks in general regard. When the city has laid low its walls, men *need* not enter by the gate.

Then is the decrepitude and decay of Christian

truth. Then it is held to be superstition to think o
spiritual presence; narrow-mindedness and bigotry t(
suppose that the Church has limits and boundaries
priestcraft to hold that her ministers have spiritua
powers. Nothing can hold its ground when thing
have come to this pass. Not truth—for truth whicl
is neither demonstrative nor superficially experimen
tal, above all things truth of ancient revelation,—no
even supported by the unanimous voice of such as pos
sess invisible, and are the successors of visible divin
powers,—is at once frittered away, and philosophize(
away, or held unimportant in comparison of othe
things: not spiritual graces,—for spiritual graces, un
less the Church and its sacraments be a divine reality
are the mere delusions of a superstitious brain; no
holiness,—for all holiness beyond what the commo:
standard of morality requires or praises, must need:
if the Church with its past and its future be for
gotten, melt away soon, and sink down to the world'
level.

But when this mighty doctrine of the sacred Scrip
tures is preached and believed in its force and in
tegrity, when the Church, the temple of the Mo:
High God, in which, according to His promise, H
walketh and dwelleth, is regarded in that its divin
character, then at once begin those two effects whic

this sacred narrative records. The crowding world is scared, and shrinks away. What has it to do with the awful temple of the great God, and all its spiritual wonders? But as it shrinks away, the humble, earnest, childlike souls throng near. They have found what their hearts did hunger and thirst for—the fountain of God's righteousness. Out of all languages of the nations men take hold of the skirt of him that is a Christian, saying, We will go with you, for we have heard that God is with you. The temple is seen to have walls, and to have a gate. It is indeed exclusive; but it offers a world-wide invitation to all that are weary and heavy-laden to enter.

Such were in the primitive days, such will be in all days, the external effects of the full exhibition of this great doctrine. Nor were the effects external only: "Great fear," also we read, "fell upon all the Church, and upon as many as heard these things."

A sacred, holy, quickening, sanctifying fear! To the minds of those primitive Christians was brought by a visible and awful miracle (to ours may be brought by the recital and meditation of it) the vivid and soul-subduing sense of *who* they were, and *where*. Born of the Holy Ghost by a divine new birth, having drunk into one Spirit, and thenceforth searched, probed, known,—for good or evil, for inexpressible good or inexpressible evil,—tried and tested by that fiery and omniscient Spirit in all their lives. Not shadowed now in type or prophecy, not dimly discovered in the works of outward nature, no longer a subject of speculations or doubtful reasonings, but truly and really, from the great Pentecost to the end of the world, He dwelleth, a Spirit of purifying or consuming fire, in the hearts of all those who by the due administration of water have been grafted into the immortal Body of Christ.

Think, brethren, when anything should bring this great doctrine really home to our hearts, should transform it from a speculative tenet into an awful consciousness, think what a fearful light it would shed upon those hearts, how it would bring out and exhibit all those sins and imperfections of thought, word, and work which, indeed, we all pass over with very little notice. To be suddenly awakened to the practical consciousness of the Almighty Spirit dwelling in us, witnessing our innermost thoughts, permitting and watching all our secret heart-troubles, suggesting we know not how much of our better wishes, grieved continually by our perverse preference of evil and sin to that which is holy and good, at one time cherished, and at another checked within us, at one time inspiring us more and more, and at another withdrawing and leaving us more and more to our own wretched guidance,—to be suddenly, I say, awakened to all this, and to feel that it has been going on in all those years when we were children, when we were boys, when we were young men, ever since,—going on so mercifully, so patiently, with such unspeakable long-suffering, through all those sad and bitter recollections, *those sad and bitter recollections* of time misspent, and heavy, *heavy* sin committed, oh! how would this awakening strike the coldest and most awful fear (yea, despair!) into our souls, if we did not remember that all the riches of this goodness, and forbearance, and long-suffering are designed by the goodness of God *still* to lead us to repentance? if we did not know that this very trial and indwelling is itself the most wonderful and undeniable proof of the yearning and love with which, even now and in spite of all our provocations, our heavenly Father desireth our salvation?

And consider, brethren, how together with this subduing yet ennobling fear would come an altered view, and rule, and standard of all earthly and heavenly things!

How could the fear of man, or the fashions of man, or the common objects and hopes of man, continue to form the rule of him, who had thus seen with his eyes, as it were, and felt with his hands the very presence of God within him? Surely he would feel himself utterly changed and altered; he would *feel* himself the new creature which he *is*.

Think, again, what the effects of such a doctrine forcibly brought home to the mind would be upon the inner life of a man, upon all that inner, secret life of a man which goes on in the retirement of his own breast, nor often passes beyond the activity of thoughts and wishes. Not only would this doctrine, thus brought home to the mind, be effectual to rule and order all that otherwise turbid scene of feelings and images, but we may safely say that nothing else could do so.

And here, brethren, suffer me to make more distinct allusion to some dangers of this place, particularly as they assail those who are young and inexperienced in the habits of it. Consider, then, for a moment the trial of collegiate life to one who comes either from home or school, in respect of the single point of *loneliness*,—the single point of being suddenly thrown upon his own resources for mental occupation and materials of thought in the long solitary times when for the first time he occupies his own apartments, living, indeed, under a rule which bounds any extreme extravagancies of outward behaviour, under governors and tutors who here and there, now and then, furnish advice or caution, reproof or help in study; but in the main, on the whole, in respect of society, habits, tastes, private occupations, books, in respect of his real inner life, his real self, his own master. Here is a great trial. Which of us, who are older, does not remember what a trial it was to himself? Which of us does not remember how ungoverned, how casual, how unsatisfactory in the retrospect were many of the associations and occupations of those days, how heavy the falls, how unrepressed the imaginations of all that time of bewildering self-direction? Then, brethren, I say that in the doctrine of Whit-Sunday, in the doctrine of the presence of the Holy Spirit of God among us and within us, is the real and only secret of hallowing all this irrepressible, onward, perpetual activity of lonely thoughts and feelings. It is the true and only talisman of secret imaginations,—those secret imaginations which make up so large a portion of our real lives, which determine so much of our real character on earth, and prospects after earth.

Think, again, of words, and consider with what power and efficacy the ever-present recollection of God in us, the all-searching fiery Spirit dwelling in our hearts, would tend to check and purify, to control and restrain from unseemly exaggeration, from wild and random paradox, from all the heavy sins of an unruly tongue, the multitude of words which naturally belong to the society and intercourse of this place. Brethren, there is a simplicity of words, a penetrating veracity, if I may so call it, or balance of speech, when the expressions are fairly proportioned to the well-ordered thoughts, which is not more characteristic of mature years and experience, than it is of a spiritual mind, and one, even in youth, habitually conscious of the hallowing presence of the Holy Ghost. It is a great grace of modest and strong-minded youth; and in the contemplation of this sacred doctrine it may be best cultivated.

And once more, brethren, think of the simple, strong consistency of act and life which would follow on the full realization in the heart of this divine Presence! Once let a man be fully possessed of this great truth, and who cannot see how instantly it would give vigour, force, and straightforward direction to all his conduct? How readily would he *see his way* among the perplexing considerations which constantly embarrass the conscientious well-wishing of commoner men! How spontaneously the various interests and apparently conflicting duties by which he was surrounded would fall into their own due subordination, and arrange, as it were, their own perspective, as he moved boldly and simply onward in the strength of the indwelling Spirit! Nothing would be indifferent to him. There would be significancy in every act. Nor would men fail to understand, and, understanding, to acknowledge, his greatness. There is always a force in the simple acting out of a truth realized. In such a truth, so acted out, there is force irresistible.

And in that truth so realized, brethren, is the true leaven of the world. In that truth, more plainly taught, more deeply held, more thoroughly pervading the heart and soul and conscience of Christian men and women, is that which might spread among the millions of the unfaithful and indifferent, and alter the whole look and course of things among us. But is it so now? Does not the Church of God, to all appearance, fail of penetrating and subduing the masses of ignorance and infidelity by which it is surrounded, in this age, in every part of Christendom? Is it not openly scoffed at by the infidel, its doctrines and constitution undermined and betrayed by the self-called philosopher, its divine sanctions and authority put aside by the rulers of the world, so that in almost every Christian land it is at this moment of unexampled political disorder and overthrow, if not actually disowned, yet certainly exercising no apparent influence *at all* either on the councils or the minds of nations; so that in our own land, favoured and blessed as it is with every outward blessing that can make a nation great and happy, and still more blessed with the soberest, truest, most apostolical faith and worship which the world knows, it does not cope with the populations of the great cities, nor address itself with its own salutary and divinely given discipline to the repression of notorious sin within its own pale, nor have a voice to speak either on Christian doctrine or Christian discipline,—is not the Church, I say, thus apparently fighting an unequal battle even here, and much more every where else; gaining apparently thousands while it is losing millions; witnessing the madness of the nations, but not venturing to protest against it, much less able to check or control it?

Brethren, *do we believe* the doctrine which we teach? Do we believe that God the Holy Ghost, who descended as on this day upon the apostles, dwells yet, and will dwell to the end of the world, in the Church, so that we and all who are duly baptized into that Church have drunk into that one sacred Spirit? that however imperfectly we cherish and cultivate His influence, yet that there is *that* in us and among us which, duly cherished and cultivated, is divinely powerful to the utter overthrow of evil, and the con-

GOD IN THE CHURCH. 217

version of the world? Surely if we, and the rest who believe this wonderful and ennobling doctrine, did in any considerable degree take it into our hearts, in its own true height and depth, we should be *felt*, felt sacredly and irresistibly, in the world which is about us.

We desire no position but that in which we stand. We wish for no help but that which is our own. The sword of the Spirit is ours; nor is there principle, nor true union, nor anything but the combination which covers real fear, on the other side. In this we must conquer. Men in their own spheres, secular and spiritual,—each one who hears me this day, and ten thousands of others, yielding themselves up to the absolute guidance of the cherished Spirit who dwelleth in them, and becoming by that Spirit the source of help and comfort, the encouragement of good, and discouragement of evil in all those with whom God gives them influence; each one of you, young men, born of the divine Spirit in your sacred new birth, and now preparing yourselves, or bound to be preparing yourselves, by study and self-discipline, by the conquering strength which is the special virtue of the young men in Christ, for your own various posts and places in the very forefront of God's host: feeble women, now shedding round their own homes the gentle light of high spiritual example, now embuing their own children's minds with the deep early lessons of the indwelling Spirit, now carrying the light and warmth of most heavenly charity, by the same Spirit, into the darkest abodes of squalid poverty and ignorance; even simple children, beginning early, and living on under the continual consciousness of the Spirit of God, and thereby giving in their simplicity the most touching example that older people can receive, and often winning their companions to holiness and the culture of the Spirit,—there is not one who, if he be deeply conscious of his spiritual birth, and bent by God's grace on cherishing the Spirit, doing the Spirit's work, yielding himself up to the Spirit's guidance and direction in all his life, may not be the instrument of untold and unlimited blessing to the Church of God which is the divine temple and body of his Lord.

SERMON XI.[a]

St. John xiii.

18. "*I speak not of you all: I know whom I have chosen: but that the Scripture may be fulfilled, He that eateth bread with Me hath lifted up his heel against Me.*"

THERE is not in the whole compass of the New Testament a more melancholy passage than the one which begins with these words, and extends to the thirtieth verse of the same chapter. It is the passage in which the traitor is, for the first time in the sacred narrative, brought actually out to light. The holy Lord was troubled in His spirit to speak the sad words; but for the sake of the other apostles, and of the Church in all time, He testified beforehand that one of them was about to betray Him. Then when He had, by the dipping of the sop and giving it to Judas Iscariot, shewn plainly both to himself, and probably to the rest of the apostles, which was

[a] Preached at St. Mary's, Oxford, in Lent, 1857.

the traitor, He bade him, in that tone of melancholy but stern calmness which nothing but the immediate possession of Satan could have steeled him to resist, do quickly that which he was doing. The traitor went forth into the darkness, never again to rejoin the company with which he had been so long associated. Immediately upon his departure the troubled spirit of the Lord seems to have been soothed, and He broke forth into that unchecked strain of divine love and comfort which, extending through the next three chapters, rises to that solemn and most affecting prayer of the seventeenth chapter,—that prayer which is the very same that He is still continually offering at His Father's right hand, in the strength of which *we* pray, and hope, and are in peace.

Most melancholy, I say, is this passage of Holy Scripture; for the words sound like the words of bitter, heavy disappointment; they sound like the mourning of the kindest and most loving of pastors, fathers, friends, brothers, over the final loss of one who will not be saved; they seem to tell of hopes crushed, opportunities lost, prospects gradually darkened, and all that gloomy history of wilful ruin which sometimes goes near to break the heart of a man who has utterly failed to rescue a child or friend from total and irremediable loss.

Yet they are not properly words of disappointment. They are deeper and more solemn than mere words of disappointment. Consider who is the speaker; —not one who could be deceived or disappointed, who could entertain warm and eager hopes, and then find them all overthrown by a result unlooked for. No; they are the words of deep, divine, omniscient, patient, long-forbearing love. They speak of a loss, now, indeed, total and hopeless, but not always so; long foreknown and foreseen, yet not in itself inevitable: a loss which had been gradually deepening into certainty, watched from its beginning to its end,—allowed, never forcibly cut short, and now, with accelerated speed, as the ultimate fall drew nearer, rushing, as it were, to its end.

For consider, even as far as we can trace it, the main points of the course of the fallen apostle in the previous history.

Chosen one of the twelve, out of the number of the disciples, "to be with" the Lord, to company with Him during all the time that He went in and out among the disciples on the earth, we find no indication that he was, at that time, entirely devoid of all belief. No ordinary earthly temptation, no intelligible indirect motive can be assigned why one who was totally and absolutely unbelieving should have joined the company of One who, more homeless than the foxes or the birds of the air, had not where to lay His head.

Sent, again, one of two, when the Twelve were sent out two and two to preach,—taking nothing for his journey but a staff only,—no scrip, no bread, no money in his purse [b],—we can hardly suppose that he was acting a deep part of utter insincerity and fraud, and that there was not mingled with the worldliness and weakness of his character some sort of belief in that which, with such self-denial and suffering, he preached.

Commissioned with powers not less extensive and wonderful than his brethren, he, no doubt, as well as they, had power against unclean spirits, to cast them out, and to heal all manner of sickness and all manner of disease [c]; and no doubt, again, he exercised this power, and found, as the Seventy found, that the devils were subject unto him through the name of Christ [d].

Returning, with the other apostles, to report all things, both what they had done and what they had taught, it does not appear that the Lord made any difference between his labours and those of his brethren, when, on their return, He took them, and

[b] St. Mark vi. 8.   [c] St. Matt. x. 1.   [d] St. Luke x. 17.

went aside with them privately into a desert place to rest awhile.

What, then, are we to think of him thus far? Must we suppose him a mere hypocrite? a simple infidel, totally devoid of any sort of belief,—yes, and even while he was exercising superhuman powers in his Lord's name, utterly unbelieving of that Lord's divine power and doctrine? Impossible! Surely, brethren, he was more like one of ourselves,—a man of indeterminate mind, capable of going right, very liable to go wrong; trembling, as it were, and hesitating on the edge of faith, yet not yielding himself, in heart and soul, to his Master's will; believing, (not really, nor savingly, but with a kind of belief,) working, obeying, but throughout with *reserves ;* never going into broad, intentional, professed unbelief or disobedience,—perhaps thinking of himself not otherwise than of a reasonably faithful, hard - working, obedient apostle.

But ere long a case arose which probed him deep, —the great discourse which the Lord held in the sixth of St. John, respecting the eating of His Flesh and drinking of His Blood. We find that the murmurs of the Jews at His saying that He was the Bread which came down from heaven received some countenance, and, as it were, echo, in the company of the apostles themselves; so that the Lord broke off from the flow of His discourse to say, "No man can come to Me, except the Father which hath sent Me draw him; and I will raise him up at the last day. It is written in the prophets, And they shall be all taught of God. Every man, therefore, that hath heard, and hath learned of the Father, cometh unto Me." And what was it, or who was it, that thus checked the holy Lord in the midst of one of His greatest and deepest discourses? It was *Judas*. "There are some of *you* that believe not. For Jesus knew from the beginning who they were that believed not, and *who should betray Him*. And He said, Therefore said I unto you, that no man can come unto Me, except it were given unto him of My Father." It was *Judas Iscariot*, and, as we should gather from this last passage, some other disciples, not apostles along with him, whom the great Eucharistic discourse, the great doctrine of the Holy Communion, discovered in their unbelief, as with a touchstone, and whose unbelief interrupted for a few moments the onward teaching of the Lord.

Yet he did not go away, or leave the Lord's company. Some more simple-hearted, though unbelieving men, were shocked, found the discourse hard, and walked no more with Christ. Not so Judas. He was content to let Peter speak, apparently in his name as well as that of the other ten, and say, " Lord, to whom shall we go? Thou hast the words of eternal life." He did not care to bring the matter to an issue. He was content, as a worldly man, to hold his tongue;—inwardly, he had no real belief of all these high mysteries; inwardly, he thought them extravagant, and did not really receive them; yet he held on, having, no doubt, some respect—how could he fail to have it?—for the Lord and His oftenwitnessed power, yet, really and in heart estranged by unbelief from His doctrine, and contemning the credulity and simplicity of the other apostles.

See him next as the steward, so to speak,—the man of business,—if I may be allowed the expression, the banker of the sacred company. He had the bag. It was his part to buy what the Lord and His brethren needed. He was employed to be the almoner in gifts to the poor. He took upon himself to find fault with what seemed to his poor ideas of devotion the needless waste of the costly ointment wherewith Mary anointed the Lord to His burying.

But the steward was dishonest. Professing to be anxious to save for the sake of the poor, he was really a thief, and purloined continually from the little store that was entrusted to his care.

And such was Judas when the awful season of the Passion drew near: an apostle, a missionary, a worker of miracles, an inward unbeliever in the deep spiritual doctrines of his Lord, yet not devoid, we may suppose, of some kind of regard and attachment, and belief too, in his Lord's power; a man of worldly shrewdness and experience, but secretly, and unknown to his brethren, covetous and dishonest; a mixed, dangerous, uncertain character, as we should judge him; devoid of the deep principle of faith; untrue, yet fair seeming, and with some kind of attachment; such an one as might —we might think—by possibility even yet turn and repent, and believe and be saved.

But mark, brethren, how it was that the last spark of hope was extinguished, *what* it was that hurried him headlong into the abyss of sin and ruin.

It was the touch of *reproof* that slew him, that hastened the death of which the faithless man was dying.

When Mary poured the box of precious ointment on the head of the Lord as He sat at meat, Judas—and perhaps he led some other of the apostles to concur unawares in his objection—feigned indignation, and complained of the waste of that which might have been given to the poor[e]. When the Lord calmly re-

[e] Compare St. Matt. xxvi. 8, and St. John xii. 4.

buked the objectors, "Let her alone; why trouble ye the woman?" and spoke in terms of high praise of her devotion, the other apostles who may at first have concurred in finding fault with Mary's act, received the rebuke in meekness, and said no more. But Christian reproof stings the faithless to the quick. Judas could not bear it. "Then entered Satan into Judas, surnamed Iscariot, being of the number of the twelve[f]." Instantly, as we read in St. Matthew and St. Mark, Judas sought the chief priests. He knew well what they wanted, the opportunity of seizing the Lord by night. Covetousness and the burning sense of indignation conspired together within him. "What will ye give me, and I will deliver Him unto you? And they covenanted to give him thirty pieces of silver. And from that time he sought opportunity to betray Him."

What *reproof* thus began, *exposure* completed. When at the last supper the Lord mournfully announced to the Twelve that one of them should betray Him, and in answer to the enquiry of the beloved Apostle and St. Peter, pointed out the traitor by giving him the sop, then again, and finally, Satan entered into him. He became demoniac. The spirit of revenge, added to the covetousness and indignation felt before, seized

[f] St. Luke xxii. 3.

him altogether. A strange sense of injury done to him—for he may, perhaps, have distinguished between a sin meditated and a sin executed—seems to have added keenness to the pang, and with the calm, mournful words, "That which thou doest do quickly," he passed from the scene of love, the reach of grace, and the hope of heaven, to purchase utter, hopeless death of body and soul for thirty miserable pieces of silver.

Yet even to the last, in spite of the bribe given and received, in spite of the hypocritical kiss whereby in the garden he distinguished the Lord from the apostles for the very purpose of betraying Him, the miserable man seems to have cheated himself into thinking that he meant no harm. He *only* pointed Him out in the evening, who all day long was teaching in the Temple, yet they laid no hands upon Him. What could be, he might ask himself, the serious harm of this, considering how innocent He was, so as to escape condemnation, and how powerful, so as to be able to avert it? This, it seems to me, we must naturally conclude from the fact recorded by St. Matthew [g], that within a few hours, in the course of that very night finding that neither the Lord's innocence nor His

[g] St. Matt. xxvii. 3.

power had saved Him from being condemned by the Sanhedrim to death,—even before the trial which took place in the Prætorium,—he was seized with remorse for his deed, and in some sense *repented :* repented, that is, with that ungodly sorrow of the world that worketh death[h]; for he threw the wretched pieces of money which he had received into the Temple, when the chief priests refused to take them back, and went and hanged himself; so that he actually died, in all probability, before his Lord whom he had betrayed: his soul had probably reached its own melancholy place before the soul of the Lord and the penitent thief were together on that awful day in paradise.

I know not how it is possible to exaggerate the interest, the deep and terrible interest, of this narrative. Judas is, perhaps, the only one of the sons of men of whom we seem to know for certain that his soul is lost; and yet what a life, what privilege, what station, what opportunities were his! Terrible as was his guilt,—a guilt which Holy Scripture seems to set in the very forefront of sin,—yet how different was it from much that there seems to be in the world,—from the savage, cold-hearted, unremorseful guilt which we

[h] 2 Cor. vii. 10.

often hear of in lower ranks of life; from the cold, profligate, scheming, life-long villainy which we sometimes are conscious of in the higher!

But oh! brethren, how awful is the warning which it gives to us,—to us who, by education, by station, and our various duties, approach more nearly to the fallen apostle's knowledge, opportunities, and dangers! If we might be at a loss to understand the design of God in allowing him, unchecked, to pass through his deepening course of sin to its consummation, as far as regards himself, is not the merciful purpose most clear, most patent, as regards us?

He knew whom He had chosen! He knew each one of the Twelve in all his weakness and waverings of mind. He knew the Stone, the Sons of Thunder, the Twin, the Publican, the Zealot, and the rest, not more thoroughly, nor less thoroughly, than He knew the traitor. His almighty Spirit knew what was in man, and watched, and saw, and foreknew, and helped, and traced to the end the various course of all whom He had chosen.

And not less deeply, brethren, not less thoroughly or searchingly, doth He know us,—us, whom He hath baptized, whom He hath engrafted as branches of the Living Vine, whom He hath made to drink into the one Spirit, whom He hath set in our own places in

His Church, whom it is His holy will to save eternally, if we will be saved.

But oh! let us take deep into our hearts the warning history of the lost apostle.

How closely it touches us!

1. He was an apostle, in close and constant nearness to the Lord. But who is brought nearer to Christ than we are? Have we not known Him, knelt to Him, prayed to Him, heard of Him from our infancy? Are not the very earliest recollections of our childhood mixed up with the sweet remembrances of hymn, and catechism, and church, and prayers, — the love of earthly parents blended, deliberately and continually blended, with the thoughts of Christ and heaven? Have we not been baptized into Him? have we not in Confirmation made solemn and personal acknowledgment of Him, and in the Holy Communion been continually blest with the nearest and most mysterious union with Him?

We are closer, nearer, more wonderfully near to Him now that He is in heaven, than ever was Judas when He was on earth.

But, brethren, nearness of body and closeness of station are, alas! not necessarily nearness of soul; and it is possible that we may partake of every ordinance of religion, yes, and flock in crowds to hear the words of Christian truth and warning, and yet in our inner selves be far, unspeakably far, and going farther and farther from Christ, because we will not give up our hearts to Him, that we may have life!

We read the Word of God, we study it, we hear it, we know more of it perhaps than our neighbours do, —but to accept it, to believe it, to yield ourselves up to it, to live according to it, to feed upon it, to know, and act as knowing, that "man doth not live by bread alone, but by every word that proceedeth out of the mouth of God;" this, and only this, will make all that nearness and all that knowledge the blessing that it should be, that it may be, that it *must* be, unless it is to be turned into a curse instead of a blessing, and bring us into a miserable likeness with the lost apostle.

2. But again: from the Lord's side Judas was sent forth, *one of two*, to preach, to work miracles, to announce the kingdom; and no doubt his own inner heart of unbelief was undiscovered by the poor people whom he addressed. He, no doubt, preached well, for he was a shrewd man; he did works of power in his Master's name, and he returned, unknown and undetected, except by the Lord, in whose name and power the works had been done. And we, brethren, — many of us as clergymen now, many more as de-

signing and hoping to become so hereafter, — each, may be, to be *one of two,* rector or curate, perhaps, among simple people, where we may be thought to " preach well," or otherwise to do " considerable things" in our parish or sphere, — should we not search our hearts narrowly, lest there should be in us that "evil heart of unbelief" which, even in the midst of holiest offices and fair-seeming service, would surely make us and our work utterly hollow and worthless in the sight of God? Indeed, it may be so. It is not the holiness of the service which can sanctify the heart of man. Unless the heart be kept in faith and unreserved devotion to God, unless the work be done in God, and for Him, the grace of God continually won in prayer to keep our will with His will, and to bless our efforts, the very holiness of the service might possibly operate to increase the danger, and throw into wider divergence the outward seeming faith from the real faithlessness within.

3. The first thing that, as far as we are told in Holy Scripture, probed to the quick the faithlessness of Judas, was the doctrine of the Holy Communion of the Body and Blood of Christ, as taught by our Lord in the sixth of St. John. Brethren, we live in anxious days, and the doctrine of the Holy Communion, in its lofty and blessed mystery, is still to many

the very touchstone of faith. Many find "the saying" of that wonderful doctrine "hard," and will not walk with Christ in His Church because of it. With such as thus depart from us we have at present no concern: they have their condemnation elsewhere. The case of *Judas* warns those who still outwardly walk with Christ, who do *not* leave His company, who partake of the blessed feast themselves, who even consecrate it, who are actually the instruments of conveying the true spiritual food of souls to many a simple and faithful communicant, and yet in their hearts rebel against the vital and mysterious truth, and believe it not,—to whom the glorious doctrine of the spiritual eating of the Body and Blood of Christ, of the indwelling of Christ, and of the union with Him, of the cleansing of the body and the washing of the soul, of the assurance of God's favour and goodness, of our being very members incorporate in the mystical Body of Christ, and heirs through hope of the kingdom, and of the preservation of our bodies and souls to everlasting life, in the sacred communion of the Lord's Supper, sounds like empty words of vain superstition, which in their inward heart of hearts they do not entertain or believe. Are there such among us? God knoweth. Brethren, be warned and watchful. The poison of such unbelief is secret and slow; it takes many disguises; it looks at one time like philosophy, at another like liberality, at another like pure spiritual religion,—but it is indeed the working of the evil heart of unbelief, and it secretly divides the inward soul from God. In the case of Judas, the particular doctrine which acted as the touchstone of his faithlessness was the doctrine of the Holy Communion of the Body and Blood of Christ. In other cases it may be the doctrine of holy Baptism, or the docrine of the Atonement of Christ for sin, or the doctrine of the Holy Trinity, or the doctrine of the Church, the Body of Christ; but whichever it be of those things which the Holy Spirit hath revealed for the salvation of men, such resistance to the truth of God operates to carry away the soul, and divide it off from Christ, and even under external circumstances of apparent nearness, to remove it far away from His grace, and the vital fellowship of the Holy Spirit.

4. But there was a moral canker in the heart of Judas, too,—a corroding, deep-seated moral evil, which worked with his want of faith, encouraged and deepened it, which was partly cause and partly consequence of it; he was *coretous and dishonest;* and his covetousness and dishonesty, acting in constant tamperings with the small store committed to his keeping, made

it impossible for him to yield up his whole soul to faith and devotion.

Brethren, I have spoken of the danger which we, and such as we, may possibly incur, of latent want of faith, deep-seated unbelief, even though we be brought so near to Christ as we are in education, knowledge, and duties. Believe me, that in such secret *moral canker* as we read of in Judas Iscariot, lies the strength, the support, the incurable hopelessness of this unbelief. If there be in the heart of those who come *ever so near* to Christ and His service, hoarded and housed, the secret plague of moral sin—be it dishonest love of money, as it was with Judas—be it restless ambition—be it the busy devil of lust, soliciting the secret imagination, and not driven out—be it sullenness and swelling discontent—be it fierce and angry temper—be it what it may, that inwardly tyrannizes over the heart of him who outwardly approaches near to his Lord, and is to all appearance busy and faithful in His service—if there be such, and it be not conquered and driven out in the strength of prayer, and inward combating with evil by the grace of the Holy Spirit, *faith cannot be;* faith, even if it have begun to spring, even if to some extent it have been real, (as in some sort we may suppose it once to have germinated even in the traitor's mind,) *faith must die.* Invisibly, secretly, the heart of faith is chilled, and it dies. Others do not suspect it—the unhappy unbeliever does not half realize it. He keeps his learning, his logic, his eloquence, his powers of argument, his station, his duties; he is outwardly just what he was —he is, perhaps, a strong, perhaps a successful, vindicator of the truth—able to say, Lord, Lord, have I not preached in Thy name, and in Thy name done many wonderful works? but the secret soul is cold, the well of living water is dried up in his heart,— *faith is dead within him.*

Brethren, I speak as unto wise men; judge ye what I say. I will not dilate upon it. I speak to consciences—to those who would fain have peace in believing—to those who feel in their heart of hearts that they do desire to live the life of the faithful, and die the death of the righteous. If you do not do battle with your own secret plague of heart, your love of money, or power, or lust, or sloth, or falsehood, or temper, or whatever other inward evil you are conscious of—do battle with it, and in the strength of grace *conquer* it, it will eat out the very heart of faith within you, and leave nothing there but a hollowness, an ache, a void, which is despair.

5. In the lost apostle all this fatal decay was unseen, save by the eyes of God, till, as I before ob-

served, the touch of *reproof* first, and then *exposure*, brought on the crisis. Then unbelief broke out into open rebellion; and the dishonest steward tried to comfort himself in detection by revenge.

And O! brethren, think how deadly to the faithless is the word of Christian reproof! Think what a trial, what a test it is of the meekness, the faithfulness, the soundness of our heart, when anything brings upon us the voice of rebuke—faithful rebuke, and others hear it! Could not any person whose position or duty calls upon him sometimes to reprove —could not the parish clergyman—could not the college tutor, tell you how poisonous and deadly to the faithless, public words of reproof are? Even to such as are faithful at heart, though erring, they are a fierce trial; but the grace of God working upon such as are really right within, may so support and uphold the better feelings as to overcome the dangerous rising of the rebellious spirit; and so reproof may only kill the sin, and help to save, instead of killing, the sinner. But if the inward heart be faithless, if a moral canker, such as I have spoken of, have been allowed to eat out the very core of divine faith within us, then the touch of Christian reproof operates as the touch of death. It is like the touch of the angel's spear, at which the evil spirit, before latent, starts forth in his full and hideous dimensions. It transforms the fair-seeming but hollow-hearted servant into the open and energetic rebel. O! let us watch our hearts, brethren, when rebuke—and I would use the word 'rebuke' largely, so as to include all serious and thoughtful reproof, from whencesoever it arises—when rebuke comes upon us, for indeed it is a fiery trial. Nothing searches more closely, nothing shews more clearly what manner of spirit we are of,—whether we can yield, and amend, and pray, and bear, or whether we rise up in furious wrath against the voice of reproof, and exhibit in our rage the absence of true, meek, and patient faith within us.

Such, then, brethren, seem to be the main points of Judas's character, as shewn in Holy Scripture. I have regarded him as the apostle, the missionary, the faithless man, the covetous, dishonest man, the traitor. Much, much more might I have said on each point, to shew how near to ourselves dangers are, very like to those which ruined him, and how careful and full of prayer must be our watchfulness if we would avoid them.

For indeed, brethren, our position as persons of intellectual cultivation, brought very near to God by our station in His Church, and our partaking in the studies and devotions of this Christian place of study, is one which is not more eminent in privilege than in danger. And there is *that* in the free habits of *thought* in so large a community, and still more there is that in the free habits of *life* too current here among many young men, — habits, I mean, of expense, and idleness, not to speak of more distinct profligacy and sin,—which throws the *danger* of such cultivation and nearness to God into most striking and fearful light. We may become lamps of God in the world, lighted from the Source of light, and shining,—honoured, and effective instruments in the hands of God, to spread and make winning His worship and obedience among tens of thousands of our countrymen; but we may be so living, yes, even now and here, as to kill the spark of faith within our hearts, and become, even though men may not see it or suspect it, traitors in heart, false and lost apostles, aliens really, however externally looking like honoured citizens of the commonwealth of God. And these are the seasons, brethren, to search our hearts as in the sight of God, and assure ourselves that we are not wandering away from grace and faith. These are the solemn penitential times to examine our own ways, and confess our sins, and turn to God in true confession, and earnest unreserved devotion. What is the good of all our learning, or anything else that we possess, if faith dies within us, and we lose our souls? or what shall a man give, or take, or win, in exchange for his soul? I thank God that He has put it into the heart of those who have authority among us, to call us together in this holy season, and that He gathers so many thus to hear the solemn words which belong to this time; but, brethren, beyond and above such things as this, far beyond and above these outward ordinances of religion, the real battle of faith is to be waged in our separate hearts. The real conquering of doubts, the real mastery of sin, the real subjecting of our spirits to the Holy Spirit of God, and of our wills to His will, is the work of our secret souls before God. It is to be done in our chapels, in our chambers, on our knees, in our secret turnings of soul to God by night and day, alone and in company, in work and refreshment.

All the apostles were weak. We may have shared the impetuosity of Peter, the doubtfulness of Thomas, the angry temper of the sons of Zebedee, the love of money of Matthew, the weakness or evil which may have tempted other apostles. But they turned, they repented, they yielded themselves up in faith, they devoted themselves in body and soul to Christ, their Redeemer and their God.

Christ knew those whom He chose. He knew

them in all their various wilfulness and wanderings, and led them safely—for they were willing to come to Him, that they might have life—through repentance to salvation.

And he knows *us* too: each single one here present, in his own place, and station, and duties, He knows as deeply and as thoroughly as He knew them. He knows what He has given us. He knows our opportunities, and the use we have made of them. He knows how far we have resisted His gracious design to sanctify and save us. He has noted down our sins. There is not a thought in our hearts, nor a word on our lips, nor has there been a secret act in all our lives, but He knoweth it altogether.

And as truly as He knows, so truly does He love us still. For does He not spare us? does He not call us to repentance? Is it not His love which opens our hearts to think sorrowfully of our sins? Does He not even now pray for us? *for us,* who have offended against Him so often and so deeply,—that *yet, even yet,* we may have the heart to turn away from sin, and be won, by His unwearied and most tender yearning love, to faith and repentance!

Can it ever be that He should say of us, 'I pray not for you all? There are some of you who have persisted in grieving My Holy Spirit, whereby ye were sealed to the day of Redemption,— who have shut your ears to warnings, who have chosen death. I pray not for you all. I pray for those who, though they have often been weak and wilful, yet do receive My words, do desire to repent, do really wish to work out their own salvation by My freely offered grace in holy fear and trembling.'

Brethren, may God grant that we may be counted among such as these,— followers of the repentant, faithful, saintly eleven; and that, turning away from our sins, and rendering ourselves up to Christ in simple, devoted, honest faith, we may by that grace escape from the faithless spirit, the moral canker, the fierce rebellion, the treason, and the despair of the lost apostle!

SERMON XII.[a]

REVELATION ii.

14. *But I have a few things against thee, because thou hast there them that hold the doctrine of Balaam, who taught Balak to cast a stumbling-block before the children of Israel, to eat things sacrificed unto idols, and to commit fornication.*

THE character of Balaam, the son of Beor, is commended, brethren, to our consideration this evening.

We have no occasion to enter into any examination now of the many questions which arise in considering the various circumstances of his story: all enquiries respecting his country, the amount and origin of his knowledge, his worship of the true God, and the like, are beside our present purpose.

We have to regard him as *a man;* a man whose character is exhibited in certain acts divinely recorded in the earlier books of Holy Scripture, and *stamped,*

[a] Preached at St. Mary's, Oxford, in Lent, 1858.

indelibly and infallibly, by the terms in which the later inspired writers refer to it; and to draw from that character, so shewn and so stamped, such lessons as it may seem to yield for the instruction of Christian people.

The forty years' wandering of the children of Israel in the wilderness was now done. From Mount Hor, where Aaron died, on the edge of the land of Edom, they had traversed the eastern coasts of the Dead Sea, and being forbidden of God to injure the Edomites, the Moabites, or the Ammonites, the children of Esau and Lot, and having utterly destroyed the two kings of the Amorites, Sehon and Og, were now peaceably encamped on the plain of the Acacia trees, the 'meadows' which lay between the mountains of Moab and the spot where Jordan mingles his waters with the Dead Sea.

The king of Moab, Balak, alarmed at the destruction which had fallen upon his powerful northern neighbours, and, no doubt, unaware of the command which had left him unharmed, did not venture upon open violence against the "desert-wearied" tribes, all young men, who lay, "abiding in their tents," each by their own separate standard, with "the ensign of their father's house," in sight of their own long-promised, long looked-for Canaan.

He bethought him of a more skilful mode of attack. He sent the elders of Moab and the elders of Midian, laden with presents, the reward of divination, to the 'diviner,' or 'soothsayer,'—to Balaam, who lived far away eastward on the banks of Euphrates, saying,— "Behold, there is a people come out of Egypt: behold, they cover the face of the earth, and they abide over against me. Come now, therefore, I pray thee, curse me this people, for they are too mighty for me. Peradventure I shall prevail that we may smite them, and that I may drive them out of the land; for I wot that he whom thou blessest is blessed; and he whom thou cursest is cursed."

Balaam, the diviner, waits upon God for direction. The word of God comes to him by night, "Thou shalt not go with them: thou shalt not curse the people: for they are blessed." Balaam obeys the word of God. He refuses to go, and the messengers return.

Balak, however, is importunate. He sends again, princes, more and more honourable than they, with larger and richer offers of wealth and honour.

Why did Balaam hesitate? Why did he bid the princes tarry yet that night? Why did he tempt God by desiring to know "what the Lord would say unto him more?"

He asked *in madness:* and he received the permis-

THE CONVICTIONS OF BALAAM.

sion he coveted from God *in anger*. It was madness in the servant of God to wish to go against God's will, —to have hopes, interests, likings other than those of being God's faithful, simple, obedient servant. It was in anger that God bade him have his wish, and go, to be the honoured, trusted prophet at the king's court.

The incident of the miraculous voice of the ass brought him to a sense of his sin; and he said unto the opposing angel, "I have sinned: for I knew not that thou stoodest in the way before me: now therefore if it be evil in thine eyes, I will get me back again."

However, he is bidden to proceed on his mission. Then follow those remarkable scenes of the three solemn sacrifices offered in the midst of the princes of Moab on three separate heights of the Moabitish mountains,—the princes anxiously expecting a divination against Israel, the seer, in heart desiring it too, and half-expecting to obtain it, yet resolved to utter nothing but the word which God should put into his mouth: until, at last, finding that God was pleased to bless Israel, and that all his efforts to obtain a contrary voice were ineffectual, he left off to seek for enchantments, as at other times, and setting his face towards the wilderness or wild level on which the Israelites were encamped, once and again he took up his parable, and spoke aloud the Lord's blessing, and His words of holy promise to the chosen people.

Thus far, brethren, we read in Balaam's history the struggle between the love of the world and the overwhelming consciousness of truth in the same mind. His first answer to the Moabitish princes may have been given in perfect simplicity and faithfulness. But after their return to him with richer offers and greater promises, his whole course is that of a man divided against himself. His love, his wish, his effort is to curse the people, and by cursing to win wealth and honour. But the controlling consciousness of God's immediate presence and will is irresistible. He blesses them in spite of himself; not, indeed, involuntarily, nor without a sense of religious satisfaction in doing it; not without a sort of sympathy with God's servants, and a kind of æsthetical wish to be like them, ("Let me die the death of the righteous, and let my last end be like his!") but without love, without personal will, without conversion of heart, under moral compulsion.

It is an instructive lesson! How often do we feel ourselves placed, more or less, in the same position; our liking, our ambition, our heart, all set one way,— our reason, our consciousness of truth, our intellectual faith distinctly calling us the other!

THE CONVICTIONS OF BALAAM.

To Balaam, indeed, the case was thus far different from ours, that he *could not*, in so broad and obvious an instance as the one of which we have been speaking, go directly against God. The voice of God in his ears compelled him; miracles dragged him; his inspiration overbore him. He was, as it were, forced into speaking the truth: just as one might imagine an unholy man *forced* into doing and saying holy things by the continual compulsion of miracles, even though his heart was unconverted, and longing to rebel all the time. To us, alas! the danger is, in such sort, greater, that our consciousness of truth, our intellectual faith, are in themselves less imperative, and are sure to sink and die away if they be smothered by want of love, if they be not honestly carried out into act, if we love and will continue to love the very things which they distinctly and pointedly forbid. Yet we also know only too well what it is to speak out faithfully, to stick to the truth in outward words, to be, it may be, its staunch defenders and admirers, while our hearts neither love it nor obey it; holding on, as it were, by our knowledge, or our logic, or our consistency, while our heart and love would fain rebel against it.

A dangerous antagonism! yet one out of which there is a safe and holy escape: if those who are at all conscious of it in themselves, and sad in the consciousness, will throw themselves, heart and soul, into confession, and win by prayer that great and precious gift, never denied to those who pray in earnest, the heart to *love*,—the simple, godly heart to *do* the thing that they know to be right, and nought beside.

Let us see how it fared with Balaam.

He had gone home "to his place" by the Euphrates in disgrace. The Lord had kept him back from honour. How he returned again to the court of Moab, whether summoned again by Balak, or of his own irrepressible ambition, we are not told. But he came. He found the children of Israel still holding their encampment on the acacia-plain of the Jordan. Wearied as they were with the desert life,—where by far the greater part of their whole number had been born, entirely unused to comfort or softness,—not an old man among them,—surrounded by heathen rites that were full of luxury and temptation, might they not be easily led to bring upon themselves the curse, which in his unwilling lips had been turned into a blessing? Were it not a fine stroke of policy to make them curse, so to speak, themselves? No word, probably, would need to be spoken, no formal scheme proposed. A look, a gesture might suffice. Balak would be able to understand a slight hint. There were the women of

Midian, they took part in the dances and plays of the sacrifices. Would it be Balaam's fault,—could he be justly blamed,—would any one think of blaming him, if those hardy desert warriors, so young, so impetuous, so dangerous in their fidelity to the true God, were led by skilful and unseen management to partake in the feasts of the idol-sacrifices, and by degrees, losing their allegiance to the true Jehovah, and breaking the first of His laws, to break the seventh also, and unite themselves to the wanton women who had used every artifice to lure them to rebellion and ruin? The scheme answered only too well. The people began to commit whoredom with the daughters of Moab. They ate the offerings of the dead; they bowed down before the idol-gods. Israel joined himself unto Baal-peor. And the anger of the Lord was kindled against Israel, not to be slaked till the zeal of Phineas, the son of Eleazar the high-priest, after twenty-four thousand had died, stayed the plague from the children of Israel.

But what of the crafty politician? what of that cunning prophet, who speaks so well and so truly, who has managed so skilfully to keep his words all faithful and obedient, and yet to gain—apparently, to gain—his worldly objects as well? What of him? Is he to triumph in secret? to compass his ends, and keep his character too? to cheat God,—to get the people accursed, even while he blessed them, to sustain the reputation of the faithful seer whose eyes were divinely opened, and at the same time to be the wealthy, honoured counsellor of the wicked king?

How his advice and double-dealing became known to the Israelites we are not told. In some way, no doubt, God, whom his cunning had outraged, revealed it to them. And, therefore, in the slaughter of Midian, which by the command of God immediately followed, when all the men and most of the women were put to the sword, Balaam too met his reward. "Balaam also, the son of Beor, the soothsayer, did the children of Israel slay with the sword, among them that were slain by them." And from that day forth, Balaam the son of Beor is known throughout the Holy Scriptures, in the writings of prophets and apostles, as the type of those who for the sake of the wages of unrighteousness, of wealth, reward, honour, in defiance of better knowledge, wilfully sin by casting a stumbling-block before the children of God.

And what a strange course was his! strange, I mean, regarded theoretically, and without reference to the weakness and wilfulness of men,—not, alas! either strange or uncommon when we think of men as they really are. He first asks the direction of God, and, receiving it, follows it implicitly. He will not go,

THE CONVICTIONS OF BALAAM. 253

for the Lord has forbidden him. When the "more honourable" ambassadors press him further, he sins by soliciting God again, and endeavouring to alter His will. He receives His permission; but it is given in anger. See how the worldly leaven is working in his heart, and how nearly, but for the rebuke his madness wonderfully received, he had lost his life for it! But he acknowledges his fault, and is ready to return home;—again a partial return to duty and repentance. Sent forward by God, he still attempts divination, and would fain steal a curse, where he knew that God designed to bless. How long he struggles against the light and truth of God! till at last inspiration overbears him; and he pours out the full voice of prophetic utterance, and seems to lose all hopes of worldly honour and advancement from the faithful fulness with which he speaks cordially forth the divine blessing.

Had he gone home then, and stayed there; poor, but true; unhonoured of Balak, but faithful at the last and in the main to God, we should have drawn a different lesson from his story; we should have magnified the grace of God which had interposed so wonderfully and so often to rescue one who had so long and wilfully endangered himself, and we should have read the lesson of hopefulness and encouragement to those who have often felt tempted to give way, drawn from the example of one who had tottered and staggered, over and over again, on the very edge of fatal sin and worldliness, but had at last yielded himself up to the guidance of God's grace, and in the strength of that grace had conquered, and was faithful in the end.

But alas for the deadly gift of cleverness! alas for the danger of that sharpness of wit which leads us to endeavour to compass our ends by indirect and circuitous means! The politician, who could not forego true words, tried his craft. He succeeded, and he failed. He succeeded against man; he failed against God. The evil that he planned, by means of other men's sins he brought about. The personal advancement that he sought was overthrown by a miserable death, and a name blasted to all generations in the inspired oracles of God.

Oh, brethren, let us turn our eyes upon ourselves! Can we not read ourselves in much, at least, of this history? How apt we are to totter thus and stagger upon the edge of truth and duty! Not indeed visibly, intentionally, distinctly giving it up and forsaking it; but trying to hold it together with as much of worldly indulgence and prosperity as we can; trying to serve God and mammon, God and our own heart's lusts;

trying by all sorts of cunning self-deceit to keep truth (so at least as not to abandon it) and be prosperous, to keep truth and be rich, to keep truth and be popular, to keep truth and be comfortable.

But if a man does thus allow himself to palter with that which ought to be the foundation and basis of all else; if he divides his aim between two objects in his life; if he goes on so, venturing to the very edge of duty and truth continually,—going, so to say, as near to the wind on every occasion as he possibly can, without actually disowning and forfeiting the truth which he believes, and thinks that he is holding fast, —do you suppose that that conflict will continue long? do you imagine that so painful a balance and inward battle can last? No; by no means: that which the intellect holds will yield and give way; that which the heart loves will gain strength and have victory. At last it must needs be so, whether the ultimate condition of the man be produced by the gradual dying away of the intellectual hold of truth, or by some sudden device of cleverness, like the counsel of Balaam, designed, by a stroke of policy and skill, to gain both objects at once. One way or the other, the worldly heart will have its way. It smothers the intellectual faith. It necessarily kills it. The world cannot be taken in to share the empire of the heart without becoming, ere long, the sole ruler and tyrant in it.

It is, I think, not to be denied that the particular sin of Balaam, the sin, I mean, which consists in yielding to worldly temptation in defiance of better knowledge, as it was the characteristic sin of the Church of Pergamos, so it is a very particular danger in the Church of England. Owing to the Protestant doctrine which lays so much stress upon individual faith and holiness, and to the effect of early teaching in Christian homes, and Christian schools, and the habit of attending church and hearing sermons, it cannot be questioned that there is among a very large proportion of our countrymen a general knowledge of religion, however much it may be overlaid in general and forgotten in the midst of the tumult and interests of our common life. You see it, now and then, come out very strikingly when sudden and disastrous circumstances forcibly remove the temptations which ordinarily smother it, and lay bare the heart. You see it sometimes, for instance, in a case of shipwreck, when Christian English people,— and not always those who have been religious before,—not in despair or wild outcry, but in sober, earnest religiousness pray to God, and act in His sight bravely, simply, faithfully. You saw it abundantly in the war of the

THE CONVICTIONS OF BALAAM. 257

Crimea, when officers and soldiers alike, to a surprising extent, shewed under the pressure of extreme distress and danger, I do not say *bravery*,—that they were sure to shew,—but *Christian bravery*—faith in the truth of God, the traces of the faithful teaching of the Church of England in her homes, her schools, her churches, her confirmations. You saw it astonishingly in the terrible details of the Indian mutiny; when all those mixed multitudes, of an average and surely a luxurious and self-indulgent community, were suddenly called upon to testify to their faith, and seal it with their blood: were called upon, I say, and *obeyed the call;* so that among the whole English population, civilians, artizans, servants, women, children, we did not hear of so much as one attempt to purchase life by apostasy, or any voluntary disowning of the name of Christ, but, on the contrary, many instances of a personal heroism of faithfulness and constancy in maintaining the truth, which make one's heart glow with Christian joy and emulation in thinking of the grace given in their need to our Christian brothers and sisters.

Yes: it is true. There is in very many of us more or less of an inward hold of truth derived from Christian parents, teachers, clergy, which, when the world is forcibly removed, as in such cases as I have men-

s

tioned, or on a death-bed, often becomes clear: becomes clear to shame us who, in the midst of the comfort, the peace, the blessings of God, allow so many cares, and thoughts, and interests, and lusts of the world to eat silently away that faith which, under other, apparently sadder, circumstances, might have won the victory, and turned the whole heart round to God.

But, oh! brethren, we who are still in the sunshine of life, whom no terrible storms force thus upon our knees, and compel to the presence and thought of God, how carelessly are we apt to let our likings and our lusts, our idleness, our ambition, or whatever else it be, *crust over* our real knowledge of God and His truth, and making it unproductive of its due acts, gradually eat it away and destroy it! In outer life,—luxury, fashion, idleness, company, business, politics,—think, brethren, what multitudes of men and women, who know what truth is, and have a sort of wish to be good and true in the end, these things do keep from anything *like* a real conversion to God, a real yielding of themselves up, in body, soul, and conscience, to the direction of the Holy Spirit! Then blessed be sickness! blessed pain! blessed adversity! blessed sorrow! for what would become of this poor world if these things did not come upon us, now and then, to waken us up from this worldly incrustation, this growing of stone round about our hearts, and force us to lay our consciences bare, and sore, and naked before the merciful eye of our heavenly Father!

But, brethren, you particularly, I mean, who belong to this University, I beg you to consider how very prime a danger to yourselves this is of which I am speaking. To know, and not to love; to know, and not to obey; to hold more or less fast the intellectual side of truth, and to profess it by word of mouth, and yet to let the heart, the affection, the liking roam freely over to the enemy's side,—how closely this danger presses upon those who live, like you, at a University where sacred truth is a special subject of general study! You read, in the way of study, the Holy Scriptures; you become familiar with them, you learn the sacred doctrines which they contain; you are able to pass examination in them; you can teach them to others; you can distinguish keenly between shades of orthodoxy and heterodoxy in opinions respecting them. But oh! how far is all this in itself from loving the truth, from yielding ourselves up to it, from giving our hearts, and our true, deep heart's love to the obedience of the will of God! How possible it is, how easy, to have the one, and not

to have the other! To be clear, learned, not doubtful, in the hold of intellectual belief; and to be cold
and unmoved, or, still worse, to be self-indulgent and
rebellious, in the actual and practical life!

This is the danger: a danger great in itself, and
to all men, especially great, as I think, to ourselves.
I said just now that there is in English people much
of knowledge of truth, much latent acquaintance and
belief of Christian doctrine, which, under particular
circumstances, not unfrequently shews itself in a remarkable way. Let me add, what is surely not less
true, that in our ordinary outward ways of life there
is very little appearance indeed of our being a religious people. Is there any nation, professing Christianity, in Europe, where the common habits of life
except in the single article of shutting up the shops
on a Sunday, bear so little the visible impress of our
being in earnest to hold fast and carry out in life the
one, revealed truth of God in Christ? And all this
exterior neglect and worldliness makes common cause
with our poor, weak, tottering hearts, and encourages
them to indulge themselves in all those free and
pleasant ways which by degrees threaten to smother
and kill the faith that is in us.

Oh! believe me, when a Christian young man, bred
up in the knowledge of God and His truth, whose

very studies make him day by day more intimately acquainted with the outside of that truth, allows himself to do what he knows to be against the law of God, if he allows his hand or his eye to offend him by leading him to sin, or his imagination to be stained with impureness,—if he lets words of bitterness, unholiness, or deceit fall from his lips, if his sloth leads him to omit his prayers, if he neglects public prayer and sacred Communion, if he idles away his time, or spends his money in riot and extravagance, or runs dishonestly into debts which he knows he cannot pay, —if, I say, he does any of these things, which are apt to be only too common among young men in such a place as this, and does not forcibly bring himself back by distinct and painful repentance to the devotion and entireness of obedience which he has thus wilfully departed from, what is he doing but deliberately cutting off the practical powers of his faith, strengthening, fatally strengthening the hold of evil upon his corrupt affections, educating himself, as it were on purpose, to become that most unhappy of all beings, a man enlightened in mind but dark in love and will, a man in whom the darkness must at last swallow up the light, and the faith expire in the practical unbelief?

And, brethren, if as we grow older, and perhaps

have known more or less of such youthful sin as I have alluded to; if, I say, we surround ourselves with comfort and ease, till these things become necessary and of prime importance to us; if we scheme for promotion or advancement, let this or that be done amiss and against the law of God which we might prevent or lessen, because we like to be popular, easy, comfortable, letting the cause of God, the cause of truth and holiness slip, because we cannot part with our self-indulgence or idleness, are we not in like manner fatally weakening, imprisoning, destroying such faith as we have, running into the very likeness of the sin of Balaam?

Oh! brethren, my elder brethren! think of Balaam's sin! Look forth upon these young men, *all young men*, whose tents are pitched around you, by these "willow-shaded streams." The sacrifices to idols, the pleasant games and plays which are not of God, are soliciting them daily. The women of Midian are around them to lure them into sin. What if any of the old prophets, who know the truth, should be so fond of his ease, or so careful of his popularity, or so busy with his comfort, or his preferment, or I know not what else, as to shut his eyes, to wink at Israel's sin, and let God's children bring down upon themselves a curse, which *he* would not *utter* with his lips

THE CONVICTIONS OF BALAAM.

for all the world? What if his neglect to act upon his own convictions should give encouragement to them to forget the truth that is in them, and practically and finally to desert God?

Oh! blessed seasons of humiliation and confession, which are given to us to prevent this crust of selfish, ungodly worldliness from creeping over all our soul, and deadening all the faith that is in it! Blessed Lent! which brings us more continually into the presence of God, and calls us to repent of all the sin which our souls know of, and all the secret sins which God only knows!

Let us obey the holy calling. Can any one suppose that he is in earnest, if he does not during this Lent open his heart to God in full penitential confession and prayer? Obey the calling both now, and whensoever the preparation for Holy Communion or your own private self-examination brings you on your knees before God. Remember the exceeding danger of those who know the truth, and yet follow their own evil likings. Beware of the gradual and imperceptible on-coming of that fatal worldliness,—like the sleep of the weary traveller among the Alpine snows,—in which faith inevitably dies. Statedly, regularly, and really search your own consciences before God, with earnest and contrite confession, and may the

Holy Spirit of God keep all our hearts so true to God, so obedient to His will, so watchful against the surrounding dangers of the world, the flesh, and the devil, that God may not write it up against us that we, at least, in an evil and self-indulgent age, have followed the doctrine or example of the unholy prophet of Moab.

SERMON XIII.[a]

ROMANS viii.

9. But ye are not in the flesh, but in the Spirit, if so be that the Spirit of God dwell in you. Now if any man have not the Spirit of Christ, he is none of His.

TO be in Christ is to be within the scope and influence of the Holy Spirit of God. None can be in Christ without partaking also of that sacred and mysterious indwelling of the Holy Spirit; nor can any, so far as we are informed in Holy Scripture, have that sacred indwelling in its true, full, sanctifying vitality, unless he be planted into Christ, a member of the sacred body in which the Holy Spirit is as the circulating and life-giving blood, a branch of the Vine in which He is as the sap. The Body and the Spirit are correlative, the one to the other. To be a member of the Body is to be made to drink into one Spirit; just as by one Spirit we are baptized

[a] Preached at St. Mary's, Oxford, in Lent, 1859.

into one Body. The one Body answers to the one Spirit, and neither is, nor can be, without the other.

To be in Christ, then, is to be within the scope and influence of the Holy Ghost. It is an estate; it is the Christian estate, or condition. Every Christian man, insomuch as he hath been planted into the Body of Christ, and still remaineth in it, hath also in him the indwelling of the Holy Ghost. His condition is not that of a poor weak creature holding out his hands to a powerful good Being outside of himself, proclaiming for ever his own utter helplessness, calling on God to approach him from without, receiving intermittent helps of God in answer to intermittent or occasional applications of prayer,—his condition, I say, is not such as that. It is the condition of one who ought to be strong; for *he* dwells in a strong tower who dwells in Christ, and he ought to be growing stronger and stronger in whose heart is the indwelling of the most strong and Holy Spirit,—who, if he has not the Spirit of Christ continually within him, is surely none of His; who, if he is not growing on in the growth and strengthening of the Spirit, is surely risking the loss of his Christian condition, and his place in the Body of his Lord.

This, I say, is the Christian estate, and we build up our Christian teaching best and most truly by founding it upon this basis. This is the language of our Lord and His apostles respecting it. How, for instance, can any man read that most precious of all the discourses of Christ, written in the fourteenth, fifteenth, sixteenth, and seventeenth chapters of St. John, and doubt that this is the Lord's own gracious teaching, that they who abide in the Vine (that surely is, who continue in the Body of Christ) shall have the Comforter dwelling with them and in them; and, having the Comforter, shall see Christ, who will manifest Himself to them by the Spirit, and shall have the peace of the Holy Ghost, and that rejoicing of heart in the Holy Ghost which no man can take from them?

Or how can any doubt that St. Paul, in the eighth chapter to the Romans, teaches the same doctrine, that is to say, that they who are in Christ must needs have the Spirit of Christ, so that if they have not the Spirit they are none of His; but that, having the Spirit and being His, they have in the Spirit life and peace, and sonship and adoption, and the witness of the Spirit with their own spirit that they are heirs of God and joint-heirs with Christ?

Or how can any person doubt that this is the teaching of St. John, who bids us "hereby know that we dwell in God, and He in us," which is surely none other than that we are very members incorporate in the Body of His Son, "because He hath given us of His Spirit?" And observe that this is the way the apostles describe the estate and condition of Christian people to whom they write, whether, as in a special Epistle, they are addressing the whole Christian population of a single city, or, as in a general one, the whole Christian Church throughout the world.

But is it indeed, brethren, the sacred revealed truth of Holy Scripture, that all we baptized people into the Body of Christ, which is the Church of God, that all we, without exception, are thus made to partake of the Holy Spirit of the Most High God? Is it the very truth, not to be pared away, or explained or diluted away, that as we are Christians, so the blessed indwelling of the Holy Ghost is surely in the heart of every single one among us? that in my heart, and your heart, and the heart of every one, the Almighty Spirit of God dwells with our own spirit, searching, sanctifying if we will,—any way, whether increasing or grieved within us, there dwelling until the spark of divine life grow strong, and burn, and purify us even unto fitness for the presence of God and the kingdom of heaven, or be by final impenitence quenched in any soul, so that he be lost absolutely and for ever? And is this not the language only of hope and charity, the hypothetical language which is compatible with ever so much uncertainty in each particular instance, but the very language of Holy Writ, so that we must build our teaching absolutely upon it, and speak so and none otherwise respecting it?

I know not how any person who studies the words of Holy Scripture faithfully can doubt that this is indeed the way, the only way, in which the Lord and His apostles speak of the condition of Christian people in regard to the Holy Spirit of God. But oh! brethren, what a lofty, what an awful teaching it is! how awful in its loftiness! To think that we, every one of us baptized into the Church of God, have in our hearts the true presence of the Holy Spirit of God, so that whether we sleep or wake, whether we are alone or in company, whether we are at our prayers, or busy with the most secular and least religious of our employments, He is with us, not seeing us from outside, but secretly and within, as spirit may dwell with spirit, seeing, searching, not controlling, not coercing, but yearning to help, sanctify, and save us; and that all this has been going on within us from the very font, so that thoughtless or thoughtful, heedless or watchful as we have been, that Almighty searcher of hearts has known and traced, yea, and felt, if I may speak so, our whole history of growth or decay in grace, that history which by God's great mercy in Christ is not closed yet, but may still, whatever be its dark passages hitherto, end in repentance and full pardon, and entire sanctification in Christ. Is not this a lofty teaching, brethren? Yes, and utterly awful and humbling in its loftiness, when we turn one by one to ourselves, and endeavour to remember honestly and deeply how it has been with us in all those years that are passed, and how it is now that they are gone by for ever.

Brethren, this is a time for very faithful and simple words, and I desire by God's help to speak to you most plainly and unreservedly on this great subject, that we may think together for awhile, and still more seriously afterwards, if we will, severally, of our own condition in respect of this sacred indwelling.

The Holy Spirit of God is a delicate thing. In Him, and in His continual and increasing presence within us, is our only hope, or strength, or salvation; without Him we cannot resist temptation, or refrain from sin. If we be in the flesh, which is inevitable if we be not in the Spirit and the Spirit in us, we cannot please God. We are not naturally subject to the law of God, neither indeed can we be. But we were early placed by God's mercy within the sphere and scope of the Holy Spirit, so that in the language of

Holy Scripture the work is begun in us, the seed is sown, the spark of life is lighted; but oh! how does it fare? Is the divine inmate occupying more and more of our hearts, so as to be making them more and more holy; or is He in any of us losing hold of them, and gradually in grief withdrawing Himself from them who will not have Him?

We know not how spirit acts upon spirit; we cannot discriminate, amid the continual risings of thought and feeling within our breasts, how much or what is the natural growth of our own minds, or what is suggested, fostered, or checked by the operation of other spirits upon ours. And I believe that we do harm to ourselves by attempting too close scrutiny into these things. Faith, and love, and other spiritual graces will not grow well when we are for ever trying to watch their growth, trying as it were to feel the pulse of our soul, trying as it were to see the seeds growing, and to analyze what is ours and what is God's, what is the effect of the soil and what of the rain, interfering with the natural and orderly processes of growth rather than helping them, by attempting to dive too deep, and to search too narrowly the manner of the mystery of the spirit of man influenced by the Spirit of God.

No: we must not pry too closely into the manner of that mysterious operation. Rather cover up the soil in which that sacred seed is deposited, and leave it to germinate by its own holy working. Enough for us to know that He who alone in all the world baptizeth with the Holy Ghost, surely blessed His own ordinance with His own mysterious gift, so that in our hearts that Holy Ghost dwelleth, a spark of sacred fire never to be extinguished, unless, which God forbid! we should sin fatally without repentance, and be cast forth, as branches cut off and destined for the burning. Yes, brethren, one fire, or the other fire: either the fire of purifying grace, or the fire of destroying anger. The Holy Spirit comes with fire, and He will either save our souls by sanctifying them in Christ, or He will burn them up with utter destruction if they will not abide His searching, holy, purifying fire. But though we may not too narrowly pry into the *manner*, very carefully must we watch the *fact* of the sacred growth of the Holy Spirit in us.

In that sacred growth we are alone with the Spirit. Neither father nor mother, neither brother nor companion, neither husband nor wife, can either grow for us or directly help our growth; no, nor directly impede it. The lonely spirit of a man in its depths hath none with it but God. None can pluck it out of His hand, nor ruin it, unless it consents to be ruined; but neither can any make it grow, or impart directly one spark of life to it. No things outward, no Church ordinances, nor daily prayers, nor knowledge, nor opportunities of any kind, can of themselves, or directly, make us grow in the Holy Spirit. The work must go on within, deep in our separate souls. None can penetrate to it, or directly touch it. We are alone with the Spirit of God. We mingle outwardly, and know each other's faces in the flesh, and judge more and less correctly of each other's minds, but how slight and superficial at the best is all this knowledge and judgment! How little can our nearest friend or neighbour really know the secrets of our heart, the real thoughts, the secret wishes, the mingled feelings, or fathom the secret well which each carries within him of memory and consciousness! But to the divine indwelling Spirit the very depths are clear; He does not wait for the wordings of the lips or the actings of the hand; He knows, He searches, He would fain sanctify the deepest and most inward stirrings of thought, wish, and will. We are in the deep of our hearts, alone, with the Spirit. *Alone with the Spirit!* And He must gain the separate victory with each separate soul. Quite alone, quite apart from all others, except in the way of outward and superficial helps, the Holy Spirit must triumph separately in the depth of each man's spirit. And each such victory will be gained, not by the exercise of irresistible or coercing power, but by the voluntary yielding of the spirit of a Christian man to His loving leadings, to His loving leadings who is the one only Witness, the one undeceived, unbaffled, infallible Witness of all we truly are, of all we have been, and of all that in our hearts we truly wish and purpose to be.

Brethren, when we think thus of the Holy witnessing and searching Spirit, does not the thought come forcibly, and as it were startlingly, into each of our minds, How does He then fare in me? In the midst of the forgetful world, wandering on, as I have been, all my life, at one time thinking more seriously of such things, but at another thoughtless, and falling into all manner of sin and folly, oh! how has the sacred witnessing Spirit fared in my wilful heart? Is He there still? Have I not quite banished Him by neglect and forgetfulness, and worse? Is He striving yet to win me to the life of Christ, to sanctify me, and save me, or has He quite yielded me up, grieved finally, and gone from me for ever?

Happy he who is so far startled by this thought as to take it deep into his heart, and dwell upon it with true prayers and honest self-examination.

For, brethren, how lightly, else, do we seem to live; we, the spirit-bearing souls whom Christ has purchased for immortality; how lightly, I say, do we seem to live, and how lightly to hold of this indwelling Spirit in all our common lives! Talking so freely; reading all sorts of light and sometimes debasing things; letting our minds loose, in wild, and wanton, and unkind thoughts; idling our time, spending our money, eating, drinking, playing beyond the bounds of Christian refreshment and recreation; thinking, alas! little enough of the eternal Inmate who witnesses and searches all, who must pray from our hearts if we are to pray really at all, who is to keep us in Christ, and so bring us to our everlasting inheritance. How apt we are to substitute for the thought of the inwardly searching Spirit our outwardly seeing neighbours, comforting ourselves in our fair external seeming, or our generally good character outwardly among men, instead of welcoming the salutary pain which comes of the thought of the inward, undeceived Spirit. For men are blind, and men can be cheated, and men are very indulgent, seeing that they need much indulgence themselves, and men make very great mistakes; but the Spirit of God is surely like the Word of God, "living and powerful, and sharper than any two-edged sword, piercing even to the dividing asunder of soul and spirit, and of the joints and marrow, and is a discerner of the thoughts and intents of the heart." Can a spirit-bearing soul be otherwise than manifest in His sight? Are we not helpless and open —even as a victim with its throat exposed to the knife—unto the eyes of Him to whom our account is to be rendered? Can we deceive the Spirit? Can we neglect the Spirit, even to the quenching of the spark of divine fire within us, and not utterly lose Christ?

Oh, my brethren, met as we are in this season of Lent to remind one another of the evil of sin, and, if it may be, to encourage one another to turn to God with more and more faithful repentance, shall we not take to our hearts this most sacred and awful truth which I have been unfolding? How fearful sin is when we thus regard it, as done in the very face, so to speak, of the witnessing and indwelling Spirit! When St. Paul speaks to the Hebrews of the hopeless case of such as finally do despite unto the Spirit of grace, what can he mean more expressly than this, that the Spirit is in the hearts of Christian men, and that when they advisedly sin without repentance, they deliberately reject Him? that where He and the spirit of a man are met alone in the deep of a heart, and He desires to guide that heart and sanctify it, the wilful spirit of a baptized man is mad enough to disown His guidance deliberately, and to resolve to have none of His sanctification!

Oh, brethren, it is nothing less than *ourselves*, ourselves entire and without reserve, ourselves in soul and body, ourselves down to the most secret and inward wish of our heart, that God will have of us. He will not accept half-service, or outward, or only half-devotion. No, this searching, indwelling Spirit utterly rebukes and abashes the idea of such unreal obedience. " My son, give Me thine heart," give it Me all, hold none away, hide nothing away in the deepest corner, lie not to the Holy Ghost who is in thee. Didst thou bargain to give less than all thou hadst for that heavenly treasure, of which the Holy Ghost within thee is the divine earnest and guarantee? Nay, then, let not Satan tempt thine heart to lie to that infallible Witness that is within thee, that thou shouldest try to keep back part of the price of that inestimable inheritance.

Oh let us not shrink and fear, or hesitate; let us yield ourselves up willingly, lovingly, to the guidance of Him whom we cannot shun, and who will most lovingly guide us. That Holy Spirit will Himself give us the power to fulfil His own sacred claims upon us; only let us frankly, and faithfully, and loyally render ourselves up to His discipline. Does it seem like a lofty and unattainable strain of doctrine to teach of the indwelling Witness, and to tell you how the divine and infallible Spirit of the Most High God sees, tries in the balance, and would fain sanctify, every the most secret wish and thought of the heart? Does it seem to clash, too violently to be practical or practicable, with the light current of ordinary life and conversation, with the true consciousness of our own hearts, to be told of this sacred law of thorough saintliness, of unreserved and entire devotion, which the truth of the indwelling Spirit thus lays upon us? Indeed, brethren, it were a doctrine far too lofty, and too terrible in its loftiness for us and such as we are, if it did not carry with it its own remedy, its own soothing, sacred, precious antidote. The fire of God's presence will not devour us if we will let it purify us; His Holy Spirit will not condemn us, if we will, even now, let Him guide us and have us for His own. The indwelling Spirit, much as He knows of our weakness and our sin, will not utterly abash and confound us at the judgment, if we will yield ourselves up to Him, even now, with true, penitent, undissembled purpose.

The Holy Ghost is not the witness only against sin, God forbid! nay, He is even still more our strength against sin, our only strength, our only possible strength, against sin.

Does not sin solicit us on every side, within us and

without? Is not sin in our hearts, yea, and in every member of our bodies? Is not sin in the books, in the newspapers we read? Is not sin in our lightness of talking, in our lonely times, and in our times of company? Is not the defiling knowledge of sin forced upon our too willing ears and thoughts by everything that goes on round about us?

And what is the talisman against all this danger? What is the antidote which is to keep us unharmed amid all this infection,—made all the more dangerous because men will not believe in its existence,—except the Holy Spirit of God, ruling, ruling alone and absolutely in our hearts?

Oh, brethren, I would not speak mere words, mere sounding words; I would, if by the grace of God I may, speak to the true consciousness of each Christian here, of every single Spirit-bearing soul that hears me.

Can you bear to think, really and seriously, of your own heart, of that deep well that is within you of conscience and memory, and to recollect that as the Holy Spirit of God which is in you knows all now, so will all, absolutely all, all that you would not for your life betray to the nearest friend you have on earth, be brought out into the fullest light at the day of judgment? It is not more certainly revealed that our secret sins are now set in the light of God's countenance [b], nor that He searcheth the heart [c] and trieth the reins of man [d], and understandeth his thoughts long before, than that when He cometh to judge the world He will "bring to light the hidden things of darkness, and make manifest the most secret counsels of the heart [e]." And if this thought, fairly faced and contemplated, be, as in itself it is, overpoweringly painful to any one, how can you then hesitate to do the only thing that can possibly offer you an escape from the pain of it? that is, to yield yourself up in body and soul, absolutely up, to the guidance of that Holy Spirit of God who is still yours?

Is sin still too strong, or does the memory of former sin wind itself still too closely round your thoughts, and seem to forbid you, to make it impossible for you to detach yourself from it, and turn thus to the simple and entire obedience of the Holy Spirit? Nay, (if there be any such who hears me now,) let him turn all the more, memory and all, to the loving, gracious Spirit within him. I know well that he cannot kill at once, nor by any effort of immediate will, that serpent-memory of sin that coils round the heart of one who has gone far from God in his youth, and

[b] Ps. xc. 8.
[d] Jer. xvii. 10.
[c] Ps. xliv. 21; cxxxix. 1.
[e] 1 Cor. iv. 5.

has not yet altogether repented. I know well how it clings, and coils, and threatens, suggesting despair at one time, and at another bringing up the thoughts of old sin, till the soul is apt to sin again in thinking of it, and how long it keeps its fangs and its poison, strong and venomous enough to ruin the soul that allows its mastery. But let him turn all the more, *memory and all*, and he will find at last that in the strength of the Spirit—by slow degrees, it may be, but at last—the fatal strength of that serpent-memory will uncoil itself from his soul, and die away around him.

But believe me, brethren, that for one who has not yet gained this victory over memory, but is sore and distressed for his sin, it is an unspeakable comfort to feel in his heart of hearts that whatever be his past offences, which he does not wish to extenuate before God or conceal, and for which he desires to have grace to repent worthily, yet at this moment he really is ready to yield, *does yield* up his heart to the Spirit, and without any reserve of feeling, thought or wish, does inwardly, yes, this moment does, a real act of inward surrender, and gives his secret self to God.

And let a man so wounded reflect on that comfortable word, (oh, how comfortable to an anxious soul!) that if a man, a Christian man, sin, and repent of his sin, we have a Paraclete with the Father, the same Jesus Christ the righteous, who is the propitiation for our sins. And remember, brethren, that there are two Paracletes, one in our hearts, and one on the Father's right hand; one suggesting repentance and crying in holy prayers from within ourselves, the other offering those holy prayers for His own precious sake to the Father. They never act asunder: the Paraclete in heaven only offers what the Paraclete on earth inspires. If, then, you have sinned, and have grace to desire to repent; if at this very moment, as this message of God sounds in your ears, the desire to render yourself up to God, to be holy and sanctified by the Spirit, moves in your heart, is not that, think you, the movement of that very Paraclete within you, giving you one help more, one hope more, one opportunity more of entire sanctification and salvation? And is not the other Paraclete at this moment ready to offer to His Father, for His own sake, the silent prayer your soul is breathing now, and the worded prayers which this night before you sleep your lips will earnestly and repentantly pour out before God? And how many more such helps and opportunities, if you neglect this one, can you reckon upon? Indeed, these are not mere words, brethren, they are most deep and most important truths; shall we not lay them to our heart? shall we not this night, before we lie down to sleep, pray in some such petition as this?

O Holy Spirit of the Most High God, who, ever since I was made to drink into Thee by holy Baptism, hast dwelt in this heart of mine, who alone hast known it in all its wayward and wandering thoughts, who hast been grieved, alas! how often and how heavily, by my wanton, repeated, and presumptuous sins; yet who still, blessed be God for His mercy, solicitest my heart, and movest me to this desire of repenting and returning unto God again,—O Holy Spirit of my God, fill my spirit with Thy grace: accept it, take it, mould it, sanctify it. Never may I forget Thy searching, purifying, awful presence; never may I attempt or wish to conceal one thought or wish from Thee. Alone or in company, by night or by day, may I feel and realize Thee, penetrating and sanctifying my inmost soul. Strengthen me to resist sin, and to bear meekly the pain which the memory of sin brings, but never to be led by it to despair, or to repeat my sin by dwelling on the thought of it. Teach me to pray; pray for me and with me; teach me to use aright all the means of grace which Thou givest me in the Church.

And lead me on thus, O holy, sanctifying Spirit,

from strength to strength, that, kept in Christ to the last, and made holy in my body and my soul, He may confess me to be His before the Father, His for ever when He returns with His holy angels to judge the world.

SERMON XIV.[a]

REVELATION V.

9. And they sung a new song, saying, Thou art worthy to take the book, and to open the seals thereof; for Thou wast slain, and hast redeemed us to God by Thy blood out of every kindred, and tongue, and people, and nation;

10. And hast made us unto our God kings and priests; and we shall reign on the earth.

SUCH is the glorious ascription of praise to the Lamb of God, offered by the four living creatures and the twenty-four elders, when they fell down before Him, having every one of them harps, and golden vials full of odours, which are the prayers of saints:—
"And they sung a new song, saying, Thou art worthy to take the book, and to open the seals thereof; for Thou wast slain, and hast redeemed us to God by Thy blood out of every kindred, and tongue, and people,

[a] This and the following Sermon were preached at Winchester College on All Saints' Day and the 5th of November, 1850.

and nation; and hast made us unto our God kings and priests; and we shall reign on the earth."

It was a *new song;*—new, because its topics were new; for what so new and strange as God incarnate shedding His blood upon the cross, and by virtue of that offering redeeming the most distant kindreds and nations of the earth, and making them, however low in estate and condition, to reign kings and priests upon the earth?—new, because it is the song of the new creation; the song of those to whom "behold all things are become new," new hearts, new lips, new hopes, new graces. And so it is new, and shall be new for ever; no newness to grow old some day; no name of newness to become an anachronism when a few years or generations are gone by; but new with an eternal newness, like the everlasting strength and undecaying youth of the Most High [b].

One point of this heavenly song, thus sung and to be sung for ever "new in the kingdom of heaven," I propose to consider, with the assistance of God, this morning; a point touching nearly upon the solemnity of this day, the festival of All Saints; a point of great importance to the true doctrine of the constitution of the Church upon earth; and, by consequence, a point

[b] "*ᾄδουσιν*, id est, assiduè cantant et jugiter."—*Corn. à Lapide, in loc. Apoc.*

which is connected most closely with some of the main and most anxious controversies with which the Church is agitated in this time of distress and trouble: —I mean that men are made by the Blood of Christ to be kings and priests upon the earth. From every kindred, and tongue, and people, and nation; however distant from the central spot where God had placed His name for so many centuries, and from whence the new light burst to irradiate the nations; however distant, barbarous, and unknown to the then civilized world, (and who more separate and barbarian than we, who are hardly mentioned by the politest writers of the age, except to be designated as the people "utterly separate from the whole world[c]?")—from the north and south, and east and west, from rich and poor, from high and low, from freemen and from slaves, we are made by the Blood of the Son of God to be kings and priests of God upon the earth.

By the Blood of Christ: that is, meritoriously and efficaciously by the infinite value of the one perfect, never-to-be-repeated Sacrifice of the Cross; instrumentally by Holy Baptism, wherein when our bodies are washed with pure water[d], our hearts are inwardly

[c] "penitus toto divisos orbe Britannos."—*Virg. Ecl.* I.

[d] Heb. x. 22, which passage, combined with Tit. iii. 5, seems to complete the baptismal doctrine, the one shewing how regeneration, the other how remission of sins, are inwardly attached by God's grace to the outward administration of water.

sprinkled with the spiritual Blood of Christ from an evil conscience, by the gracious dispensation of God, who bindeth His divine inward gift to the duly-administered external ordinance.

We by this Blood receive these great things: *we*, that is, all baptized Christian people, to whom this outwardly-administered washing hath been the means, and remaineth the pledge, of the inward divinely-given sprinkling of the conscience: *we*, that is, *all;* not one, nor a few, nor a class; not here a bishop, and there a pope; not here a prince, and there a potentate; not the clergy; not the learned; but all, in every land, kindred, estate, tongue, people, and nation; the children of noble and priestly houses in the midst of light and civilization at home, the child of the New Zealander newly reclaimed from nakedness and cannibalism, or of the Hindoo a convert from the bloody worship of Juggernaut: one and all; all whom the due outward washing of pure water, carrying by God's wonderful mercy the inward sprinkling from an evil conscience by the Blood of Christ, all become in Christ,—

(1st.) *Kings:*—that is, half, the lasting, eternal half of their Christian greatness.

They are kings, because they are members of that Christ who is King of kings and Lord of lords: not separate kings,—not having each a single royalty,

ALL SAINTS KINGS AND PRIESTS. 289

determined to his own separate person from God the fountain of all power; but kings, as members of the King, as partakers of that eternal royalty which is His, and His Body's. This royalty of Christ on earth, thus partaken by the Church His body, is clearly stated in many passages of Holy Scripture. To Christ as man, all "power was given both in heaven and in earth [e];" and again, "all things are delivered unto Him by His Father [f]." He is "the heir of the world," so that all is of right His. And it is the Father's good pleasure to give this kingdom to His little flock [g], that is, the Church; whereby the meek, that is, the little ones [h], the saints of God, become in Him the rightful inheritors of the earth.

Thus are they kings; but they are also priests. In earlier days, before the blood of sprinkling had been shed, and men made members of the great High-Priest, they had no access to God themselves. If they desired to approach Him, it could only be by some intermediate help, some priest, who, deprecating the wrath of God by the blood of victims, might on their behalf offer prayers for them, and, if it might be, become the channel of blessing to them. But Christ being come, the only true Priest [i] and the

[e] St. Matt. xxviii. 18.   [f] St. Luke x. 22.   [g] St. Luke xii. 32.
[h] St. Matt. v. 5.   [i] Heb. ix. 7—14, 24; x. 19—22.

single Victim of price, the access to God is opened the veil rent, the entrance to the holiest unclosed. Thenceforth may every member of His Body exercise a child's right of approaching his Father,—laying before Him his weaknesses, wants, and sins, with the assured hope that He who is his Father will, more than any earthly father to his own children, give His pardoning and sanctifying Spirit to those that ask Him.

Such, shortly, is the doctrine of the royalty and priesthood of all Christians; which is testified in two other passages of the New Testament besides the text: in Rev. i., "Unto Him that loved us, and washed us from our sins in His own blood, and hath made us kings and priests unto God and His Father; to Him be glory and dominion for ever and ever. Amen[k].' And again, in the second chapter of St. Peter's first Epistle: "Ye are a chosen generation, a royal priesthood, a holy nation, a peculiar people[l]."

In connexion with this great doctrine, which in its consequences is obviously of great importance to the whole theory of the Church, its powers, and privileges, there are, in these distracted and unquiet days

[k] Rev. i. 5, 6.   [l] 1 St. Peter ii. 8.

two main errors, held on two opposite sides, both of which are of extreme and imminent danger. The one of these is the doctrine of some of the Liberalizing, or Neologian party, the other, that of the Roman Catholics. The former [m], or Neologian party, so hold fast the doctrine of the separate priesthood of Christians as to deny and disown altogether all authority and power and priestly offices as exercised towards some Christians by others; thus making each single Christian his own standard of doctrine, life, authority, and worship. The latter, or Roman Catholic party, so hold the existence of authority and priestly offices within the Church, exercised towards Christian people, that they really deny, in a great many important points, the royal priestliness of single Christians. The former reject lawful and necessary authority, for the sake of vindicating the personal rights of baptized people; the latter tyrannize over the just and inalienable rights of baptized people, for the sake of maintaining an excessive and unscriptural authority. Between the two stands the orthodox and primitive doctrine of the Church of England; maintaining against the Neologian school the divine origin

[m] Bunsen's Church of the Future; Arnold's Fragment on the Church.

and authority of powers and priestly offices within the Church; maintaining against the Roman Catholics the sacred and indefeasible priestliness of all the baptized, whose representatives, and not whose lords, are the divinely-descended priests who minister in sacred offices among them.

(1.) The Neologian heresy proceeds, as it appears, from a superficial and faulty reasoning upon true grounds. Because, they say, each single Christian is a prince and a priest in the Church, therefore it is impossible that there can be any others exercising such offices towards him. Because, as a member of Christ, each has a free and unimpeded access to God in Him, therefore all claim whatever of authority and priestly powers over him must needs be tyrannical and usurping.

A most faulty and dangerous inference!

For let it be remembered that the single Christians are only in so far kings and priests in Christ as they are, and remain, members of the Church, which is His Body [n]. The Church is not an aggregate of many individual powers, combining for purposes of mutual help or joint operations. Not so, by any means. She

---

[n] Cf. Christian Remembrancer, No. LIX., Jan. 1848, "On the Church of the Future."

is the one royal and priestly Body of Christ, so that the separate members obtain these great names and privileges solely as partaking in her life, which is the Holy Spirit of God, and in her being, which is the Body of the Lord.

On them must operate, in divers ways, the collective royalty and priestliness of the whole Body. Who shall admit them to the Body? Some person, doubtless, who shall have the authority of the whole Body to admit. Who shall teach and train them? Who shall judge for them in the many questions which may arise of life and doctrine? Who shall rebuke them, if they need rebuke? Who shall build them up in the faith? Who shall, if the need arise, reject them from the body of the faithful, and terminate by authoritative act every claim which they can possibly have to their high and exalted titles?

Doubtless, there must be those who, acting in the person of the whole Church, the Body of Christ, duly commissioned and empowered to discharge these various offices, wherein the collective priestliness controls and limits, confer and withdraw the priestly powers of individuals, are priests over priests, stewards, governors, rulers as being representatives, of the household of God.

Nor can any reason be assigned why, this kind of

power within the Church being granted, the individuals exercising it should not be appointed in the way of a *succession* from the apostles, and possess, by the grace of apostolical ordination, personal gifts for the discharge of the peculiar offices of the collective priesthood which are not shared by their fellow-Christians.

And such, precisely, is the doctrine of the Church of England in this matter, as against the one error and its supporters. She believes, with them, that every baptized Christian has in Christ a free and immediate access to God the Father, that in Him he may offer filial prayers, confess and mourn over his sins as a child before a tender parent, assure himself of the gift of the Holy Spirit, and the pardon of his daily sins, in answer to his prayers.

But whereas he needs many offices to be exercised towards him which he cannot exercise towards himself,—to be admitted, trained, taught, edified, rebuked, if need be, and, if need be, expelled,—and whereas the still more special offices of the collective priesthood, the administration of the Sacraments, and the absolving power, were specially delivered to the apostles, representing the Church, by her holy Founder, she believes that there is, and ever has been, a succession of men authorized and empowered, by a solemn selection and ordination, to exercise upon all the single, ordinary lay-priests, if I may so term them, of the Church, these sacred functions.

Selected by their predecessors in the same duties, ordained by the Holy Spirit of God, by an assured descent from the apostles, they exercise *upon* the Church of God the priestly powers of that very Church of God herself. They represent her while they rule her; and they rule her with a perpetual acknowledgment that in her, at large,—in her, the royal, priestly Body of Christ, the Church diffusive,—reside ultimately those divine powers of which they are, in each generation, the appointed and empowered organs.

(2.) But here we find ourselves in direct opposition to the Roman Catholic theory upon the same subject. According to that view, all these powers reside *properly*, not representatively, in the priestly *rulers* of the Church. The separate lay-members of the Church have no portion, not only in the right of exercising, but not even in the real possession of them. To this assumption of a distinct and original power in the priesthood, they have added an imaginary historical basis, by which they have arranged the priestly authority into a complete and independent system, in which lay-Christians have no sort of part.

Supposing, quite without a shadow of support in ecclesiastical history, that among the equal apostles

St. Peter alone had the gift of succession, so that while the apostolic powers of the other thirteen expired with their own lives, his were continued on in his successors to last through the whole history of the world, they conclude that in the line of the popes the apostolic grace, authority, and power has remained in the Church in every age. Every point in that line, according to this view, has been in its own time the centre of light, truth, authority, commission, grace. Thus have the powers of the priesthood been arrayed into a complete theory. In each separate generation all are held under the Bishop of Rome, who is the St. Peter, or rather the whole of the apostles, in his own time, to the whole Church; and this line they claim to trace back to St. Peter himself, the first occupier of the apostolical see of Rome. The consequences of this portentous theory are not few nor distant.

Hence at once it follows that Rome must be infallible: for how can the sole channel of light, commission, power, and truth, how can the whole college of the apostles, be conceived to be involved in error?

Hence it follows that the bishop of Rome is superior to all councils: for how can any accumulation of derivative and borrowed light be equal to that which is the source and fountain of light in each generation to them all?

Hence it follows that all other bishops in all lands are not successors of the apostles at all, but deputies of the bishop of Rome, the single successor of all the apostles.

Hence, alas! it follows that all the corruptions and additions to the primitive faith which the ignorance of one age and the superstition of another, the fanaticism of one pope and the ambition of another, have at various times sanctioned, are embodied and imbedded so deeply into the Roman Catholic creed, that they cannot part with any of them without parting with that which they have made the very mark and characteristic of their Church.

I do not scruple to say that this priestly system, as so taught in the Church of Rome, and now, by a most extraordinary act of aggression, attempted to be imposed upon this nation, is utterly baseless in point of historical truth, and a most grievous usurpation and tyranny over the rights of all Christian people, who by the repeated declarations of the Holy Scripture are themselves, one and all, the ultimate holders of the sacred privileges of the royal priesthood. So that, let Rome say what it will, nothing is infallible in the Church, except the universal voice of Christendom, in long time and with full accord testifying to the doctrines which were entrusted to the entire Church by its Lord, that is, the doctrines of the ancient creeds:—not pope, not council, not saint, not doctor; each of which may surely be true, in so far forth as they ask and receive the Holy Spirit's aid upon their researches or decrees; but none are of full, plenary authority to rule the faith of the Church, unless the Church herself, the Church diffusive, the Church in all the world, the Church of all saints, do by her final acceptance ratify and acknowledge the decree or doctrine as a part of that sacred deposit which *she* received of her Lord º.

Brethren, we live in very dangerous days, and perils of all kinds and on all sides threaten our stedfastness: we are assailed from without in divers ways; by those who, like the Neologian, try to do away with all power, and order, and succession in the Church, and make it a great aggregate of individuals, each of whom is pope, council, and church to himself; or like the Roman Catholics, would rob him of all personal share in the lofty powers of the priestly Church, and subjecting him to the mere domination of an usurping hierarchy, take from him the high personal responsibilities too, which do really attach to the membership of the Body of Christ. And we are assailed most grievously from within,—by indifference, worldliness,

º Cf. Laud against Fisher, § 33, p. 228, seq.

and sin; and we are imprisoned by state-bonds, which cramp the spiritual powers and being of Christ's Church within the narrow and inconsistent limits of state policy and worldly convenience, taking from us, at least for the present, liberty of counsel, security of doctrine, assurance of soundness in our spiritual fathers.

In all these pressing and various sorrows, which make thoughtful men sad and anxious every morning as they rise from their pillows, to think what melancholy things each day may bring to their knowledge, I hardly know any single doctrine which, when fully taken in and digested, seems to offer so much comfort and strength to us, as the doctrine of this day, the doctrine of our text,—the royalty and priesthood of all saints.

If we take deeply into our hearts the recollection that we have each one of us been baptized into that glorious body, so as to be true members of Him who is the single and only King and Priest in earth and heaven, which priesthood, exercised *by* us in those points in which it can be exercised by a man for himself, and *upon* us by a succession of delegated priests in such as require the office of the whole body, or collective priesthood, of the Church,—if, I say, we take this view of the royal priesthood of all saints deeply into our hearts, we shall be *intellectually* able to withstand all these various assaults which I have spoken of. For this doctrine, the doctrine of the Holy Scriptures, of the primitive Church, and of the Church of England, has a firm and solid foundation which is, in itself, strong against every assault, whether of philosophy, or of wilfulness, or of usurpation, or of Erastianism and worldly policy.

Intellectually, I say: but, brethren, *we must live* as becometh all saints, we must repent of our sins, and try to model ourselves by the example of the King of saints, and His holy servants of old; we must love, obey, pray to Him, in all our days upon the earth, if we desire that that intellectual position be a blessing to us, or that we, favoured so far by being born and bred in the apostolical and reformed Church of England, should (in the day when controversies shall be done, philosophies, and usurpations, and policies gone by) be found at last in the triumphant Church, among the true and accepted saints of the most high God.

Such living alone will help to make our intellectual position clear and strong, and save us from being entrapped by one or other of the insidious foes by whom we are surrounded.

And let us remember that the faith which in the saints of God hath subdued kingdoms, wrought righteousness, obtained promises,—the faith which hath done, and may yet do, the mightiest of all works, the maintaining and spreading of the kingdom of God, and the subduing of the various hosts of superstition, impiety, and infidelity, which surround it,—the faith which, by the mercy of God in Christ, shall save our own souls in the great day, is the humble faith of daily prayers and daily self-control, of daily work and daily love; the humble faith of guarded lips, desires checked, feet and eyes withdrawn from evil, the Spirit's spark of fire cherished in the heart; the humble faith of those who, in whatever age or rank of life, strive modestly and steadily in the strength of grace, and in the consciousness of their lofty priesthood in Christ, to do their duty in that state of life to which it hath pleased God to call them.

SERMON XV.

REVELATION v.

9. And they sung a new song, saying, Thou art worthy to take the book, and to open the seals thereof: for Thou wast slain, and hast redeemed us to God by Thy blood out of every kindred, and tongue, and people, and nation;

10. And hast made us unto our God kings and priests: and we shall reign on the earth.

TO a superficial observer the question of the independence of the sees of England upon the bishop of Rome may seem in itself a slight and unimportant point. He may suppose, in ignorance or in scorn, that it is merely a question of the extent and limits of a diocese and patriarchate. When he finds, therefore, Anglican writers insisting on the independence of the English communion before the days of Gregory[a] and Augustine, and quoting ancient canons to

---

[a] Cf. the 7th Canon of the Council of Ephesus; Bramhall's Just Vindication, Disc. II. Pt. I. ch. v. p. 156.

prove that a local Church may not subsequently be intruded upon by a jurisdiction to which it was not subject from the first, he may consider the whole question as trifling and unworthy of regard except to the persons whose authority is immediately in question. But in truth, while the papal authority is of necessity the actual *point* of conflict, nothing less than the whole theory of the Church, the nature and origin of its authority, the liberties and graces of the baptized, together with a great number of usages of practice and doctrines of faith, are really at issue in that conflict.

The Roman Church, in setting out her dioceses in England, and claiming the submission of all baptized people within the territorial limits of those dioceses, is, I grant, only acting out her own lofty and consistent theory of usurpation over the Church universal.

But if we should allow that claim, or, out of respect to a venerable and apostolic see, refrain from entering our most earnest protest against it, we should simply yield up the true doctrine of the royalty and priesthood of Christians, submit ourselves and our children to a yoke which our fathers were unable to bear, and become partakers in the sin of imposing upon Christendom a system of doctrine which, if it be not, as we hope it is not, destructive of spiritual life and the grace of sacraments, is at least widely removed, by addition and corruption, from the pure faith and practice of the apostles.

Thus the recent act of the bishop of Rome throws us back upon the Reformation; and we are called upon to vindicate the Church of England from the charge of schism, in having in the sixteenth century resumed the ancient and claimed the inherent independence of the British sees upon that of Rome.

We do not indeed stand in the position of the Greek Church, which from the first has disowned "the Western pride,"—the words are St. Basil's [b],—which never gave way, no not for an hour, to these uncatholic claims of later times,—which never heard, except to smile at, that palmary argument of the Papacy which, acknowledging perforce the equality of the apostles among themselves, confines to St. Peter only the gift of succession; we have not maintained that silent protest of eighteen centuries which stands unanswered and unanswerable against the modern arrogance of Rome; but we maintain that the position of independence in which we stand is one justified by the true primitive constitution of the Church of Christ, and that, whatever personal guilt or evil motives may have led some of those who were foremost in the

[b] ἡ δυτικὴ ὀφρύς.—*S. Basil. Magn.*, Ep. ccxxxix. vol. iii. p. 533.

Reformation to detach our national Church from the obedience of the Pope, the act itself was just, necessary, and catholic; that no such subjection is due on the part of a national Church to a foreign patriarch as shall require or enable it to forego its own solemn judgment of primitive truth, or make it rebellious to reform itself from clear and notorious abuses in doctrine or practice; and that it was possible on principle, and necessary in fact, for the sees of England at that time to detach themselves from an authority not itself originally canonical in England, maintaining a solemn protest and appeal to the universal Church in justification of that separation.

For was there not a cause?

(*a.*) Had not the bishops of Rome [c] gradually transformed a primacy of ecclesiastical order into a sovereign supremacy, involving infallibility and absolute dominion in this see over the whole Church, so as to drive away the whole East, with all its bishops, from the communion of the West [d]?

(*b.*) Had they not, in one nation after another, laid claim to powers, such as that of deposing monarchs and giving away thrones and countries, in themselves

[c] Bp. Burnet's Hist. of the Reformation, vol. i. pp. 131—140, (Lond. fol. 1715.)

[d] Laud against Fisher, pp. 216, seq.

unreal, and absolutely inconsistent with the separate existence and security of nations?

(*c.*) Were they not notoriously and shamelessly selling, from one end to the other of Europe, their pretended indulgences of sin for money [e]?

(*d.*) Had they not deprived lay-Christians of the cup of the Lord in the Holy Communion [f]?

(*e.*) Had they not allowed the gradual perfection of a system under which practically, if not theoretically, the Blessed Virgin and the Saints received the worship due to God only?

(*f.*) Had they not, for generation after generation, drained this land of treasure [g] to an amount hardly

[e] Robertson's Charles V. (Works, vol. iv. pp. 14, seq.)

[f] "Licet Christus post cœnam instituerit, et suis discipulis administraverit sub utrâque specie Panis et Vini hoc venerabile sacramentum tamen hoc non obstante non debet confici post cœnam nec recipi nisi a jejunis. Et similiter quod licet in primitivâ Ecclesiâ Sacramenta reciperentur sub utrâque specie a fidelibus, tamen hæc consuetudo, ut a laicis sub specie Panis tantum suscipiatur habenda est pro Lege, quam non licet reprobare. Et asserere hanc esse illicitam est erroneum, et pertinaciter asserentes sunt arcendi tanquam hæretici." — *Concil. Constan.*, Sess. 13. Cf. *Laud against Fisher*, p. 260.

[g] "First, therefore, the Archbishop of Canterbury paid unto the Pope for his *annates*, or 'first-fruits,' at every vacation, 10,000 florins, besides other 5,000 florins for the use and right of his pall.

"The Archbishop of York paid likewise for his first-fruits 10,000 florins, and, as it is thought, other 5,000 florins for his pall.

ALL SAINTS KINGS AND PRIESTS. 307

conceivable, in the shape of fees, tributes, and other payments to Rome, so that for centuries the land had groaned under the burthen?

(*g.*) Had they not added many fond things vainly invented to the primitive Creed of the universal Church?

Brethren, I cannot doubt for a moment that there was abundant cause, in these and many other reasons, for the detachment of the sees of the Anglican communion from the Roman obedience at the time of the Reformation; cause so abundant and adequate, that

"The Bp. of Ely paid for his first-fruits 7,000 florins.

"The Bp. of London paid for his first-fruits 3,000 florins.

"The Bp. of Winchester paid for his first-fruits 12,000 florins.

"The Bp. of Exeter paid for his first-fruits 6,000 florins.

"The Bp. of Lincoln paid for his first-fruits 5,000 florins.

"The Bp. of Lichfield and Coventry paid for his first-fruits 3,000 florins.

"The Bp. of Hereford paid for his first-fruits 1,800 florins.

"The Bp. of Salisbury paid for his first-fruits 4,500 florins.

"The whole value of the Pope's first-fruits throughout Europe, as I find in one record, (although very imperfect,) ariseth to the sum of 2,246,843 florins. Here I leave out the yearly perquisites that the Pope made of his elections, preventions, dispensations, pluralities, trialities, totquots, tolerations; for his bulls, his seals, his signatures; for eating flesh, for eggs, for white meat, for priests' concubines, and for other like merchandize, I know not what. The sum whereof amounteth notwithstanding to 900,000 florins."—*Bp. Jewell's Defence of the Apology*, Pt. VI. 734—738.

none but such as have convinced themselves that Rome is the centre and sovereign of the Church, so that there is no grace nor salvation except for such as obey her, can reasonably doubt of it; and I will add, that evil as probably were the motives and character of the prince [h] who effected this detachment, and possibly imperfect and unworthy as may have been those of others who, in the next generation, repeated and completed it, yet any person who looks carefully into the ecclesiastical Acts of Henry VIII., and the transactions of Archbishop Parker on the accession of Queen Elizabeth, will be struck with the evident carefulness with which the true principles of the Church were kept in view in many of them. I allude particularly to those which recent events have caused to be the most closely examined, the Acts relating to the royal supremacy and the confirmation of

[h] "Non ignoro varias esse hominum sententias de occasione quam arripuit Henricus VIII., magni incepti perficiendi; sed mihi gravissimè errare videntur qui in Henrici facto hærent, neque ad priora tempora animum revocant. Quemadmodum enim mortis caussam nemo sapiens ultimæ, quæ hominum rapit, horæ tribuit: sed prioribus vitæ temporibus, per quæ moriendi caussæ paullatim sunt contractæ; sic repudiatæ, et tanto cum omnium ordinum applausu rejectæ authoritatis Pontificiæ altius repeti caussæ debent in antiquis Anglorum Historiis inveniendæ."—*Casaubon, Ep. ad Fronton. Ducæum*, p. 401.

bishops[i]. Certainly the intention of the prelates who directed the measures whereby the Anglican communion was, in those reigns, withdrawn from the obedience of Rome, was to frame them on the model and the principles of the primitive Church.

But the question whether the motives of the prime movers in the English Reformation were better or worse, or whether the precise arrangements made by them, in vindication of the just liberties of the Anglican Church, were more or less perfect, is to us, in respect of the claims now made upon our submission by the see of Rome, of comparatively little consequence.

The question is, Is Rome changed? Are her claims juster, more moderate, better founded, than they were? Has her course, during the three centuries that have elapsed since the Reformation, made those claims more plausible, so that her argument might seem to have been bettered by the exhibition of her spiritual virtues?

Is Rome less fettered by the political interests of the secular world than she was?

(1.) It has been observed, that the position of a universal bishop, such as the Pope claims to be, requires

[i] Gladstone's Remarks on the Supremacy; and Strype's Life of Abp. Parker, bk. ii. c. 1.

him to have a temporal sovereignty. No bishop, the subject of another secular prince, could be conceived to have the independence and freedom of action which the so-called infallible head of the Church on earth must necessarily require. To this observation it is added, that he must also be a despotic sovereign[k]; the political servitude and civil degradation of the people of Rome is necessary to the ecclesiastical order of the rest of the Roman communion. Let a third observation be added to these two. There has hardly been an instance, since the Reformation, of any considerable struggle between the Roman Catholics and the Protestants in any part of Europe, in which the political necessities of the Pope's temporal dominions have not engaged him in operations and intrigues on the Protestant side, against what he of course regarded as the only true faith in Christ. The princes of the Smalkaldic league were encouraged by Clement VII. in their resistance to the Emperor Charles V.[1] It was with the full concurrence of Urban VIII. that Gustavus Adolphus invaded Germany, and recovered half of that country from the grasp of the most faithful son of the Roman Catholic Church[m]. The court of Innocent XI. was cognizant of, and indirectly sup-

[k] Gladstone on the Supremacy, p. 28.   [1] Ranke, i. 120—123.
[m] Ibid. ii. 572.

ported, the invasion of England by William of Nassau, and the dethronement of James II.[n] So tortuous, complicated, and contradictory have been the operations of that secular polity, the existence of which is an essential incident to the spiritual claims of the Romish see.

(2.) Again, how has it fared in respect of piety and religion with those countries in which the Roman Catholic obedience has been maintained since the Reformation? What force or power, what effort of force or power, did Rome make with all her boasted completeness of discipline and authority, to stay the unequalled profligacies of the reign of Louis XV. in France, when her highest ecclesiastical dignities were prostituted in the person of the abandoned Dubois[o],

[n] Ranke, iii. 181.

[o] "The Abbé Dubois, afterwards Cardinal and Prime Minister, was at this time sixty years of age; his father was a poor apothecary near Limoges. Young Dubois came to Paris in hopes of a bursarship at a college; but failing in this object, he combined an opportunity for learning with the means of livelihood by acting as servant to the Principal. A more favourable turn of fortune afterwards assigned to Dubois a subaltern post in the education of the Duke of Chartres, and the prince and the preceptor soon became inseparable friends. A ready wit, undaunted assurance, and sagacious counsels recommended Dubois, who, moreover, did not scruple to augment his favour by the most shameful services. His profligate character was so notorious, that when Philip became Regent, it was not without much opposition and clamour that he could appoint him a councillor of state. The Regent's own words on that occasion shew his true opinion of his favourite;

or to check the terrible atrocities of the first Revolution? What power has she now over the highest, or the middle, or the lowest classes of that unhappy nation? How far has she been able to stem the torrent of infidelity which has poured over Germany, and which is said to have poisoned the minds of the priesthood of Spain [p]? What did she do in Ireland, where her power really was great, and might have been efficient if it had been honestly exercised, to put down midnight murder and organized assassination? Did we hear of counties put under interdict, or secret organizations denounced with the single-minded zeal of those whose object was to win souls to God? Alas! no. These boasted powers have been reserved for political objects. Rome can excommunicate her rebels. But she has had a mother's heart for the worst of sinners. Now, as ever, personal holiness has been sa-

'Let me beg of you, my dear Abbé, to be a little honest!' The gross vices of Dubois, and his shamelessness in the high ecclesiastical dignities which he afterwards attained, have justly made his name infamous with later times."—*Lord Mahon's History of England,* i. 328.

[p] The late Mr. Blanco White (who had the melancholy experience of first relinquishing the Roman Catholic communion for that of the Church of England, and afterwards deserting the Church altogether, to become and die a Socinian,) having no love for the clergy of either of the communions which he had left, has spoken strongly of the infidelity prevalent among the clergy of Spain, and as strongly of the faith (bigoted and blind as he esteemed it) of the clergy of the Church of England.

crificed to the maintenance of power; so that the most common laws of honesty and morality have been made to bow, and Rome is the same Rome which was in former ages the unblushing advocate of equivocation [q] and falsehood, and celebrated in solemn services of thanksgiving the awful massacre of the eve of St. Bartholomew.

(3.) Of pretended miracles I would fain speak carefully; for God only knoweth what powers [r] He may be pleased to grant to prayer and faith in any portion of the Church. But how can we speak patiently of that image of the Blessed Virgin at Rimini, with its winking eyes, crowned by the present Pope, and thus sanctioned by his authority; and afterwards—I speak only from the common sources of public information—discovered and exposed as a cheat?

(4.) And again, has not the present Pope, in the exercise of his pretended infallibility, actually created a new point of faith? added to the already burthened creed of Rome the doctrine of the Immaculate Conception of the Blessed Virgin? and thus required

[q] Cf. Pascal, Lettres Provinciales VII. and IX. des restrictions mentales.

[r] "Videamus utrum habuerit caritatem. Crederem, si non divisisset unitatem. Nam et contrà istos, ut sic loquar, *mirabiliarios* cautum me fecit Deus meus, dicens, *In novissimis temporibus exsurgent pseudoprophetæ*, &c."—*S. August. Tract.* xiii. in c. iii. *Evang. Joann.*

his subjects to believe, on pain of damnation, what seems to be directly opposed to the plain words of Holy Scripture?

Nay, brethren, Rome remains, in this generation, and must needs remain, till she gives up her unscriptural pretensions, the same Rome as she was in her darkest and boldest days. She has forged herself chains in her very claims. The spell of her ancient guilt is on her. Every stain and wrinkle of her persecutions, tamperings with the faith, and usurpations, is, by the very force of these usurpations, and as long as they are retained, made indelible.

Brethren, being such as she is, has been, and, alas! seems likely to remain, how is it to be explained or understood that she has succeeded in winning from their allegiance to the Church of their Baptism so many of our honoured, learned, and conscientious brethren? I do not speak of weak women or silly youths, in whom it is idle, well-nigh ridiculous, to speak of argument or conscience; but of those who could weigh reasons, search authors, recognise duty; how *can* they have found themselves able to accept all these things to which they have bound themselves by submitting to the see of Rome? Brethren, I believe it is mainly because they have allowed themselves to be so vexed and fretted by the imperfections and difficulties of the Church of England, not few, alas! nor small in these Erastian days,—that they have forgotten or ignored the real character of the Church to which they have clung. On the English Church, its documents, public acts, rulers, usages, history, even its current conversation and temporarily prevalent expressions, they have learned to fix their eye like a microscope. Nothing so small, so trifling, as not to be brought in to swell the catalogue of the offences of England. But they have *turned the glass* when they have looked on Rome; if, indeed, they have consented to look on her at all, except in distant admiration of her high pretensions. They have forgotten that here in England every difference of opinion, every impropriety and offence comes to the surface, and is known in the whole length and breadth of the land, so that every imperfection of the Church and its people is spread, commented upon, and exaggerated by a hundred writers; while there, all is smothered and concealed, except what it may be convenient to bring to light, or may become accidentally known; and that, (as in the parallel case of social order and protection, there is certainly no country where life and property are so well secured as in this, in spite of the continual publication of the details of crime in our courts of law and police,) so it is probable that there is no part of Christendom where so much of intelligent faith, or so much of family devotion leavening the hearts and directing the lives of men and women, exists as in our own. God forbid that we should boast, when indeed our shortcomings, as compared with our opportunities and graces, are fearful and most humbling,—but really as compared with the countries of the Roman Catholic obedience, or the less perfectly constituted Protestant communities of the continent, our own shortcomings do seem less considerable. And if there be any who doubts whether or no the living grace of God is really withheld from our Church, let him consider whether the increase of the colonial episcopate, and the eighteen hundred new-built churches in the last fifteen years, do not indicate at least a beginning of better things, which should be a comfort and encouragement to us to believe that God has not left us even in our dark and troubled times.

Then may God pardon those who have gone, or who shall go, from us to join the Roman communion! and as we believe them still to be within the grace of His Sacraments, give them repentance for the scandal and the schism which they have caused, and for the encouragement of recklessness and infidelity which such acts must always give to the weak and wilful!

But for ourselves, brethren, let us remember that

the difference between Rome and England is not only a difference founded on arguments of ecclesiastical history in past days, great and important as these are. It is a moral difference.

In Rome, the single Christian is the mere subject of a hierarchy. His duty is summed up in one word, he must obey,—not conscience, not the word or law of God, but *his priest*. Hence follows to the good, feebleness of mind and want of skill and strength in personal direction; to the bad, recklessness and facility of sin. A perfunctory confession, a hasty absolution, and the Christian man believes himself at peace with God, though the inward work of deep repentance and self-government be unlearned. The priest meanwhile obeys his superiors; and as ambition, or temporal interests, or endless indirect objects bias, from time to time, and sway the superiors, so the consciences of the mass of people are drilled, and controlled, and swept in any direction that may be desired.

The doctrines of the Church of England recognise in all her baptized children, according to their means and powers, a sacred right and responsible duty of judgment. She regards them, as the Holy Scripture regards them, as made kings and priests in Christ. In their various degrees, and according to their opportunities, they must search their Scriptures, like the

SERMON XV.

noble Bereans, and see if these things are really so. They must not be kept in ignorance, nor withheld from forming a judgment whether the modern claims of the Church and her teaching have or have not departed from the pure models of the first ages. They must learn the deep inward lessons of heart-repentance, of mortification of their own lusts, and they must gain the strength of self-direction by the light of a well-instructed conscience, to keep their steps straight along the path of divine duty and holiness. In all these duties they have the divinely-descended priesthood by their side, to assist, but not to supersede, their own personal graces; to teach them the ancient faith of the pure Church; to administer to them the Holy Sacraments; to give them, in their sorrow, the benefits of absolution; yet not, in teaching them, to direct them to forego their own intelligent reason in recognising and embracing truth; nor, in sacraments, to deceive them into thinking that the mere imparted sign gives grace, without repentance and faith in the receiver; nor, in absolution, to pretend that the priest's sentence can supersede the necessity of a full outpouring of a really contrite spirit before the throne of God.

And so, I do from my heart believe that there is no position in the universal Church where a baptized

Christian soul may be more sacredly, more healthily, more truly trained and strengthened to grow in grace and reach the heavenly inheritance, than in the Church of England.

There are, I well know, imperfections in it, which, when God is pleased to give the time and the means, we desire to amend.

There are also, in these days, dangers arising from the interference of the State in spiritual things,—such as I referred to on All Saints' Day,—which (if such interference should be obstinately maintained, and the free exercise of the essential powers of the spiritual Church be fully and finally denied, and the denial fully and finally accepted and acquiesced in) would, I cannot doubt, make it difficult to believe that the Anglican establishment remained a vital branch in the sacred Vine which the Lord hath planted.

Yet, if ever so doleful a day should come, (which God forbid!) if ever those who now labour cheerfully and happily in the Church of their fathers, feeling that her troubles and distresses are indeed great, but by patience, and prayer, and greater diligence of duty, and more earnestness of faith and devotion, even these troubles may, by God's mercy, be lightened, and that meanwhile they are a means and occasion of humility, penitence, and trust,—if ever, I say, so doleful a day should come, as that well-instructed Christian men should be compelled to quit her, who is their mother till she ceases to be God's daughter, will *Rome* be the alternative? Rome, the usurping, worldly power, which has claimed to depose princes, and dispose of realms? Rome with her system of indulgences, of compulsory confession and celibacy with all their terrible dangers, of equivocations, and dispensations? Rome with her purgatory, her Mariolatry, her mutilated Eucharist, her sacraments depending for their efficacy on the intention of the priest, her developements of corrupt doctrine?

Nay, then must they be content to pass their lives, like our own beloved and apostolic Ken, in even a more dreary isolation than they have yet known; bearing silent witness to the world of the sacred original truth of Christ's holy Church; living more near to heaven, as the spiritual (alas!) as well as temporal brotherhood of mankind is withdrawn from them; endeavouring to be all the more earnest and deep in prayer and devotion in their heavy affliction; trusting that when the eternal morning breaks upon their night of loneliness and affliction, it may shew their place still to be among the countless multitude of the redeemed, thronging in white robes to follow the Lamb whithersoever He goeth.

But God forbid that such a day of grief should *ever* come! nor, if we are all in earnest in our devotions and prayers now in the times of trial, need we fear it.

If we mortify our lusts, devote ourselves to our separate duties, and are really instant in all our lives in prayers, and Communions; if we are charitable, careful, and wise, neither giving offence needlessly, nor taking it, nor *playing* with serious things; if each in our separate sphere, — we teaching, you learning, some in being confirmed, others in the position of communicants,—if we, all and one, brethren, should really render and yield up ourselves, our souls and bodies, a reasonable, holy, and lively sacrifice to God, that His will may be done in us, and by us, then, no doubt, grace and comfort, and growth in the love and favour of God will be the sure and only result of the present sorrows of our beloved Church of England.

www.ingramcontent.com/pod-product-compliance
Lightning Source LLC
Chambersburg PA
CBHW050611300426
44112CB00012B/1451